New Millennium Woes and Livelihood Struggles in Africa:
Begging to Survive by Zimbabwe's marginalised

by

Fidelis Peter Thomas Duri & Ngonidzashe Marongwe

Langaa Research & Publishing CIG
Mankon, Bamenda

Publisher:
Langaa RPCIG
Langaa Research & Publishing Common Initiative Group
P.O. Box 902 Mankon
Bamenda
North West Region
Cameroon
Langaagrp@gmail.com
www.langaa-rpcig.net

Distributed in and outside N. America by African Books Collective
orders@africanbookscollective.com
www.africanbookscollective.com

ISBN-10: 9956-551-23-6

ISBN-13: 978-9956-551-23-1

© Fidelis Peter Thomas Duri & Ngonidzashe Marongwe 2021

About the Authors

Fidelis Peter Thomas Duri is a Professor of History in the Department of History, Archaeology and Development Studies at Great Zimbabwe University in Zimbabwe, where he is also the Research Coordinator in the Simon Muzenda School of Arts, Culture and Heritage Studies. Previously, he had started off his professional career as a History teacher at St David's Girls High School, Bonda, before becoming a History lecturer at Marymount and Mutare Teachers' Colleges, both in Zimbabwe. He was also a part-time lecturer in History and African Studies at Africa University in Zimbabwe during his full-time tenure at Marymount and Mutare Teachers' Colleges.

Duri is a holder of a PhD in History from the University of the Witwatersrand in Johannesburg, South Africa (2012), where he was also a part-time History tutor while pursuing his studies. He also holds a Bachelor of Arts Honours degree in African Experience (1986), a Graduate Certificate in Education (1988), and a Master of Arts degree in African History (1999), all from the University of Zimbabwe.

He has more than 50 academic publications, which include books, book chapters and peer-reviewed journal articles which focus on environmental history, socio-cultural dynamics, subaltern struggles, African border studies, and Zimbabwe's socio-political landscape during the colonial and post-colonial periods. Among his most popular and best-selling books are: *The relentless governance by the sword: Situating Operation Murambatsvina in Zimbabwean history* (2010); *Resilience amid adversity: Informal coping mechanisms to the Zimbabwean crisis during the new millennium* (2016); *Contested spaces, restrictive mechanisms and corridors of opportunity: A social history of Zimbabwean borderlands and beyond since the colonial period* (2017); *The end of an era? Robert Mugabe and a conflicting legacy* (2018); *Violence, peace and everyday modes of justice and healing in post-colonial Africa* (2019); and *Mugabeism after Mugabe: Rethinking legacies and new dispensations in Zimbabwe's 'Second Republic* (2020).

Duri is also a reviewer of articles for international academic journals such as *International Migration: A Journal of the International Organisation for Migration*, and *Dzimbahwe: Journal of Humanities and Social Sciences*. In addition to reviewing scholarly articles of several local and international journals, he is also a member of the editorial boards of the *Zimbabwe Journal of Historical Studies* and the *International Journal of Developing Societies*. He has also been engaged on a number of occasions by the Zimbabwe Council for Higher Education (ZIMCHE) to review proposed regulations of History degree programmes offered at various Zimbabwean universities.

Ngonidzashe Marongwe is an Associate Professor of History in the History and Development Studies Department at Great Zimbabwe University in Zimbabwe. He holds a PhD in African History from the University of the Western Cape (UWC), South Africa. He is a past Andrew Mellon Foundation Doctoral Fellow at the Centre for Humanities Research, UWC (2009-2010 and 2012); and a SEPHIS Fellow at the Centre for the Study of Culture and Society, Bangalore, India (2011). His research interests include African governance, political violence, gender, military history and terrorism. Marongwe has edited several books such as *Myths of peace and democracy: Towards building pillars of hope, unity and transformation in Africa* (2016); *Violence, politics and conflict management in Africa: Envisioning transformation, peace and unity in the twenty-first century* (2016); *Contested spaces, restrictive mechanisms and corridors of opportunity: A social history of Zimbabwean borderlands and beyond since the colonial period* (2018); *End of an era? Robert Mugabe and a conflicting legacy* (2018); *Violence, peace and everyday modes of justice and healing in post-colonial Africa* (2019); and *Mugabeism after Mugabe: Rethinking legacies and new dispensations in Zimbabwe's Second Republic* (2020).

Acknowledgements

We are profoundly grateful for the various forms of assistance that we received from various individuals and corporate organisations. First, we would like to thank the many interviewees whose views form the bedrock of this book. Many of these would like to remain anonymous. A big thank you also goes to the various photographers from different news sources whose pictures we have used in this book. We also would like to acknowledge the help we received from our employer, Great Zimbabwe University. We had unlimited access to internet and library resources. Professor Extraordinarius Munyaradzi Mawere, thank you dearly for meticulously editing this book and for the intellectual mentoring that you have given us and indeed continue to provide to both of us. To the Duri and Marongwe families, keep up the moral and socio-economic support.

Table of Contents

List of Figures & Maps

List of Maps

List of Abbreviations and Acronyms

AIDS: Acquired Immune Deficiency Syndrome
ATM: Automated Teller Machine
AU: African Union
BBC: British Broadcasting Corporation
BEAM: Basic Education Assistance Module
CAZ: Child Aid Zimbabwe
CIA: Central Intelligence Agency
CNN: Cable News Network
DRC: Democratic Republic of Congo
DC: District of Columbia
ESAP: Economic Structural Adjustment Programme
EU: European Union
FAO: Food and Agriculture Organisation
FGD: Focused Group Discussions
GAPWUZ: General Agriculture and Plantation Workers Union of Zimbabwe
GDP: Gross Domestic Product
GMB: Grain Marketing Board
GNU: Government of National Unity
ILO: International Labour Organisation
IMF: International Monetary Fund
HIV: Human Immunodeficiency Virus
MDC: Movement for Democratic Change
MDC-M: Movement for Democratic Change- Mutambara
MDC-T: Movement for Democratic Change- Tsvangirai
MSF: Médecins sans Frontières
MTN: Mobile Telephone Networks
NCA: National Constitutional Assembly
NCDPZ: National Council of Disabled Persons of Zimbabwe

NGO: Non-Governmental Organisation

NRZ: National Railways of Zimbabwe

NSSA: National Social Security Authority

OECD: Organisation for Economic Cooperation and Development

RAU: Research and Advocacy Unit

RTGS: Real Time Gross Settlement

RBZ: Reserve Bank of Zimbabwe

SABC: South Africa Broadcasting Corporation

SADC: Southern African Development Community

SAMP: Southern African Migration Project

SAPES: Southern African Political and Economic Series

SAQA: South Africa Qualifications Authority

SAWIMA: South Africa Women's Institute of Migration Affairs

ST1: Sexually Transmitted Infection

UK: United Kingdom

UNICEF: United Nations International Children's Emergency Fund

UN: United Nations

US: United States

VISTZP: Visually Impaired Strategic Trust of Zimbabwe People

VOA: Voice of America

VOP: Voice of the People

WFP: World Food Programme

ZANU-PF: Zimbabwe African National Union - Patriotic Front

ZBC: Zimbabwe Broadcasting Corporation

ZCTU: Zimbabwe Congress of Trade Unions

ZDHR: Zimbabwe Doctors for Human Rights

ZDI: Zimbabwe Defence Industries

ZETDC: Zimbabwe Electricity Transmission and Distribution Company

ZIMCODD: Zimbabwe Coalition on Debt and Development

ZIMPARKS: Zimbabwe Parks and Wildlife Management Authority

ZIMSTAT: Zimbabwe Statistical Agency

ZNA: Zimbabwe National Army
ZRP: Zimbabwe Republic Police
ZTV: Zimbabwe Television
ZUPCO: Zimbabwe United Passenger Company
ZWD: Zimbabwean Dollar

Introduction

Conceptualizing begging and methodological underpinnings

Historical background

Begging or panhandling is an ancient practice that was noted, for instance, in Luke Chapter 18, Verses 35-43 in the Christian Bible where there is mention of a beggar living with disabilities who solicited for alms from the roadside. Begging has been a source of livelihood for some impoverished people across the globe since time immemorial but its prevalence tended to fluctuate in accordance with the socio-economic and political conditions obtaining in various historical periods and spaces. In colonial Zimbabwe, for example, most beggars were of foreign origin and were mainly from Malawi, Mozambique and Zambia. In the colonial Zimbabwean town of Umtali (now Mutare), for example, a council meeting held on 30 June 1949 discussed the increasing number of street beggars, most of them from Mozambique. Two juvenile beggars from Mozambique had recently been taken to the police and were later deported. Sometime later, one of the beggars was spotted in the streets of Umtali (*Umtali Advertiser*, 1 July 1949). During an Umtali council monthly meeting in September 1951, concerns were again raised about the conspicuous presence of African beggars in the town (*Umtali Advertiser*, 2 October 1951). Throughout the 1950s, some destitute Mozambican children, including those aged between seven and 11 years, frequently crossed into Umtali to beg with the full knowledge and approval of their parents (Duri, 2012b). Colonial statutes such as the Natives Accommodation and Registration Act of 1946, the Vagrancy Act of 1960, and various pass laws were enacted to control begging by Africans in urban areas which were regarded as the preserve of the white people (Patel, 1988; Rugoho and Siziba, 2014).

From 1976, there was a significant rise in the number of local beggars in colonial Zimbabwean towns, most of who had fled the armed struggle for independence in the rural areas. At independence in 1980, most of them returned to their rural homes to join family members and relatives leaving beggars of foreign origin predominant in Zimbabwe's urban areas (*Standard*, 16 January 2005). In 1984, the Zimbabwean government rounded up beggars in Harare, the capital city, ahead of the Non-Aligned Movement summit and dumped them in an empty land more than 100 kilometres away (Bourdillon, 1991). As socio-economic hardships besieged the country from 1991 as a result of the implementation of the Economic Structural Adjustment Programme (ESAP), the preponderance of local beggars became more visible, particularly in Zimbabwe's urban areas (*Standard*, 16 January 2005).

From the onset of the new millennium, as will be noted later in this book, the number of beggars shot up as the majority of Zimbabweans became overwhelmed by a surfeit of socio-economic maladies of unprecedented magnitude. In actual fact, what became unique about Zimbabwe from 2000 was that the proportion of street beggars to the population of the major cities became probably the highest in the developing world (Dabudabu, 11 December 2009). In September 2002, as reported by Rudo Makunike, a *Mail and Guardian* journalist, "Street kids and beggars on the roads are an increasingly common sight and they have become more brazen in proportion to the compassion fatigue of motorists and pedestrians also reeling from a wayward economy" (Makunike, 27 September 2002: 1). By 2006, a myriad of grinding socio-economic privations had turned Zimbabwe into "a nation of beggars" (Koinage, 19 December 2006: 1). In May 2014, the number of beggars crowding the streets in most urban centres was reportedly "increasing at an alarming rate" (Kariati, 19 May 2019: 1). In February 2017, Walter Mzembi, the then Minister of Tourism, expressed alarm at the increasing number of beggars, particularly children, in Zimbabwe's urban centres (Mawire, 7 February 2017). In October 2019, Michael Chideme, the then Harare City Council Spokesperson, acknowledged the increasing number of beggars but stated that it was the responsibility of the national government through the Ministry of Labour and Social Welfare to cater for them, otherwise the council could not do anything about it

(Bamu, 21 October 2019). By early January 2020, beggars had become "owners of the city, roaming the streets" (Ntali, 9 January 2020: 1). As Dhliwayo (18 January 2020: 1) observed in most of Zimbabwe's urban centres, "begging at street corners has become more of a trade" and in Harare, "street urchins have invaded almost every corner". In February 2020, as Lopez (1 February 2020) reiterated, hundreds of street children, mostly beggars, roamed Zimbabwe's urban areas, particularly Harare. By early March 2020, Zimbabwe had gained notoriety for having "more people begging on the street than elsewhere in the (Southern African) region" (Sanderson, 1 March 2020: 1).

From the foregoing, it becomes quite apparent that begging in various parts of the world in general, and Zimbabwe in particular, has a long history. The practice is still quite visible, and perhaps more widespread, in the contemporary world as the ever-increasing number of marginalised people seek livelihoods. Thus, despite being an old survival initiative, begging is very much a contemporary pursuit and this is why the continuous present tense is mostly used in discussions throughout this book.

Conceptualising begging

Begging is an informal means of earning livelihoods through charity. It is an undertaking by impoverished and marginalised individuals or groups of people, including the young and the elderly, the disabled and those who are not, boys and girls and men and women. It is not restricted to public places such as streets, shopping areas and religious institutions and buses, but also takes place in private premises. According to Namwata, Mgabo and Dimoso (2012), it involves soliciting for a voluntary gift that is usually in the form of money, food or clothes. Begging as a survival strategy depends largely on the mercy of strangers where the governments and other welfare institutions have failed. In many ways, begging is a of the "gift economy" largely sustained by people's sympathies (Swanson, 2007: 709).

In the academic literature, scholars have categorised beggars in

3

various ways, some of which will be discussed in this section. There has been a tendency by many scholars and organisations to view begging as an urban phenomenon centred along the streets (Mhizha, 2010; Namwata, Mgabo and Dimoso, 2012; and Mihalache *et al.*, 2013). The United Nations International Children's Emergency Fund (UNICEF) (2001), for example, classified panhandlers into beggars-of-the-street and those on-the-street. Similarly, Mhizha (2010) has categorised them as street-living and street-working beggars to refer to individuals who permanently live on the streets and those who use the streets as a place of begging while they have residence elsewhere.

Correspondingly, in their study of municipalities of Dodoma and Singida in Central Tanzania, Namwata, Mgabo and Dimoso (2012) established four categories of beggars: 'those on the street', 'of the street', 'in the street', and 'of street families'. According to this classification, beggars 'on the street' have permanent homes and maintain contacts with their families. They beg during the day and return home during the evening. Those 'of the street' live and sleep on the street and their contacts with home and family are remote and occasional. Beggars 'in the street' are completely isolated from their families and immediate communities. Beggars 'of street families' are born and bred on the streets mostly by parents who are beggars. Together with their parents, they engage in begging. Most beggars 'of' and 'in' the street live rough lives such as sleeping in sewers and drainpipes (*Eye Net*, 8 July 2004).

Some scholars also categorised beggars in terms of their degree of need. Stone (1984), for instance, classified beggars into deserving and undeserving cases. Undeserving cases are those believed to be capable of earning livelihoods through other productive means but simply take advantage of situations to beg. These belong to the category of 'mental poverty' in the Munyaradzi Mawere formulation (Mawere, 2017) for being lazy to utilize their capacities to earn alternative livelihoods to begging. The deserving cases are viewed as those who lack the ability to survive without begging due to a number of factors such as extreme conditions of visual, mental or physical disability and other forms of deprivation. This category includes widows, abandoned women with children, the frail and the elderly (Groce, *et al.*, 2013).

4

Presently, begging is a worldwide phenomenon visible in both developing and developed countries. Although begging is a universal phenomenon, it is more prevalent in developing countries (Namwata, Mgabo and Dimoso, 2012). South Asia, particularly India, Bangladesh, Cambodia and Nepal, for example, has the largest population of beggars (Mihalache et al., 2013). While this book broadens the spatial limits of begging beyond urban settings to include even the rural and peri-urban areas, both within national borders and beyond Zimbabwe, the population of beggars is generally more spatially concentrated in urban than rural areas. In the urban areas of developed countries such as Britain (Ogunkan and Jelili, 2010) and China (Hanchao, 1999), for example, beggars are a common sight. Several factors account for the prevalence of begging in many urban areas around the world. The concentration of beggars in urban areas is always high because impoverished people usually drift from the countryside to the towns in search of greener pastures such as employment and other livelihood-earning opportunities. Urban society is largely heterogeneous in composition; people are comparatively more isolated and know relatively less about their immediate or distant neighbours than their rural counterparts. In sprawling cosmopolitan urban settings, the chances of sharing in times of need are very scarce resulting in increased incidences of begging. Ironically though, it is in these very urban settings where potential alms-givers from the affluent and the workers are found. In addition, it is in the urban cosmopolitan milieu that beggars sometimes take advantage of their anonymity to beg without being noticed, despised and stigmatised by close relatives and acquaintances (Groce et al., 2013). As a result, in times of severe adversities, beggars tend to be more concentrated in urban areas than in other parts of the country (Arshad, Kamal and Arif, 2014).

In Zimbabwe in particular and the world in general, the begging population is, and has always been, far from being homogenous but complex and diverse. Children, mostly comprising orphans, those of school-going age, school dropouts and unemployed school-leavers constitute a significant population of beggars. Impoverished adult men and women, most of who are unemployed, the elderly and the disabled also make up a considerable number of beggars. Most of the disabled are physically handicapped, deaf, dumb and blind (Cheneso, Marapa, Mukonda and Zikina, Separate Interviews: 2014). The mentally ill are, and have always been, part of the begging community around the world. They are, however, not part of this study because it would have been very difficult, if not impossible, to derive data from them in view of their mental condition. In addition, the book is preoccupied with people who are driven to beg by their vulnerable condition in socio-economic terms and does not include those who are sent to beg for fund-raising purposes by institutions such as churches and schools. That said, the core of the argument advanced in this book is that begging is one of the several critical features of human resilience to calamities. Given their poverty-ridden condition, largely characterised by mendicancy and pauperism, begging becomes a key survival option for some marginalised and downtrodden sections of the society.

Research methods and theoretical framework

A multi-pronged methodological approach was utilised to collect data for this book. Firstly, library research was undertaken at various Zimbabwean universities and teachers' colleges, and on the internet in an effort to review relevant literature. This secondary data comprised published and unpublished documents with the academic literature largely derived from the fields of Development Studies, Health, Economics, History and the Social Sciences. Secondary written sources which include newspaper articles and documents from the Zimbabwean government, NGOs and the donor community were also valuable sources of information pertaining to begging dynamics in Zimbabwe and the neighbouring countries.

The methodology employed during fieldwork was largely participatory or interactive, comprising observations, oral interviews and focus group discussions (FGD), most of which were conducted at marketplaces, bus termini and along the streets and pavements in Zimbabwean towns and cities. Interviews were conducted with beggars in urban areas (for example, Harare, Mutare, Chitungwiza, Masvingo, Chipinge, Rusape and Chimanimani) and peri-urban business centres (such as Odzi, Birchenough Bridge and Nyika) and non-beggars who included local government officials, councillors, businesspersons, and people from the community. The selection of participants from the begging community was largely based on their availability.

The data collected was analysed qualitatively and phenomenologically using two distinct but complementary theoretical frameworks. These are the Human Capabilities Approach to Poverty and the Social History Theoretical Framework. While poverty can simply be defined as the lack of material needs such as food, shelter and clothing, this book includes the incapability of some marginalised people to meet their basic needs as an important determinant of poverty. The definition of poverty by the Human Capabilities Approach was aptly summarised by the Poverty Reduction Forum Trust (2011: 7-8) as follows:

> Poverty is seen not only as a lack of certain material things (such as food and shelter) but also as the lack of the capability to meet one's needs. Capability…refers to a person's opportunity and ability to generate or produce desired particular outcomes so as to meet one's needs. Thus, this approach would consider a person to be poor when s/he lacks the ability to satisfy his/her needs at a minimal adequate level. The Human Capability Approach therefore looks at the ends (meeting of needs), as well as the means (the ways through which people meet the ends). For example, food is an end while the ability to acquire needed food is a means. The capabilities approach also considers the internal and external factors that influence a person's capabilities. An advantage of this approach is that it allows the definition of poverty to emerge from the context of the study. In addition, the Human Capability Approach facilitates the identification of poverty indicators, influencing factors and impact in a particular context. Using this approach, people in a particular context are able to construct their own meanings of poverty and describe their experiences of it as opposed to them responding to an imposed definition of poverty.

The Social History approach, popularly known in the academic discourse as history 'from below' or 'from the ground up', articulates history from the perceptions of the subaltern paying particular attention to their peculiarities (Kros, 2007). It essentialises the marginalised people, in terms of their experiences, interests, emotions and behaviour, and emphasises and legitimises their agency in history (Stearns, 2003). The primacy of this approach lies in its focus on how ordinary people make creative choices to survive, sometimes in ways that contravene institutional dispensations, dictates, contexts or structures (Kaelbe, 2003). In this book, the Social History approach contextualises begging in the socio-economic and political quagmire that gripped Zimbabwe from 2000 and illuminates the initiatives undertaken by impoverished people, particularly beggars, to alleviate the challenges emanating from the crises.

The utilisation of the Human Capabilities Approach to Poverty and the Social History Theoretical Framework in this book illustrates that despite having a long history, begging is very much a phenomenon of the present. This is largely because the gap between the rich and the poor continues to widen and many people worldwide are struggling to survive through various informal means owing to the rising poverty levels.

Summary of chapter contents

This book consists of five chapters. The first chapter discusses Zimbabwe's socio-economic and political crisis[1] from the year 2000 in considerable detail in order to contextualise the prevalence of begging. Chapter 2 examines the broad range of livelihood initiatives of beggars in Zimbabwe which involved, among other things, managing space and time, and exhibiting competency to communicate effectively with potential alms-givers in order to induce their sympathy. Chapter 3 focuses on the various challenges faced by the begging community in Zimbabwe. Chapter 4 dwells on the influx of Zimbabwean beggars in neighbouring countries and pays

---

[1] We use the term crisis instead of crises in the mode as deployed by B. Raftopoulos (2009). In this modality we still acknowledge the multifacetedness and plurality of the crisis, which for some can be considered as crises.

8

particular attention to their survival mechanisms in harsh diasporan enclaves. Chapter 5 looks at the positive and negative effects of begging on Zimbabwe's socio-economic fabric. Overall, this book illustrates the importance of begging in the struggles of survival for many Zimbabweans, particularly from the onset of the new millennium, as socio-economic calamities gripped the country.

Chapter 1

Contextualising the Prevalence of Begging in the Zimbabwean Crisis from 2000

Introduction

Considering the fact that begging is a complex phenomenon undertaken by a population whose composition is heterogenous, its causes are equally diverse and depend on a multiplicity of variables that are closely linked to the conditions and experiences of an individual or individuals concerned (for example, disability, mental dislocation, deprivation, exclusion, insecurity, frustration, and poverty) and the manner in which they are determined by longstanding and/ or prevailing socio-economic and political influences of the immediate and/ or wider community. A number of arguments on the causes of begging have been raised in the academic discourse. Mental health problems and low self-esteem, for example, have been cited by psychologists (Fawole, Ogunkan and Omoruan, 2011). Social scientists have tended to place more emphasis on socio-economic determinants such as social exclusion, homelessness and poverty (Kennedy and Fitzpatrick, 2001).

This chapter is not concerned with the origins of begging in Zimbabwe but seeks to explain why it became more prevalent and widespread in the country from 2000. It locates the upsurge of panhandling pursuits in the debilitating socio-economic and political crisis that besieged Zimbabwe from 2000 (Raftopoulos, 2009), plunging the majority of its population into abject poverty for decades to come. The characteristic features of the crisis include international isolation, waning investor confidence, depletion of foreign currency reserves, record hyperinflation, deindustrialisation, shortages of food and other basic commodities, unprecedented unemployment, starvation, virtual absence of social services, and general poverty (Raftopoulos, 2009; Richardson, 2005). This catastrophe largely emanated from the disastrous policies and practices of the then President Robert Mugabe's Zimbabwe African National Union- Patriotic Front (ZANU-PF) party which had been at the helm of government since independence from British colonial rule in 1980. The plight of the country's ordinary people was exacerbated by negative ecological developments, particularly chronic droughts that alternated with floods that were also experienced (Duri, 2014).

The central argument of this chapter is that begging has always been one of the critical informal strategies of survival employed by impoverished Zimbabweans to salvage an existence in a harsh socio-economic and political environment. The moral economy of such informal pursuits also lies in the failure by the state, non-governmental organisations and socio-cultural institutions to provide meaningful support to these people to enable them to adequately address their plight (Tignor, 2005). The upsurge in begging in Zimbabwe from 2000, as studies in other parts of the world also show, is an index of abject poverty (Adebibu, 1989); it is "a question of survival" (Gossling *et al.*, 2004: 145), and "a major way out for the helpless poor" (Jelili, 2013: 53).

Socio-economic hardships in Zimbabwe during Mugabe's reign, 2000-2017

The Zimbabwean crisis was sparked off on 26 February 2000 by the government's seizure of commercial farms, mostly white-owned, and redistributing them to indigenous Africans. This was part of the ruling ZANU-PF party's desperate attempts to restore its waning legitimacy ahead of parliamentary, local government and presidential elections that were to be held between 2000 and 2002. ZANU-PF's support base had significantly shrunk during the last decade of the 20th century when various sections of the society, particularly the workers, were disillusioned by the government's implementation of the World Bank and International Monetary Fund's (IMF) ESAP from 1991 (Duri, 2010; Hill, 2003; Masunungure, 2004). Among other things, the programme reduced government spending on social services, removed state subsidies on basic commodities, deregulated prices resulting in high costs of living, and raised unemployment levels through job rationalisations and retrenchments (Bond and Manyanya, 2002; Hill, 2003). It was in these conditions of general discontentment across the country that the opposition Movement for Democratic Change (MDC) was formed on 11 September 1999 largely through the efforts of the Zimbabwe Congress of Trade Unions (ZCTU), the umbrella body for all workers' unions in the country, and several other civil organisations such as the National Constitutional Assembly (NCA) with financial backing from local commercial white farmers and international donors mostly from the United States (US), Western Europe and Australia (Masunungure, 2004; Meredith, 2002). In its desperate effort to cling to power in the face of fierce competition from the opposition MDC which made significant inroads among the disgruntled electorate during the first few months of its formation, the ruling party sanctioned the seizure of commercial farms, the majority of which belonged to the whites and reallocated them to indigenous people, mostly ZANU-PF supporters (Duri, 2012a; Meredith, 2002).

From 26 February to 8 March 2000, about 400 white-owned farms were seized (Meredith, 2002). The number of farms confiscated rose to 1 500 by June 2000 (Meredith, 2002). At the end of June 2000, the Commercial Farmers Union reported that 1 525 farms had been grabbed (Pilossof, 1 December 2010). The year 2000 saw more than 1 600 commercial white farms being seized (Moyo, 2000). By the end of 2002, 11.5 million hectares of land had been seized inside the space of 36 months (Sachikonye, 2003). By 2007, more than 4 000 farms had been grabbed (Duri, 2014; *Financial Gazette*, 26 July- 1 August 2007). Land invasions continued after the setting up of the Government of National Unity (GNU) in February 2009 soon after which the General Agriculture and Plantation Workers Union of Zimbabwe (GAPWUZ) estimated that around 225 farms were seized (Poverty Reduction Forum Trust, 2013; Zimbabwe Human Rights NGO Forum, 2010).

The land grabs plunged the country into the throes of a deep socio-economic crisis. Among other things, Zimbabwe became critically food-deficient. Agricultural production fell dramatically as most farms were redistributed to privileged persons on the basis of political patronage. Most of the new farmers either lacked the

13

technical knowhow for commercial farming or were simply not interested (Hammar and Raftopoulos, 2003). Agricultural production for domestic consumption nose-dived and hunger stared in the faces of most Zimbabweans. In addition, the country's foreign currency reserves increasingly became depleted because of the decline in the production of export crops. This had several negative repercussions on the ordinary people. The decline of export earnings meant that the government faced increasing difficulties in procuring imports from abroad such as food and medicine that were critical in the survival of ordinary citizens

As a result of the commercial farm seizures, Zimbabwe nose-dived from being "a bread-basket to a basket-case" (Hunt, 3 August 2011: 1). The production of maize, the staple grain, for example, declined by 90% between 2000 and 2003 (Mamdani, 2008). By 2004, the country's agricultural output had fallen by 75% largely as a result of the land seizures (Cross, 2004). The contribution of agriculture to the total exports fell from 39% in 2000 to 13% in 2007 (Fischer, 2010). In March 2008, the commercial farming sector was producing less than 10% of the maize it harvested in the 1990s, and less than 5% of the country's total maize production (*Irin News*, 13 March 2008). Compared to 2000 statistics, the 2010 agricultural production levels plummeted as follows: maize, 50%; cotton, 45%; tobacco, 50% (Hunt, 3 August 2011); dairy products, from 187 000 tonnes to 31 000; and livestock, from 605 000 animals to 230 000 (*BBC*, 29 August 2014). This cost Zimbabwe £7 billion in lost production during the first decade of the 21st century (Hunt, 3 August 2011).

The seizure of several parts of the Hippo Valley Estate comprising 49 plantations, the country's biggest sugar producer located in the province of Masvingo, in 2002, for example, clearly illustrates the demise of the Zimbabwean agricultural industry (Kahiya and Mukaro, 22 July 2005). The estate was owned by the South African Anglo-American Corporation and extended over 70 000 hectares. Before the farm invasions, it produced an average of 236 000 tonnes of sugar per year and together with the nearby Triangle Estate, produced all of Zimbabwe's sugar for local consumption and export (Meldrum, 4 February 2004). When it was seized, close to 180 new farmers subdivided among themselves part

14

of the estate into plots ranging from 20 to 60 hectares in size while 140 others, most of who were connected to the ruling ZANU-PF party, took over privately-owned plots within and around the sugar plantations. Production levels plummeted over the years since most of the new farmers lacked the skills of managing and harvesting sugar. Consequently, there was a 440% decrease in the hectarage of sugar cultivation and there was a national shortage of sugar in shop shelves from 2002 (*Zimbabwe Independent*, 20 March 2006). In March 2006, Hippo Valley was producing only 50% of its mill's output (Ibid).

Negative ecological developments also exacerbated the decline of agricultural production. Devastating droughts and subsequent crop failures aggravated the critical shortage of food and spurred the incidence of begging even in rural areas. The drought of the 2001-2002 agricultural season, for example, was regarded as the worst in 50 years (Oxfam, 10 June 2002). Together with the collapse of commercial agriculture as a result of farm 'invasions', the drought significantly contributed to the fall in maize production from 2000 to 2003 (Richardson, 2005). It was partly because of the drought that only 25% of maize needed for food in the country was harvested in 2001. The situation worsened in 2002 when cereal production fell by 57% and more than 5 million people out of a total population of over 12 million were in desperate need of food aid (Meldrum, 1 June 2005).

Droughts and resultant crop failures persisted during the decade. The government declared 2007 a drought year after people from most parts of the country failed to harvest enough crops to meet their subsistence needs (Duri, 2014). During the 2012-2013 agricultural season, late rains and long mid-season dry spells resulted in 45% of the maize crop being written off (Mudzungairi, 19 September 2013). As a result, the country's grain harvest of 968 000 tonnes in 2013 fell far short of a demand of 2 million tonnes by both people and livestock (Kwaramba and Mtimba, 31 October 2013). In October 2013, hunger and poverty gripped most people in the dry rural district of Gutu in Masvingo Province to the extent that people were competing with wild animals to get scarce food from wild fruits (Ibid).

As if the ravaging impacts of recurring droughts were not enough,

15

the country also experienced cyclone-induced floods with almost equally debilitating consequences during the same period. To illuminate this, Zimbabwe, together with many other Southern African countries, such as Zambia, Mozambique and Malawi, entered the new millennium on the back of a major ecological catastrophe, Cyclone Eline. The cyclone ravaged most parts of Zimbabwe between 9 February and 2 March 2000 (*The Herald*, 12 February 2015). Cyclone Eline resulted in massive floods, which were considered as the worst in living memory and resulted in the death of 136 people. Additionally, 59 184 houses and 14 999 toilets were destroyed while 538 schools and 54 clinics were partially or completely damaged. Furthermore, 230 dams burst while a total of 20 000 head of livestock were lost (Ibid).

Another notable cyclone that rampaged Zimbabwe was Cyclone Japhet in March of 2003. The cyclone affected three provinces of Zimbabwe namely Mashonaland Central, Masvingo and Manicaland. Among other things, the cyclone resulted in the loss of human life, destruction of infrastructure, land, agricultural activities and livestock. Another cyclone that had a devastating impact was Cyclone Idai that affected Zimbabwe, together with Mozambique and Malawi between 4 March and 21 March 2019. In the three countries, Cyclone Idai cumulatively led to some 1 000 deaths and left some 2.6 million people in desperate need of humanitarian assistance, destroyed homes and livelihoods (Oxfam International, 2020). In Zimbabwe, up to 700 people were either dead or missing as a result of the cyclone and a further 50 000 homes were destroyed (*VOA News*, 18 March 2020). What made the situation worse was that the international community and donors failed to alleviate the impact of Cyclone Idai by failing to raise the required funds for reconstruction. To this extent, Amnesty International pointed out that less than half of the US$450 million it needed for relief and recovery in Zimbabwe and Mozambique had been secured by March 2020 (cited in *Aljazeera*, 15 March 2020). What needs to be noted is that the US$450 million still fell short of the US$622 million Zimbabwe required to replace the significantly damaged infrastructure, properties, crops, and livestock (World Bank, 19 September 2019). This resulted in many affected and displaced residents in Zimbabwe failing to access food, cash and clothing (*Aljazeera*, 15 March 2020).

As Zimbabwe became chronically food-deficient largely as a result of the ZANU-PF government's disastrous land reform programme, droughts and floods, hunger and poverty marked the lives of significant sections of the population. Aid agencies reported that 25% of Zimbabweans were in critical need of food aid in May 2002 (*BBC*, 31 May 2002). In October 2003, 50% of the nearly 14 million people in Zimbabwe were food-insecure (Human Rights Watch, 25 October 2003; Mamdani, 2008).

In September 2007, the WFP indicated that at least 3.3 million Zimbabweans were in urgent need of emergency food aid (Manwere, 14 September 2007). As starvation gripped Zimbabwe, Save the Children, an international aid agency, reported in September 2008 that some children in the rural areas "were eating rats and inedible roots riddled with toxic parasites to starve off hunger" (*Reuters*, 25 September 2008: 1). In rural Matabeleland in December 2008, as Dugger (21 December 2008: 1) observed, "barefoot children stuff their pockets with corn kernels that have blown off a truck as if the brownish bits, good only for animal feed in normal times, were gold coins" while in various parts of the country "destitute villagers pull the shells off crickets then toss what is left into a hot pan". Nearly 7 million Zimbabweans, constituting about 75% of the population which was well over 12 million, were in need of emergency food aid in January 2009. In terms of critical food-deficiency levels among its citizens, Zimbabwe with the nearly 7 million starving citizens, became ranked third in the world after Afghanistan (8.82 million) and Ethiopia (8.67 million) ahead of the Democratic People's Republic of Korea (5.58 million) and Bangladesh (5 million) (*Irin News*, 29 January 2009).

In late October 2010, the Federation of Red Cross and Crescent Societies estimated that 2.17 million Zimbabweans, about 25% of the population, were in urgent need of food aid (*Associated Press*, 3 November 2010). In November 2011, the WFP reported that more than 1 million Zimbabweans were on the verge of starvation and in urgent need of food aid (*Voice of America*, 20 November 2011). In September 2012, 1.6 million Zimbabweans out of the country's total population of about 13 million were in desperate need of food aid

(WFP, 13 September 2012). During the period January to March 2013, about 19% of Zimbabwe's rural population or around one in every five people were in need of emergency food aid. These food insecurity levels were the worst in four years (WFP, 14 March 2013).

Some famished citizens managed to obtain food aid from the international community. This clearly exposed the Zimbabwean government's failure to cater for the welfare of many of its citizens. In October 2003, for example, close to 7 million people, out of the nearly 14 million Zimbabweans, were surviving from humanitarian assistance offered by international donors (Human Rights Watch, 25 October 2003; Mamdani, 2008). As starvation wreaked havoc in various parts of the country, the WFP managed to provide food assistance to 2.4 million people in February 2008 (*Irin News*, 13 March 2008). By November 2008, the WFP was feeding 4 million Zimbabweans, constituting more than 40% of the country's population (*Independent UK*, 7 December 2008; Quist-Arcton, 25 November 2008). In March 2013, the WFP was providing emergency food aid to more than 1.4 million Zimbabweans (WFP, 22 March 2013).

The land seizures also impoverished many former farm workers after the new owners failed to reemploy them, let alone to have their gratuities paid up. This was partly because some new farmers either lacked the technical skills for both intensive and extensive commercial farming or were not interested at all. In 2005, more than 50% of the seized farms were not being utilised (Duri, 2014). At Stockdale Farm near the town of Chegutu, for example, the former white owners employed more than 60 000 workers but less than 50% of the workforce was retained by the new owner, Edna Madzongwe, then a senior ZANU-PF official and President of Senate (Chikwanha, 4 May 2014). Charleswood Farm in the Chimanimani District used to employ more than 1 000 workers but when Zimbabwean soldiers took over in April 2004, they engaged only 100 workers (Wasosa, 28 January 2005). More than 20 000 workers lost their jobs when Kondozi Farm in the Mutare District of Manicaland Province was seized by riot police and ZANU-PF supporters on 19 July 2005 (Poverty Reduction Forum Trust, 2013).

The national unemployment levels among former farm workers

18

clearly illustrate the ruinous impact of land seizures on the livelihoods of many ordinary Zimbabweans. By December 2001, about 30 000 farm workers had lost their jobs (Food and Agricultural Organisation, December 2001). The General Agriculture and Plantation Workers Union of Zimbabwe (GAPWUZ) stated that employment for its members decreased from 500 000 in 2000 to 200 000 in 2008. As a result, the union's membership declined to 25 000 in 2008 from 150 000 before the land seizures (Chikwanha, 4 May 2014). The Internal Displacement Monitoring Centre, a Non-Governmental Organisation (NGO) based in Geneva, estimated that about 1 million farm workers lost their jobs from farm invasions during the period 2000-2010 (Zimbabwe Human Rights NGO Forum, 2010). Over 50% of the permanent female farm workers lost their jobs while 60% of the seasonal female workers became jobless and 30% and 33% of their male counterparts respectively lost their jobs. This also left between 1.8 million and 2 million (approximately 20% of the total population of Zimbabwe) dependants of former farm workers destitute (Sachikonye, 2003).

In addition to losing their jobs, most former farm workers were left homeless together with their dependants. When, for instance, Kondozi Farm in Manicaland Province was seized in July 2005, scores of displaced workers who included women, children and the elderly were stranded along the road outside the farm with their life-long belongings while others congregated at nearby business centres. On 21 July, a 70-member delegation comprising chiefs and headmen from the surrounding Marange rural area, most of whose subjects had been employed at the farm, approached the then country's Vice President, Joseph Msika, seeking a reversal of the evictions for the sake of the livelihoods of its black workers (Kahiya and Mukaro, 22 July 2005). Their pleas fell on deaf ears and a "humanitarian crisis" set in (Ibid: 1).

While some workers displaced from farms in various parts of the country returned to their homes, others had nowhere to go. Most of those who got stranded included foreign migrant workers from neighbouring countries such as Zambia, Malawi and Mozambique, constituting approximately 20% of the displaced farm labourers (Mamdani, 2008), who had lost contact with their homes and had

19

taken up permanent residence at the farms where they worked. There were also Zimbabweans who had been born and bred at the farms where they worked and had no close family members and relatives to accommodate them. To aggravate the plight of displaced workers, most of them were not allocated land. Only less than 5% of the displaced farm workers received land under the government's land redistribution exercise (Sachikonye, 2003). In February 2003, more than 150 000 displaced farm labourers and their families were homeless (Watson, 1 March 2003). By 2004, between 45 000 and 70 000 permanent farm workers had been displaced with nowhere to go (Chambati and Moyo, 2004). As the examples below illustrate, such conditions of destitution resulted in the prevalence of begging across the country.

Vasco Roberto, 72-year-old man of Mozambican origin, explained how he came to reside in a squatter settlement outside Chimanimani town in south-eastern Zimbabwe after the seizure of Charleswood Coffee Estate in April 2004. He had worked and stayed at the farm since 1968 and had lost contact with his family and relatives back home in Mozambique. After retiring, he was being looked after by his son who also worked at the farm. After the farm was seized, his son was not employed by the new farm owner who had taken over. Following their eviction, they settled in a squatter settlement on the outskirts of Chimanimani town where they initially survived from the proceeds of begging by his three grandchildren until his son began to earn substantial income from illegal gold-panning in the nearby mountains of Musanditeera (Roberto, Interview, Chimanimani Town: 2014).

Narrating his ordeal following their eviction from Kondozi Farm in 2005, James Arimenda (61) stated that two of his children had resorted to panhandling since they had nowhere to go and nothing to eat. He had been born and bred at Kondozi Farm where his parents, both of Malawian origin, worked and lived. He also became a worker at the farm from the mid-1970s. At the time of eviction in 2005, his three children aged 18, 16 and 12 years were learning at the nearby Odzi Secondary School. The seizure of Kondozi Farm left him destitute without employment, shelter, food and means to pay for his children's school fees. His children withdrew from school since he could no longer afford their educational requirements. They set up a shack five kilometres away outside Odzi Township which became their permanent home. His two elder boys eked livelihoods as gold panners along the nearby Odzi and Odzani Rivers while the youngest one begged for alms in the Odzi Township (Arimenda, Interview, Odzi Township: 2013).

Some sections of the white population also resorted to begging after being rendered destitute by the farm seizures. Between 2000 and 2001, around 3 000 white farmers were evicted from their farms (Chibber, 26 July 2014). The farm invasions reduced the number of commercial farmers in the country from 4 500 to only 450 by February 2004 (Cross, 2004). By 31 December 2009, only 300 white commercial farmers remained on their farms (*Voice of America*, 31 December 2009). The Internal Displacement Monitoring Centre reported that more than 3 000 white commercial farmers were evicted during the period 2000-2010 (Zimbabwe Human Rights NGO Forum, 2010).

While considerable numbers of displaced white commercial farmers either relocated to their remaining premises within the country or fled abroad to reunite with their families or venture into other businesses, others became destitutes in Zimbabwe. A white beggar at the corner of Leopold Takawira and Robert Mugabe streets in Bulawayo, Zimbabwe's second largest city, told the *Zimbabwean* that he began panhandling in 2007 after his grandfather's farm in Shangani had been seized by the government (Sigauke, 24 March 2015; Sithole, 28 March 2012). At a shopping centre in Eastlea Suburb, just outside Harare's Central Business District, as Benedict Unedoro (11 April 2008) noted in early 2008:

> Five destitute white men, aged between 30 and 60, have thrown pride and caution to the wind and beg openly. They marshal cars into parking bays and offer to clean and guard them while the owners do their shopping. The shoppers are mostly well-to-do black people and the poor whites do not seem to mind begging from blacks.

An informal survey conducted by the *Voice of America Studio 7* in 2015 revealed how the country's inexorable socio-economic woes

21

had seen "members of the white community in particular and other minorities, begging on the streets of Harare or doing menial tasks and even seeking treatment in public hospitals" (Chifera, 4 September 2015: 1). This clearly illustrates that, as the rates of hunger, poverty and destitution escalated in Zimbabwe, racial divisions among the impoverished people increasingly became blurred.

The socio-economic afflictions of ordinary Zimbabweans worsened during the period 19 May to 27 July 2005 when the government launched Operation *Murambatsvina* (Clean-up) supposedly to clear urban and peri-urban areas of vice and squalor. During the operation, the police, army and municipal authorities demolished squatter settlements, flea markets, tuck-shops, vending stalls and home industries (Duri, 2010). The operation severely disrupted the informal sector which was sustaining the livelihoods of more than four million citizens and contributing 25% to the Gross Domestic Product (GDP) in a country where unemployment was more than 80% (Duri, 2014). During a study conducted by Action-Aid International, an NGO, together with the Combined Harare Residents Association in August 2005, 79% of the interviewees indicated that the operation had deprived them of their sources of survival and they were living on the margins of poverty as a result (*Standard*, 14 August 2005). During the ruthless blitz, 32 500 informal sector enterprises countrywide were demolished and an estimated 97 550 people, the majority of who were women, lost their means of survival (US Government, 2009). More than 700 000 people were left homeless and without sources of survival and over 2 million were reduced to paupers (Fuller, 2012; UN, 12 August 2005; Tibaijuka, 2005). Some local NGOs claimed that more than one million people were displaced countrywide (*Zimbabwe Independent*, 17 June 2005). It was estimated that more than 2 million people, or over 15% of the country's population, were indirectly affected by loss of customers, employees or markets due to demolitions and evictions (Schaefer, 23 March 2007; Tibaijuka, 2005).

The operation left several people homeless, particularly local Zimbabweans who did not have rural homes and foreigner workers, mostly labour migrants from Malawi, Mozambique and Zambia since the colonial period, who had taken permanent residence in the country together with their descendants. In Harare alone, over 300 000 families were reportedly displaced (*Standard*, 12 June 2005). As if to add insult to injury, no immediate measures were put in place by the authorities to resettle the evictees (*Zimbabwe Independent*, 3 June 2005). As Leslie Gwindi, the then Harare City Council's spokesperson, proclaimed in early June 2005: "All we are saying is that we want all illegal structures to be removed. And we will not look for other places for them because how did they come to be where they are staying now?" (Cited in Dongozi, 5 June 2005: 6; Duri, 2010: 49). His sentiments were echoed by Edmore Veterai, the then Zimbabwe Republic Police (ZRP) Officer Commanding Harare Police Province, who commanded: "...They (evictees) must go where they belong. No one in Zimbabwe comes from nowhere. Everybody belongs somewhere" (cited in Dongozi, 5 June 2005: 6; Duri, 2010: 50). Caesar Zvayi, the then editor of the state-sponsored *Herald*, reiterated: "Zimbabweans are unique in that they have both a rural and urban home" (Duri, 2010: 50; Zvayi, 7 July 2005: 9).

Graphically, the demolition of shack settlements generated what Joost Fontein (2005) termed "negative seismic effects of tsunami proportions" given that most evictees were left stranded with nowhere to stay and nothing to eat and basically, without livelihoods. In total, about 70% of the urban population lost their shelter and/ or employment (Schaefer, 23 March 2007). In some cases, the government simply bundled destitute evictees into trucks and dumped them in the remote countryside unknown to the victims thereby creating an internal refugee crisis in a country that was not at war (Dube, 2010). In July 2005, for instance, a 40-year-old man died outside the Tsholotsho District Administrator's office where he and 100 others had been dumped by the police after their shack settlements had been destroyed in Bulawayo (*Voice of America Studio 7 News Bulletin*, 31 October 2005). Josiah Rugara, a 40-year-old destitute who was surviving on begging in Masvingo town in December 2010, stated: "We have no home, we live in a shack. Our homes were destroyed during the *Murambatsvina* (Clean-up) operation. We live on begging" (*Radio VOP*, 24 December 2010). Children were also caught up in the blitz and more than 300 000 of them dropped out of school due to the demolitions, evictions and relocations (US

Government, 2009). The operation, therefore, ranked "among the world's worst government-created humanitarian disasters" (Schaefer, 23 March 2007: 1).

As if these problems were not enough, the Zimbabwean industry was collapsing at an unprecedented rate thereby raising the levels of unemployment, poverty and destitution among the majority of the citizens. The seizure of commercial farms largely contributed to plunging the country into a phase of deindustrialisation and aggravated the impoverished situation of ordinary Zimbabweans. The compulsory acquisition of farms was a flagrant violation of property rights and this had, among other things, negative implications on the investment climate in Zimbabwe (Richardson, 2005). Many prospective foreign and domestic investors shied away. Foreign direct investment inflows into the country fell from US$103 million in 2005 to US$40 million in 2005. While foreign direct investment inflows improved to US$66 million in 2007, they slumped to US$44 million in 2008 (*Scoop Independent News*, 15 January 2010). In addition, the collapse of the manufacturing sector, particularly clothing and textiles, partly emanated from the decline in agricultural production, their basic source of raw materials, which had been disrupted by the farm seizures. Several companies downsized their operations and retrenched workers amid speculation while others shut down (Yarns and Fibres, 15 April 2011). Consequently, the country plunged into an inexorable phase of deindustrialisation.

From 2000 to 2008, the collapse of the manufacturing sector, particularly clothing and textiles, was largely caused by the prevailing economic environment characterised by the violation of property rights, increasing speculation, and viability challenges in a hyperinflationary environment. Consequently, more than 700 companies had shut down by 2001. Production in the manufacturing sector plunged by 10.5% in 2001 to about 17.5% during the following year (Richardson, 2005). From 2009, the collapse of the manufacturing industry was largely associated with the prevailing negative monetary environment. Among others, entrepreneurs were now supposed to trade in foreign currency during this period and had to inject fresh capital which banks did not have due to tight liquidity. In addition, bank lending rates during this period were unsustainably high (Yarns and Fibres, 15 April 2011).

Aggravating the situation was the Indigenisation and Economic Empowerment Act promulgated in 2007, which eroded foreign investor confidence by obliging all non-Zimbabwean companies with equities of US$5 million and above to cede 51% shares to local entrepreneurs (Marongwe and Muguti, 2017; Murigo, 6 September 2014; *Sunday Mail*, 15 July 2012). Foreign investors already established in the country either closed or scaled down operations while prospective ones conveniently kept their distance from Zimbabwe. In 2013 alone, Zimbabwe witnessed 75 company closures and 9 617 job losses (*Harare 24 News*, 6 September 2014). The mining sector also faced serious viability challenges. Examples of mine closures between 2000 and 2009 include Shabani and Mashava (asbestos) (Mugodzwa, 2017), Mhangura (copper) and Kamativi (tin) (Matikinye, 11 December 2009).

The livelihoods of many ordinary Zimbabweans increasingly became jeopardised by escalating unemployment rates as a result of farm seizures and deindustrialisation. By the end of 2000, well over 300 000 employees out of the country's formal workforce of 1.3 million had lost their jobs (Hammar and Raftopoulos, 2003). From late 2002 into early 2003, the country's unemployment rate was in the region of 50-60% (Watson, 1 March 2003; Zeilig, 2002). By the end of 2003, only 30% of the population was in formal employment (Chiriga, 16 April 2011). Formal sector employment levels dipped from a peak of 1.4 million between 1981 and 1998 to about 998 000 in 2004 (*Bulawayo 24 News*, 22 April 2013). By 2005, unemployment was way beyond 80% (US Government, 2014; Women's Coalition of Zimbabwe, 2005). Some sources estimated that only 8% of adult Zimbabweans were formally employed in 2005 (Mukaro, 3 June 2005). In November 2006, more than 8 million people, out of a total population of about 13 million, were unemployed (*Relief Web*, 22 November 2006). At the height of Zimbabwe's socio-economic malaise in 2008, only 6% of the population was employed in the formal sector. Thus, out of an estimated total population of more than 13 million people in 2008, only 480 000 were in formal employment (Chiriga, 16 April 2011). From 2009 into 2010, the unemployment rate spiked to around 94% (Ibid; *Mail and Guardian*,

29 January 2009). In 2010, hardly 7% of the population was employed in the formal sector (*Scoop Independent News*, 15 January 2010). In April 2011, only 850 000 people were formally employed. This employment figure equalled that of 1970, some 4 decades down the line. Most of the formally-employed were civil servants since most of the primary and secondary industries had virtually collapsed (Chiriga, 16 April 2011). According to the ZCTU, between 5 000 and 6 000 workers further lost their jobs in 2012. Only around 500 000 people were believed to be employed in the formal sector in the same year (Dube, 12 June 2013). In 2013, the unemployment rate shot up to a record 95% (*My Zimbabwe News*, 25 August 2013; US Government, 2014).

Such harsh socio-economic conditions led some impoverished people to seek livelihoods through irregular means such as begging since the formal sector had virtually collapsed. As Potts (2006: 279) argued: "If the formal sector cannot provide, self-employment is the answer, and if city by-laws and government policy and development agencies deem this 'informal' and 'illegal', so be it." Thus, some former breadwinners and their dependents begged for alms in order to survive.

The Zimbabwean government increasingly became bankrupt as a result of the poor performance of the economy. Revenue inflows into state coffers in the form of corporate and individual taxes, royalties and other sources related to the economy dwindled considerably as a result of farm seizures, deindustrialisation, high unemployment levels, and increasing international isolation. In addition, the international community became reluctant to bail out the government with balance-of-payment support owing to the repulsive investment climate. The cumulative effect of these developments was the decimation of the country's economy which fell by 5% in 2000, 8% in 2001, 12% in 2002, and around 18% in 2003 (OECD, 2004). Increasing international isolation, deindustrialisation, and other negative socio-economic developments resulted in the drastic fall of government revenue. Thus, from 2001, Zimbabwe recorded a budget deficit for every year up to 2008 (Bulter, 1 July 2013). The government increasingly became bankrupt and severely incapacitated to provide basic social services to the majority of its citizens. As poverty rates escalated and living standards plummeted, considerable sections of the society embarked on several informal pursuits of survival such as begging.

Worsening Zimbabwe's bankrupt condition was the government's close involvement in the war in the Democratic Republic of Congo (DRC) from October 1998 to 2002. Mugabe's unilateral decision to send troops to the DRC to assist the government of Laurent Kabila to fight rebels costed Zimbabwe about US$1 million per day (Dzinesa, 2000; Fuller, 2012). During the war, Zimbabwe deployed more than 13 000 of its troops at an estimated total cost of US$1 billion (Johwa, 10 September 2004). This was extremely extravagant for a bankrupt state like Zimbabwe. In a desperate bid to boost state revenue, the government started to print paper money, a situation that fuelled inflation (Bond and Manyanya, 2002). The involvement in a costly, unnecessary and unpopular war resulted in many international donors withdrawing funding to Zimbabwe, a development which worsened bankruptcy on the part of the government (Mamdani, 2008). Under these conditions, it was thus little surprising that in 2004, Zimbabwe's economy witnessed a negative GDP growth of - 13.6% (*Economy Watch Content*, 9 April 2010).

The economy shrunk by 34% between 1998 and 2005. Per capita GDP fell by 38% between 1998 and 2005 (Schaefer, 23 March 2007). During the period 2004-2006, the economy shrunk by 30% (Gilpin, 1 August 2008). Zimbabwe's GDP fell from US$6.86 billion in 2000 to US$4.42 billion in 2008 (Bulter, 1 July 2013). According to the IMF Report, the country's GDP slumped by 14% in 2008 alone (*Scoop Independent News*, 15 January 2010). As the government increasingly became cash-strapped it embarked on excessive borrowing to the effect that the country's debt in 2008 equalled 131% of its GDP (Bulter, 1 July 2013). Between 2004 and late 2008, the economy contracted by more than 50% (Chiriga, 16 April 2011). In the 2008 financial year, the country experienced a negative GDP growth of - 14.1% with an external debt of US$5.821 billion (*Economy Watch Content*, 9 April 2010). It was only in early 2009 that the Zimbabwean government declared bankruptcy and introduced a multi-currency monetary system (Bulter, 1 July 2013).

With the setting up of the GNU, Zimbabwe's economy somewhat rebounded in 2009 to record a yearly growth of 5.7%. It further grew by 8.1% in 2013 (*Trade Mark Southern Africa*, 1 July 2011). These positive developments largely emanated from the relative macroeconomic stability resulting from the multi-currency regime introduced in 2009, effective budgetary mechanisms, and the improvement of the security situation as a result of the establishment of a GNU. Investor confidence, however, remained marginal and liquidity challenges persisted making it difficult for the government to significantly improve the living standards of its majority citizens. In late January 2013, for example, Zimbabwe's public account had only US$217 left as cash-on-hand in the bank and had to be bailed out by an undisclosed donor (Tanquintic-Misa, 31 January 2013).

These financial developments had far-reaching negative consequences on the livelihoods of ordinary Zimbabweans. The bankrupt Zimbabwean government became financially disabled to meet even the very basic needs of most of its suffering citizens. Those famished by droughts and floods, as well as food shortages resulting from farm seizures and company closures awaited the mercy of international donors while the government's social-service institutions became white elephants. The same applied to other vulnerable people such as the retrenched, the unemployed, HIV-AIDS victims, malnourished children, elderly people, orphans, and destitute widows and widowers while the government increasingly became a helpless onlooker. It should be noted, however, that aid from donors, particularly international humanitarian organisations, did not meet all the needs of all impoverished Zimbabweans. In addition, the supply of international relief aid was erratic as it was sometimes cut by the government in a desperate attempt to conceal its battered image (Dugger, 4 June 2008), or sometimes ended up in ZANU-PF hands from where it was distributed selectively to reward its supporters and starve opposition sympathisers (Harawa, 20 August 2013; Human Rights Watch, 25 October 2003; *World Press*, 4 June 2008). Thus, voracious Zimbabweans improvised a broad range of informal strategies such as begging in order to make ends meet in a livelihood-threatening environment.

In an attempt to address its economic nightmares partly by

funding the ever-increasing budget deficit, the government blundered by routinely printing paper money up to 2009 (*Nation Master*, 4 February 2010). The currency became virtually worthless and hyperinflationary rates shattered world-record levels. The basic commodities available in the country became unaffordable to the majority of the population owing to the unprecedented rates of inflation which had rendered the local currency virtually useless. In June 2002, the country's annual inflation rate was pegged at 113 % (Oxfam, 10 June 2002). In October 2002, it rose to 144% (Watson, 2003). As the government continued to print valueless money, the most hyperinflationary period in Zimbabwean history which broke world records began in 2004 (Murigo, 6 September 2014).

In November 2005, the inflation rate hiked to 400% (Wines, 2 May 2006). Hardly a month later in mid-December 2005, it was pegged at 585% (*CNN*, 19 December 2006). In February 2006, the government admitted to printing paper money worth ZW$21 trillion to buy US dollars (Wines, 2 May 2006). The inflation rate shot up from 914% in March 2006 to 1 000% in May during the same year (Wines, 2 May 2006), developments which prompted the World Bank to declare Zimbabwe "the fastest-shrinking economy outside of a war zone" (Perryer, 7 October 2019: 1). As inflation rates continued to escalate, the prices of basic commodities increasingly became unaffordable. In 2006, for example, the price of a loaf of bread rose sharply to ZW$80 000 from ZW$35 000 in 2004 (Bulter, 1 July 2013).

Inflation rates spiralled to 1 300% in February 2007 (Sithole, 7 February 2007). In March 2007, the inflation rate reached 1 700% making it the highest in the world (Duri, 2014; *Reuters Alert*, 20 March 2007; Schaefer, 23 March 2007). It skyrocketed to around 2 200% in May 2007, 3 700% in June 2007 and over 4 500% by 10 July 2007. This escalating rate of inflation throughout 2007 implied a doubling of prices of basic commodities every month and a hike of 2.33% per day (Sokwanele, 20 July 2007). In November 2007 inflation rocketed to 8 000% (Zimbabwe Institute, 13 November 2007). Consequently, the price of a loaf of bread rose by over 300% from October 2007 to early January 2008. Between November 2007 and January 2008, the prices of white sugar, cooking oil and beef went up by between 60% and 250% (*Irin News*, 13 March 2008).

World record hyperinflation levels continued to be shattered as Zimbabwe reached the 100 000% mark in March 2008 (*Irin News*, 13 March 2008). In January 2008, ZW$10 000 could buy a full chicken but on 27 March 2008, it bought only two eggs (*Inflationomics*, 27 March 2008). As the economy reached its negative climax, inflation rocketed to an astronomical 11.2 million per cent in June 2008 (Berger, 9 October 2008). As a result of spiralling inflation, the Zimbabwean dollar depreciated three-fold in June 2008. By mid-July, the annual rate of price increases exceeded 2 million per cent (Gilpin, 1 August 2008). By September 2008, it had spiralled to more than 11 million per cent (UN, September 2008). Inflation shot up to 231 million per cent in October 2008 (Berger, 9 October 2008; Chibber, 26 July 2014). After the Reserve Bank of Zimbabwe (RBZ) had knocked off three zeros from its currency in order to make it easier to compute, a loaf of bread which cost ZW$500 in early August 2008 cost between ZW$7 000 and ZW$10 000 in early October of the same year (Berger, 9 October 2008). In November 2008, the monthly inflation rate reached a record 79.6 billion per cent, second only to Hungary in 1946 (Fuller, 2012). In December 2008, the IMF reported that the inflation rate had reached 500 billion per cent (*Thomson Reuters Foundation*, 2014). Throughout 2008, inflation reigned supreme and the currency was devalued "to such an extent that a wheelbarrow full of notes would not even buy a loaf of bread" (Perryer, 7 October 2019: 1). As salaries increasingly became eroded by spiralling inflation, several workers became paupers forcing them to seek alternative sources of survival. In 2008 alone, more than 30 000 Zimbabwean teachers left the profession and 10 000 were believed to have gone to South Africa to seek alternative livelihoods (Moshenberg, 28 January 2009).

The paradox of this rabid monetary environment was that while the Zimbabwean dollar was so difficult to get in view of the high unemployment rates in the formal sector and dwindling informal opportunities of obtaining income, it was virtually worthless because of spiralling inflation. The majority of Zimbabweans, driven to the margins of destitution and with very limited options of survival at their disposal, ventured into various livelihood-earning pursuits such as begging from the remaining few who could manage to part with some donations in cash or kind. On 28 March 2012, for example, the *Zimbabwean* reported an influx of white destitutes in Zimbabwean towns some of who were being fed by local churches while the others survived from begging. A white destitute interviewed along the streets of Bulawayo in March 2012 told the *Zimbabwean* that having retired from the National Railways of Zimbabwe (NRZ) in 2006, his pension and other benefits were eroded by inflation (Sithole, 28 March 2012).

Poverty, therefore, became endemic for many ordinary people in Zimbabwe from 2000. In 2002, it was estimated that 76% of the population was living below the poverty datum line as a result of the prevailing socio-economic problems which were compounded by droughts. As poverty rates escalated, Zimbabwe became one of the most unequal societies in the world (Zeilig, 2002). In early 2004, 68% of the Zimbabwean population was living below the poverty line (US Government, 2014). Between 2004 and 2009, more than 50% of Zimbabwe's employable population, the majority of who were wallowing in grinding poverty, was surviving from remittances brought in by family members, relatives and friends in the diaspora (Chiriga, 16 April 2011). By the end of 2006, over 80% of Zimbabweans were battling poverty (*Relief Web*, 22 November 2006; Schaefer, 23 March 2007). In mid-2008, the then Botswana President, Retired Major General Ian Khama, described Zimbabwe as a big refugee camp full of suffering and misery (*News from Africa*, November 2008). By the end of 2008, Zimbabwe had become a factory for poverty with 10 million out of more than 13 million of its people living in on the margins of destitution (Moshenberg, 28 January 2009). Despite being victims of their government's economic blunders and ecological disasters, significant numbers of impoverished Zimbabweans did not sit idly and bemoan their predicament. Instead, they improvised a plethora of informal mechanisms such as emigration, seeking refuge in foreign countries and panhandling to salvage livelihoods.

The rugged monetary and hyperinflationary terrain was significantly levelled by the institutionalisation of a multi-currency fiscal system from February 2009 (*Thomson Reuters Foundation*, 2014). Inflation was contained and prices stabilised (*Bulawayo24 News*, 18

January 2011). International isolation of the country somewhat eased and basic commodities reappeared on shop shelves (Chagonda, 20-21 December 2011). Lamentably, the livelihoods of most ordinary Zimbabweans did not improve accordingly. Unemployment rates remained high as potential investors remained speculative and without confidence. Tight liquidity remained problematic for most ordinary Zimbabweans. Liquidity challenges also continued to incapacitate the government from implementing poverty-alleviation and other welfare programmes for its people. According to UNICEF, at least 6.6 million Zimbabweans could not meet their basic needs and about 3.3 million children were chronically hungry in April 2010. In addition, 78% of Zimbabweans were absolutely poor and 55% of the population were living under the food poverty line (Dube, 8 April 2010). By the end of October 2011, Zimbabwe had become one of the poorest countries in the world where at least one in every two people lived below the poverty line (*Humanium*, 6 November 2011). In November 2011, close to 15% of Zimbabwean children were not attending school and more than 30% of all children under the age of five years were suffering from chronic malnutrition (Ibid).

Given these circumstances of dire need in which disabled persons were one of the worst affected sections of the population, begging became a critical survival option in Zimbabwe. As Watson Khupe, a Zimbabwean disability activist, noted in 2010:

> Although begging has never been legally condoned by modern societies, in present-day Zimbabwe, no rational person can condemn begging by persons with disabilities. Begging is considered as a normal way of raising some income. There is also a misconception that begging is an enjoyable venture. It is not a passion and it will never be a hobby. It must be noted that even those who are involved in begging do not enjoy it. It is simply a last resort to the oppressed, marginalised and unemployed disabled persons (Khupe, 19 April 2010: 1).

The harsh political environment in Mugabe's Zimbabwe from 2000

Zimbabwe's socio-economic degeneration took place in a political

32

environment routinely typified by violence. Much of the political violence was engineered by the then President Robert Mugabe's ruling ZANU-PF, a party that played a prominent role in the war of liberation from British colonial rule and had been in power since independence in 1980, against the main opposition MDC led by Morgan Tsvangirai. The orgy of terror from 2000 took various forms which included intimidation, torture, beatings, detentions, killings and invasion of business premises (Marongwe, 2012, Sachikonye, 2011). Besides perpetuating the condition of poverty among the majority of the population, political violence actually aggravated it in various ways. The violent political climate had negative economic implications. The government became hopelessly bankrupt as it increasingly became isolated from the greater part of the international community; inflation skyrocketed to unprecedented world-record proportions; business was severely disrupted and almost ground to a halt; many domestic and foreign investors, and tourists avoided the country; the unemployment rate soared; food and other basic services became scarce; millions of people were displaced and poverty became entrenched among the majority of Zimbabweans (Raftopoulos, 2009). The options of survival became very limited as many Zimbabweans improvised a multiplicity of informal strategies to eke livelihoods. Under such dire conditions of abject poverty, the number of Zimbabwean beggars within the country and abroad rose sharply.

What sparked off political violence in 21st century Zimbabwe were the results of the February 2000 referendum which did not go in favour of the ruling party, ZANU-PF. The plebiscite was held to determine people's opinions on a proposed constitution that had been drafted largely by ZANU-PF supporters and apologists. By implication, one of the clauses of the proposed constitution could have given the then President Mugabe, who had been in power for two decades, the right to rule the country for 10 more years. The MDC and the NCA capitalised on the discontentment among the general population over the government's implementation of austerity measures under ESAP to de-campaign the ZANU-PF-crafted constitution. The draft constitution was rejected by 55% of the 1 312 738 people who voted. A post-referendum analysis showed that the majority of the negative votes had come from the urban areas (Meredith, 2002). The results of the referendum were generally viewed as a resounding victory for the opposition MDC and a crushing defeat for the ruling ZANU-PF. The ruling party did not take the result kindly as it represented its first electoral defeat since independence in 1980. Worse still for ZANU-PF, parliamentary elections were due in June 2000 (Raftopoulos, 2003). The outcome of the plebiscite therefore set the stage for belligerent politics in 21st century Zimbabwe.

The period between the February referendum and the June parliamentary elections in 2000 was "the most violent in the country's history" (Hill, 2003: 239), worse than violence in the liberation war times. Infuriated by the results of the referendum, Mugabe, literally unleashed the "...degree in violence" (Meredith, 2002: 233) on to the population. Nathan Shamuyarira, the then ZANU-PF's Information Secretary, weighed into the justificatory discourse of deploying violence by proclaiming that violence is "an area where ZANU-PF has a very strong, long and successful history" (Ibid). Soon after the referendum, Mugabe declared war on the political opposition and went on to appoint a "war cabinet" (Churches in Manicaland, 2006: 180). He castigated the white people, particularly commercial farmers, for reversing the gains of the liberation struggle by supporting the MDC. He called upon the former freedom fighters (war veterans) and civilians to confiscate commercial farms, most of which belonged to the whites. In a statement sanctioning the seizure of white commercial farms, Mugabe said, "Our party must continue to strike fear in the heart of the white man, who is the real enemy" (Masunungure, 2004: 176). Consequently, most of the farms were taken over violently, and with loss of life in some instances, in accordance with Mugabe's instructions. A peace march organised by lawyers, churches, and civil groups such as the NCA in Harare on 1 April 2000 was disrupted by a group of war veterans and ZANU-PF supporters. The group was commanded by the then medical doctor and war veterans' leader, Chenjerai Hunzvi. Armed with dangerous weapons such as clubs, the gang chanted war songs and assaulted the demonstrators and innocent passers-by. Surprisingly, the police indiscriminately fired teargas into the crowd instead of apprehending the assailants (Meredith, 2002). At his surgery in Harare's Kuwadzana Suburb, Hunzvi went on to set up a torture camp to persecute political rivals (Feltoe, 2004).

During the run-up to the June 2000 parliamentary elections, state-sponsored violence was also extended to the rural areas and farms where the MDC was popular. In the largely rural province of Mashonaland Central, for example, Border Gezi, the then ZANU-PF Provincial Governor, declared a one-party state where the independent press and opposition election materials were not tolerated (Hill, 2003). Terror tactics in the rural areas and farmlands included general intimidation and severe beatings at public places, private premises and torture camps. The terror campaign in the countryside forced more than 10 000 people to flee to the towns (Feltoe, 2004).

The Amani Trust, a private organisation which studied the political climate that prevailed in Zimbabwe from mid-February to June 2000, recorded more than 35 000 incidents of politically-motivated violence, 91.2% of which were orchestrated by ZANU-PF supporters (Ibid). During the same period, more than 18 000 people, mostly MDC supporters and sympathisers, were subjected to a broad range of gross human rights violations (Masunungure, 2004). The pre-election violence claimed more than 120 lives, mostly those of opposition supporters (Hill, 2003). Those killed included six white farmers and 11 black farm workers (Mamdani, 2008).

These negative political developments had disastrous effects on the country's economy, image on the international arena, and the general well-being of its citizens. Political violence disrupted general peace and rendered the economic landscape virtually unsuitable for conducting normal business by both local and foreign investors and ordinary people. Political violence in general and farm invasions in particular, for example, displaced thousands of white farmers and their African employees, some of whom became destitutes. These developments created an internal refugee crisis in Zimbabwe's urban areas where thousands of people took refuge after fleeing the political violence that gripped the rural and commercial farming areas. Begging in the congested urban areas became more prevalent as some people sought to survive in a harsh socio-economic and political dispensation where both formal and informal livelihood options increasingly became fiercely contested.

State-sponsored political violence was accelerated after the June 2000 parliamentary elections largely because ZANU-PF had not won convincingly. The MDC had won 47% of the vote and taken most of the urban and peri-urban parliamentary constituencies (Feltoe, 2004). In view of its marginal parliamentary election victory largely earned though a relentlessly brutal campaign of violence and intimidation, and the local government elections that were due in 2001, a state of paranoia besieged the ruling party. Immediately after the election results were announced, soldiers and police details were deployed in Harare's residential areas supposedly "to stop any violent reaction to the election results" (Ibid, p.217). They raided bars and nightclubs where they scuttled celebrations by MDC supporters and sympathisers. They indiscriminately beat up patrons and passers-by in order "to demonstrate what the price was for voting against Mugabe" (Meredith, 2002: 194). In other parts of the country throughout 2000, ZANU-PF officials threatened the electorate with unprecedented violence if the ruling party lost the municipal elections that were due in 2001 (Ibid).

Despite the threats, intimidation and violence, ZANU-PF performed dismally in the 2001 municipal elections. In Bulawayo, for example, the ruling party lost by a humiliating margin of 12 000 votes to 60 000 (Mugabe, 2001). This set the stage for another phase of political violence ahead of the presidential elections that were to be held in 2002. As one war veterans' leader warned the electorate: "If President Robert Mugabe loses the election, you people in the cities who voted 'no' during the referendum are in for a very tough time because we will teach you and your white masters a very big lesson" (Raftopoulos, 2001: 19). Mugabe himself declared: "No matter what force you (MDC) have, this (Zimbabwe) is my territory and that which is mine, I cling (to) unto death" (Meredith, 2002: 236).

Throughout 2001, ZANU-PF supporters waged a relentless campaign of political terror. They seized copies of the independent press in various parts of the country (Ibid). The army began to retrain war veterans with a view to using them to harass opposition supporters and sympathisers. From April 2001, Hunzvi set up

36

"mobilisation bases" across the country which became springboards of waging terror campaigns in both the rural and urban areas (Ibid, p.211). In the urban areas, gangs of ZANU-PF supporters and war veterans raided several business premises in order to terrorise people ahead of the 2002 presidential elections. In Harare, the invaded premises included a transport firm, a bakery, a departmental store head office, a child-care home, a training centre, a dental surgery, a safari company, premises of a soccer club and Avenues Clinic in Harare "where fifteen (medical) operations were under way" (Meredith, 2002: 212). By May 2001, more than 300 business premises had been violated countrywide (Ibid). In addition, several MDC campaign rallies ahead of the 2002 presidential elections were often violently disrupted by state security agents and ZANU-PF supporters (Hill, 2003).

Even though Mugabe won the presidential election, the victory was far from convincing considering the concerted efforts of violence that had been instituted. Mugabe won controversially by 56% of the votes against Tsvangirai's 42%. Again, as an analysis of the election results illustrated, Mugabe had got most of his votes from the countryside while Tsvangirai virtually swept the urban areas (Ibid). Predictably, various forms of violence were improvised by ZANU-PF in a desperate attempt to regain its political hegemony ahead of the parliamentary elections that were due in 2005. Among other things, the ruling party capitalised on the 2002 drought and countrywide crop failures to deny government food aid to opposition supporters. Besides using drought-relief aid to reward its loyalists, the ruling party also employed it as bait for potential supporters. The ZANU-PF government monopolised the importation and redistribution of maize, the staple grain, though its company, the Grain Marketing Board (GMB). Abednico Ncube, the then ZANU-PF government minister, threatened the opposition electorate with state-induced famine: "As long as you value the government of the day, you will not starve...You cannot vote for the MDC and expect ZANU-PF to help you...You have to vote for ZANU-PF candidates...before the government starts thinking your entitlement to food aid" (Meredith, 2002: 231). In 2002, when more than 50% of Zimbabwe's population of more than 13 million was on the margins of starvation, Didymus Mutasa, a senior ZANU-PF official, warned: "We would be better off with only six million people, with our own people who support the liberation struggle" (Ibid, p.231). In February 2005, Gordon Moyo, the then Chairman of the Bulawayo Agenda, a local civil rights group, bemoaned ZANU-PF's increasing use of conditional food aid as a political resource ahead of the parliamentary elections (*Standard*, 6 March 2005). As opposition support bases increasingly became famished, Archbishop Pius Ncube of the Roman Catholic Church lamented: "It is criminal what the government is doing. They do not care if people die. For the sake of political power, the government is willing to sacrifice the lives of thousands" (Meredith, 2002: 231). In July 2012, Elizabeth Takawira, a visually-impaired woman, explained how the politicisation of food aid by ZANU-PF and traditional chiefs in her rural Chivi District in Masvingo Province forced her to the city of Mutare in Manicaland Province to survive through begging:

> We were labelled MDC supporters by the traditional leaders in my home area. So when the relief food was distributed, they side-lined us. I became hopeless and desperate and decided as a last resort to come and beg here. I used to sleep in the backyards and sometimes would sleep in the shop verandas in Chivi before I came to Mutare... (Saxon, 11 July 2012: 1).

The ZANU-PF government's use of social violence in the form of conditional food aid prior to the 2005 parliamentary elections caused untold miseries for the already suffering majority of Zimbabweans, some of whom resorted to begging in order to salvage an existence. In March 2003, as the conditions of living continued to deteriorate, the MDC organised "the biggest anti-government urban protest in years" (Hammar and Raftopoulos, 2003: 15). During the two-day protest, most employees stayed away from work to demonstrate their dissatisfaction with ZANU-PF rule which had impoverished the majority of the population. In the major towns, business came to a standstill. Instead of addressing issues of poverty, the government responded ruthlessly through beatings and evictions. Consequently, 250 protesters were admitted to hospital, 500 officials and supporters of the opposition MDC were arrested, and more than 1 000 people were evicted from their homes (Ibid). The response of the government to the March 2003 demonstrations clearly manifested its insensitivity to the plight of the poor. After failing to tackle fundamental issues relating to poverty, the state aggravated the situation by torturing and displacing significant sections of the population. The evictions, in particular, drove several people to the margins of destitution thereby forcing more people into informal pursuits of survival such as panhandling.

State-sponsored political violence constituted by beatings, unlawful arrests, torture, general intimidation and killings, among other inhumane treatments, continued for the greater part of 2004. Between January and September 2004, according to the Human Rights NGO Forum, 12 people were killed during incidents of politically-motivated violence, 2 002 were arrested unlawfully, 7 491 were subjected to various forms of torture and 329 were physically assaulted (Chimhete, 3 April 2005; Chimhete, 1 May 2005). As a result of the upsurge in state-sponsored political violence, the MDC announced its withdrawal from contesting in any future elections on 26 August 2004. For five months, starting early September 2004 until the end of January 2005, the country's political landscape was relatively calm. The opposition party reversed its decision not to participate in elections on 3 February 2005 owing to the fact that the incidence of overt political violence had subsided (Duri, 2010).

Violence resurfaced in February 2005 soon after the MDC decided to contest in the elections. As the 31 March 2005 elections drew closer, violent incidents of political violence, mostly state-orchestrated, took place across the country. In February 2005, for example, the police scuttled a training session that had been convened by the MDC for its 120 parliamentary candidates (Dongozi, 6 March 2005). In the Guruve North Constituency on 2 March 2005, 11 MDC supporters were unlawfully arrested by the police for distributing election campaign materials. On the same day in Harare East Constituency, groups of ZANU-PF supporters in a government-owned bus travelled to various parts of the constituency pulling down MDC election campaign posters (*Standard*, 6 March 2005). During the same month, several MDC activists and sympathisers were apprehended in various parts of the country while distributing campaign materials (Dongozi, 5 June 2005). It was also during this month that Tendai Savanhu, the ZANU-PF candidate for Mbare Parliamentary Constituency, visited the main market in Harare's suburb of Mbare where he threatened to evict the vendors if his political party lost (Chimhete, 3 April 2005; 1 May 2005).

In the town of Norton, 11 MDC youths who were campaigning peacefully were brutally beaten up by ZANU-PF supporters. Their campaign fliers and regalia were seized and burnt (Dongozi, 5 June 2005). By March 2005, more than 10 aspiring MDC parliamentary candidates had been arrested in various parts of the country while campaigning or putting up posters (Dongozi, 5 June 2005). During the morning of 30 March 2005, a group of belligerent soldiers based at the Zimbabwe Military Academy, obviously acting on orders from their pro-ZANU-PF senior officials, went round the suburbs in the city of Gweru chanting war songs (*Standard*, 3 April 2005).

Political violence flared again during the aftermath of the March 2005 parliamentary elections whose results had confirmed the MDC's dominance in urban areas. ZANU-PF launched a vindictive campaign on opposition supporters and sympathisers in urban and peri-urban areas and selected rural targets. In April 2005, for example, reports abound of rural homes of opposition officials and supporters being put to flame in the provinces of Mashonaland West, Matabeleland South and Manicaland. In the rural areas of Mashonaland West Province, some villagers fled the violence and took refuge in the town of Karoi. In the Gwanda District of Matabeleland South Province, 45 MDC supporters and sympathisers were beaten up and denied food-aid by the state-owned GMB. In early April, six MDC supporters were reported to have taken refuge at their party's provincial headquarters in the city of Mutare after their homes in Makoni East rural constituency had been demolished by ZANU-PF supporters (Muleya, 8 April 2005). In the districts of Guruve, Murehwa South and Shamva, former MDC polling agents were beaten up and their possessions destroyed. The MDC chairperson for Ward 6 in Karoi town was brutally murdered by suspected ruling party supporters in April 2005 (Chimhete, 3 April 2005; 1 May 2005). In May, ZANU-PF youths raided two schools in

40

the Chihota area of Marondera District in Mashonaland East Province and chased away nine teachers after accusing them of sympathising with the MDC (Manyukwe, 17 May 2005).

These acts of political violence in the aftermath of the March 2005 parliamentary elections, largely perpetrated by the ruling ZANU-PF party, aggravated the impoverished condition of considerable numbers of Zimbabweans. The othering of certain poverty-ridden sections of the society deemed to be anti-ZANU-PF during the distribution of government food aid was tantamount to condemning them to death. Aggravating the situation was the abject destitution brought about by the displacement of some people, mostly opposition supporters and sympathisers, as a result of political violence. These conditions of untold afflictions tended to spur informal survival pursuits such as beggary in various parts of the country.

The 2005 post-election period was politically turbulent and significantly marked by ZANU-PF's violent acts of retribution against opposition MDC leaders and their supporters. In the immediate aftermath of the announcement of election results, ZANU-PF supporters from the Mbare Parliamentary Constituency in Harare, angered by their party's defeat, evicted six MDC supporters from their vending stalls at the main market in Mbare Suburb. The police declined to arrest the perpetrators even though they were well known in the Mbare residential area (Chimhete, 1 May 2005). From 19 May 2005, the ZANU-PF government took the campaign of vengeance to new levels and evicted thousands of people from the urban and peri-urban areas. This operation, code-named 'Murambatsvina', was launched on the pretext of cleansing the urban and peri-urban areas of vice and squalor but it is a fact that these were the very areas where the opposition MDC had the greatest number of supporters and sympathisers (see earlier sections for more). The disastrous impact of this blitz on the livelihoods of impoverished Zimbabweans has been discussed earlier on in this chapter. What needs to be emphasised here is that the political expediency that is the urge to eliminate political rivals through exclusion and displacement, by the ruling ZANU-PF government sacrificed the livelihoods of many citizens. Considerable sections of the society who were pauperised by the pogrom did not sit idly bemoaning their plight but devised a surfeit of irregular strategies such as begging in order to survive.

Incidents of overt political violence continued to escalate as the March 2008 harmonised elections neared (Fuller, 2012). Reports from NGOs indicated that over 3 463 people were tortured in 2007. The number of torture victims in 2008 more than doubled the 2007 figure (US Government, 2009). In addition, thousands of women belonging to opposition political parties, mostly from the MDC formations, were reported to have fallen victim to politically-motivated rape perpetrated by unscrupulous men loyal to Robert Mugabe (*Zimbabwean*, 22 August 2011). During the March 2008 pre-election violence, therefore, "no-one was spared…not the women, not the children, not the elderly" (Godwin, 2010: 105).

During the 29 March 2008 harmonised elections, both Tsvangirai and Mugabe failed to win an outright majority in the presidential race. Tsvangirai had 48% of the vote while Mugabe got 43%. A run-off election was therefore scheduled as required by the country's electoral laws. In view of the fact that Mugabe had lost the first-round vote to Tsvangirai, ZANU-PF-orchestrated violence against MDC supporters and sympathisers attained brutal proportions ahead of the second-round vote pencilled for 27 June 2008 (Scoones, 2013). In April 2008, for example, a group of medical practitioners was reportedly treating 157 people suffering from severe floggings and other forms of brutal torture at the hands of ZANU-PF supporters. On 19 April, Human Rights Watch reported that ZANU-PF supporters and apologists were setting up terror camps across the country to harass political opponents ahead of the second-round vote Reeler, 2008). August 2013). According to Tendai Biti, the then MDC Secretary General, 500 MDC supporters were assaulted, 400 were apprehended, 10 were murdered and 3 000 families evicted during April 2008 alone (Ibid). Between 29 March and 18 April, one person was killed and 240 were maimed during incidents of state-sponsored political violence (Amnesty International, 18 April 2008).

By 27 June 2008, the death toll resulting from acts of political violence by ZANU-PF supporters had reached 193. During the same period, the MDC charged that more than 200 of its members and apologists were missing and presumed dead (US Government, 2009). This orgy of terror had serious implications on the national economy and the prevalence of begging in Zimbabwe. Various forms of violence largely perpetrated by ZANU-PF on opposition supporters displaced many Zimbabweans, several of who were rendered destitute. While others were indirectly displaced by inhospitable conditions of general insecurity and fear of political violence and threats, others were either physically driven out of their homes, or had their premises put to flame by ZANU-PF arsonists. As some displaced people wandered without food and shelter in the wilderness, sometimes in neighbouring countries, considerable numbers resorted to begging from strangers in order to earn livelihoods. Ippo Mario, a 17-year-old Zimbabwean boy who begged in the South African town of Musina, for example, narrated how he had fled Zimbabwe after the ruling ZANU-PF party began attacking supporters of the opposition MDC following the disputed elections of 2008: "First, they burnt down my father's shop and threw stones through the glass. And one time they beat my father. That is when I decided to run away after my father was dead ... my mother ... is [also] deceased" (Scott, 2 November 2009).

After citing the prevalence of violence ahead of the second-round presidential race, Tsvangirai withdrew his candidacy on 22 June 2008 (Scoones, 2013). Mugabe went ahead with the 'election' and declared himself the winner amid controversy. Politically-motivated violence continued even after the 'elections' of 27 June. Between October and the end of December 2008, for example, about 32 people were abducted by state security agents and detained for up to 60 days before trial. By the end of 2008, 14 of the abductees were still missing (US Government, 2009). On the whole, political violence, largely propelled by ZANU-PF, resulted in more than 200 people losing their lives in 2008; over 5 000 were tortured and 36 000 were displaced (Human Rights Watch, 8 March 2011). In a study conducted in 2011 by the Research and Advocacy Unit (RAU), 52% of the female respondents reported having fallen victim to politically-motivated violence during the 2008 elections (*Zimbabwean*, 22 August 2011).

Tsvangirai refused to accept the results of the run-off presidential 'election'. The European Union (EU), the US and the United Nations (UN) condemned the second-round presidential 'election' and regarded it as a farce. The African Union (AU) recommended the formation of a power-sharing government and requested the Southern African Development Community (SADC) to mediate in the political impasse. SADC intervened and a GNU comprising ZANU-PF and two MDC factions led by Tsvangirai (MDC-T) and Arthur Mutambara (MDC-M) was constituted in February 2009. Under the new arrangement, Mugabe remained President. Tsvangirai became Prime Minister with Mutambara as his deputy (Scoones, 2013; Masunungure, 2009).

The formation of the GNU in February 2009 helped to reduce cases of overt political violence for the first 12 months of its existence. Incidents of overt violence resurfaced in 2010 during the constitutional outreach programme when public hearings in some parts of the country were prematurely ended by violent politically-motivated clashes between supporters of ZANU-PF and other political parties (Marongwe, 2013). During the outreach programme, more than 2 000 cases of political violence were documented by human rights organisations (*Africa Contact*, 26 May 2011). From 2011, ZANU-PF officials went round the country urging, and often compelling, people to sign a petition against Western countries and the US for imposing economic sanctions on Zimbabwe. In January 2011, an MDC-T youth activist from the town of Chitungwiza was beaten up by ZANU-PF supporters for refusing to sign the anti-sanctions petition (*Irin News*, 31 January 2011).

Even though the GNU reduced the incidence of overt political violence, it failed to effect major changes on both the macro and micro-economic environments that would significantly alleviate the plight of impoverished Zimbabweans. The fact that the GNU was a provisional political arrangement lasting from 2009 to 2013 marked a period of political uncertainty which had negative implications on the economy. Both domestic and foreign investors remained sceptical until a final political solution was found. In addition, the investment environment remained uncompetitive partly due to the country's suicidal indigenisation and empowerment laws which either chased or scared away investors. A July 2013 National Social Security

Authority (NSSA) Harare Regional Employer Closures and Registrations Report for the period July 2011 to July 2013 showed that 711 companies closed in Harare alone leaving 3 336 people jobless (Chitemba, 1 November 2013). This is to say, unemployment, deindustrialisation, liquidity problems and general poverty persisted during the tenure of the GNU. Most of the money available in Zimbabwe continued to flow out since most of the commodities on sale in the country were imported as result of deindustrialisation (Ndlovu, 6 April 2014). Cash-flow problems were also exacerbated by the hesitancy of institutions and individuals to deposit money in banks. This was largely in view of the precedence of the pre-2009 hyperinflationary environment in which savings were corroded and the banking and insurance sectors collapsed. In addition, some sections of the banking sector continued to collapse up to 2013 due to tight liquidity and poor corporate governance. Potential depositors were also discouraged by low interest rates for their savings and high charges for banking transactions (Chitemba, 1 November 2013; Ndlovu, 6 April 2014). The liquidity crunch was also perpetuated by the establishment of the multi-currency regime, dominated by the US dollar, in 2009. Even though inflation was contained, Zimbabwe lost its monetary sovereignty and could not manufacture its own notes and coins, a situation that contributed to the worsening of the liquidity crisis (Ndlovu, 6 April 2014).

It is a fact that the GNU brought about a period of relative political harmony and prosperity in the country. As already mentioned, international isolation eased and basic commodities reappeared on supermarket shelves. Inflation was contained largely through the introduction of the multi-currency system (Ndlovu, 6 April 2014. Lamentably, however, the investment climate remained pathetic, unemployment persisted, the liquidity crunch continued to grip the country and poverty became entrenched among the generality of the Zimbabwean population.

With the four-year tenure of the GNU ending in February 2013, and a general election due later during the same year, uncertainty and anxiety gripped many Zimbabweans, most of who were wallowing in abject poverty. The 2013 pre-election terrain was distinguishable more by covert than overt cases of political violence largely because of the peace efforts of the GNU and the supervisory roles of SADC and the AU. During this period, 83.3% of the recorded cases of politically-motivated violence were instigated by ZANU-PF supporters (Heal Zimbabwe Trust, 28 July 2013). In one of the overt cases in February 2013, the 12-year-old son of an MDC-T Deputy Organising Secretary in the Headlands rural area of Manicaland Province was burnt to death when suspected ZANU-PF supporters set fire to a hut in which he was sleeping (Mushava and Nleya, 25 February 2013). From January to July 2013, there was widespread intimidation across the country as ZANU-PF supporters indiscriminately demanded their party's membership cards from ordinary citizens and forced them to register as voters (Heal Zimbabwe Trust, 28 July 2013).

From various viewpoints, 2013 was indeed an anticipated turning point in which Zimbabwe failed to turn. The country was plunged into political chaos, economic uncertainty and further international isolation after the 31 July 2013 general elections. ZANU-PF won a parliamentary majority and Mugabe was declared the winner with 61% of the vote against Tsvangirai's paltry 34% amid claims of electoral irregularities from the opposition MDC factions, NGOs, the US and the EU (Scoones, 2013). These developments plunged the country into further international isolation (Ibid).

With Mugabe again in the driving seat, Zimbabweans now had to wait anxiously for the next general elections five years later in 2018 to see if the country's political fortunes would change for the better. It was during Mugabe's term in office after the controversial 2013 elections that internal power struggles rocked ZANU-PF leading to his ouster in November 2017. It was during this term that the then President Robert Mugabe became a nonagenarian and began manipulating political dynamics within ZANU-PF so that his wife, Grace, who was 40 years younger than him, would succeed him (Duri and Chikonyora, 2018). ZANU-PF's internal strife culminated in the Zimbabwe National Army intervening during the night of 14 November 2017 and the morning of the following day by seizing state television and placing the First Family under house arrest (*BBC News*, 21 November 2017; Duri and Chikonyora, 2018; Ndebele, 17 November 2017). Some of Grace's close allies were apprehended while others went into hiding (Ndebele, 17 November 2017). Mugabe resigned on 21 November 2017 as the Zimbabwean Parliament had initiated proceedings to impeach him (Levin, 4 December 2017). With the ousting of Mugabe, the 75-year-old Emmerson Mnangagwa, his former deputy, was sworn in as Zimbabwe's Interim President on 24 November 2017 (Duri and Chikonyora, 2018; Ma, 24 November 2017).

Mugabe's reign from 2000 certainly marked a dark episode in the political history of Zimbabwe. It was a forgettable era in which his ZANU-PF party sought to monopolise political space at any cost. ZANU-PF relentlessly harassed all forms of opposition through intimidation, torture, murder, manipulation of electoral processes and rigging. In the process, gross human rights violations were committed. ZANU-PF's use of violence, displacements and food aid politics on some sections of the population, among other things, pauperised many Zimbabweans, some of whom were forced to seek sustenance through begging.

State repression and socio-economic anguish in Mnangagwa's Zimbabwe

Zimbabwe's comatose economy remained on a never-ending downward spiral after the downfall of Mugabe. In fact, the plight of many Zimbabweans worsened owing to Mnangagwa's neoliberal economic policy that was punctuated by austerity measures in a multi-pronged effort to end international isolation, lure investment, resuscitate industry, boost revenue inflows and export earnings, and create more jobs. Unfortunately, this was not to be as the greater part of the international community did not trust Mnangagwa since he had been part of Mugabe's administration for a long time. Many foreign investors remained wary and sceptical, the manufacturing sector did not significantly recover, while revenue inflows and export earnings remained pathetic. Deindustrialisation persisted, the unemployment rate continued to rise, inflation spiralled and prices of basic commodities spiked. As government coffers dried up, the country continuously ran short of foreign currency, cash, fuel, electricity, medical drugs and many other basic commodities (Duri,

Marongwe and Mawere, 2019). The ever-rising cost of living and high poverty levels further condemned many Zimbabweans to beggary as they sought livelihoods.

From late 2017 when Mnangagwa came to power, Zimbabwe's economic performance continued on a downward spiral. Investors remained wary and the prospects of industrial rejuvenation remained elusive. At least 96 companies shut down in the first 15 months that Mnangagwa was in office. The company closures, which averaged six a month, included 20 in November 2017, 13 in December 2017, 13 in January 2018, and 9 in May 2018 (Ndlovu, 17 February 2019). The Zimbabwean economy shrunk by about 6% in 2019 (Elich, 14 February 2020; *Zimbabwe Independent*, 10 January 2020). In January 2020, Zimbabwe was rated as the second worst-performing economy in the world (*Zimbabwe Independent*, 10 January 2020).

Among other problems, the country continued to experience acute shortages of basic commodities and essential services owing to the depletion of foreign currency reserves, government bankruptcy, and the long running mismanagement of the economy, among other things (*Daily News*, 18 December 2018). From late 2018, for example, there were severe shortages of commodities such as fuel, gasoline, essential drugs and other basic foods such as bread (Ibid; Pigou, 18 January 2019; Runyanga, 19 November 2018; Sguazzin, Latham and Bax, 24 January 2019). The erratic availability of some basic commodities resulted in panic buying by those who could afford, causing further shortages (Pigou, 18 January 2018).

On 13 May 2019, the critical shortage of electricity prompted the Zimbabwe Electricity Transmission and Distribution Company (ZETDC) to impose rotating blackouts lasting up to 10 hours a day, "the worst the country had seen in three years" (*Zimbabwe Mail*, 22 May 2019: 1). The imposition of power cuts was meant to avert the risk of the country completely running out of electricity. The power shortage was caused by a host of factors such as low water levels at Lake Kariba where most of the electricity is generated, the ageing equipment at the main power plant and lack of funds, particularly foreign currency, for the importation of spare parts and refurbishment (Nyathi, 4 January 2020; *Zimbabwe Mail*, 22 May 2019).

In addition to impacting negatively on industrial production, fuel shortages and incessant power cuts severely jeopardised the livelihoods of the ordinary people. In December 2019, some of the country's listed companies such as Delta Corporation and Econet Wireless Zimbabwe said their viability was threatened by the widespread power cuts and foreign currency shortages. Delta, Zimbabwe's largest beverages manufacturer, for example, reported a 48% drop in half-year beer sales compared with the same period in 2018, after output and distribution had been constrained by shortages of fuel and electricity (Nyathi, 4 January 2020). Without power and fuel, there is no production. With limited electricity, for instance, many companies either shelved production or shut down resulting in the laying off of workers, most of who had very limited options of survival. As Jason Burke (10 August 2019), a journalist, noted: "Far from seeing reform after Robert Mugabe was toppled, the country has fallen into crisis as millions are reduced to paupers".

Unemployment rates continued to skyrocket as industrial rejuvenation remained a mirage (Runyanga, 19 November 2018). Having taken over a country that was in an advanced state of socio-economic decay, Mnangagwa largely failed to ameliorate the situation. In late 2017, more than 90% of Zimbabweans were unemployed and about 80% were desperately poor (Erasmus, 26 November 2017). By January 2020, about 95% of Zimbabweans were unemployed (Bhoroma, 31 January 2020; Elich, 14 February 2020). Given this dire situation, many Zimbabweans sought sustenance through informal means such as begging.

Numerous challenges such as deindustrialisation, the slump in export earnings and the scarcity of foreign currency fuelled inflation and aggravated the plight of many Zimbabweans as prices soared while disposable incomes shrunk. In October 2018, for example, the inflation rate stood at 20.85% (*New Zimbabwe*, 20 May 2019). By January 2019, the inflation rate had risen to 42% (Sguazzin, Latham and Bax, 24 January 2019). In February 2019, it stood at a high of 59.39% while the local Real Time Gross Settlement (RTGS) currency had fast depreciated to the rate of RTGS$3.0675 to US$1 (Mugabe, 12 April 2019). Hardly a month later in mid-March, according to the Zimbabwe Statistical Agency (ZIMSTAT), a government department, the inflation rate shot up to 66.8% even though some independent

49

economic analysts insisted that it stood at more than 200% (Chakanyuka and Mhlanga, 16 April 2019).

By April 2019, according to statistics from ZIMSTAT, the inflation rate had spiked to 75.86% (*New Zimbabwe*, 20 May 2019). In late May 2019, figures from the IMF indicated that Zimbabwe had the second highest inflation rate in the world at 78%, after Venezuela's 10 000 000% (Ndlovu, 28 May 2019; *Pindula News*, 4 June 2019). The inflation rate continued to soar and in June 2019, it stood at 175% (Marima, 19 August 2019; Muronzi, 27 September 2019). In August 2019, according to the IMF, Zimbabwe's annual inflation was 300%, making it the highest in the world at that time, having overtaken Venezuela which now came a distant second after its rate had drastically declined to 135.3% (Muronzi, 27 September 2019). In January 2020, independent analysts pegged Zimbabwe's inflation rate at 470% (*Newsday*, 30 March 2020). In late February 2020, government statistics provided by ZIMSTAT put the annual inflation figure at 540.16% even though Steve Hanke, a renowned American economist, placed the inflation rate at more than 1 096% (*Newsday*, 30 March 2020). In mid-April 2020, ZIMSTAT calculated the country's annual inflation at 673.39%, the highest rate since dollarisation in 2009 (Mhlanga and Mangudhla, 15 April 2020).

From 2019, the government aggravated the misery of many citizens by implementing neoliberal economic policies that involved tough austerity measures in a bid to attract international loans and investment. Among other things, the neoliberal economic measures involved scaling down government support for public entities, local authorities and social services; freezing of salaries and benefits of workers in state entities; putting in place a market-based foreign exchange; phasing out subsidies on basic commodities such as fuel and maize meal; currency devaluation, and deregulating prices (Elich, 14 February 2020). The neoliberal economic framework, together with the hyperinflationary environment, contributed towards the spiking of prices and severely eroded the livelihoods of many Zimbabweans. The government of Mnangagwa virtually became a clueless onlooker as the prices of basic commodities and other essential services spiked thereby eroding the disposable incomes of many already suffering citizens.

It is not an overstatement to posit that many Zimbabweans will best remember Mnangagwa's reign as a forgettable period of time during which price hikes of unprecedented magnitude took place. As prices of basic commodities skyrocketed, the cost of living shot up and chronic poverty stared in the faces of many Zimbabweans. In December 2018, the prices of basic commodities shot up by 42% (Ndlovu, 17 February 2019). On 12 January 2019, Mnangagwa announced a fuel price hike of over 200%, making it the highest in the world (Pigou, 18 January 2019). The increase in the price of fuel had knock-on effects on other commodity and service costs. In January 2019 alone, the prices of basic commodities spiked by 56.9% (Ndlovu, 17 February 2019). Between March 2018 and March 2019, the prices of basic commodities rocketed by an average of 66.8% (Chakanyuka and Mhlanga, 16 April 2019). The prices of most products went up by more than 300% within the space of 60 days, in March and April 2019 (*Pindula News*, 2 May 2019). As if this was not enough, the prices of petrol and diesel rose by nearly 50% on 21 May 2019, this being the second fuel price hike since January earlier in the year. The increase came after the Reserve Bank of Zimbabwe (RBZ) effectively removed a subsidy by ending a favourable United States dollar exchange rate for fuel importers (*Zimbabwe Mail*, 22 May 2019). In February 2020, Zimbabwe's gasoline price was the highest in the world (Elich, 14 February 2020). ZIMSTAT reported that the prices of goods and services went up by an average of 540.16% between March 2019 and March 2020 (*Newsday*, 30 March 2020).

As part of its austerity measures, the government did not adjust workers' salaries accordingly in a way that cushioned workers from inflation and price hikes (Chakanyuka and Mhlanga, 16 April 2019). It is a fact that neoliberal economic policies were "an assault on the Zimbabwean people" as they tended to "shift costs from the wealthy onto working people" (Elich, 14 February 2020: 1). Thus, the Zimbabwe Coalition on Debt and Development (ZIMCODD) slammed the government's austerity measures, arguing that they enabled inequalities to thrive and relegated ordinary people to paupers (Mhlanga, 26 January 2020).

It now becomes apparent that in Mnangagwa's Zimbabwe, economic dislocation reigned supreme while the majority of citizens endured a rude reality of misery and despair. The plight of the already-suffering Zimbabweans was aggravated by ecological disasters such as droughts and floods which rendered many of them food insecure. The severe drought during the 2018-2019 agricultural season, variously described as "the worst in living memory" (Corcoran, 28 November 2019: 1) and "the worst dry spell in a century" (Nyathi, 4 January 2020: 1), left most rural Zimbabweans critically food insecure, forcing many to seek sustenance through begging. Together with Cyclone Idai of early 2019, the drought caused serious food shortages and plunged the country into a humanitarian crisis at par with countries such as Yemen, Syria, the Democratic Republic of the Congo and South Sudan that were currently besieged by major internal conflicts (Corcoran, 28 November 2019). In August 2019, the UN estimated that about 30% of Zimbabwe's 16 million people needed humanitarian food aid due to drought and the worsening economic crisis (Marima, 19 August 2019). In January 2020, aid agencies estimated that 2.2 million Zimbabweans in urban areas were at risk of starvation while 5.5 million others in rural areas did not have adequate food (Nyathi, 4 January 2020). According to the World Food Programme, approximately 7.7 million people, nearly 50% the population, were in need of food aid until the end of 2020 (Corcoran, 28 November 2019). As an illustration, in November 2019, Georgina Zomba, a 62-year-old grandmother with six dependants who stayed in the Marange Communal Lands in the Manicaland Province, said the drought forced her to become a beggar: "I have two blind children, and since August we have begged at the bus station every day to get some money for food" (Ibid: 1).

As many Zimbabweans wallowed in poverty, Mnangagwa's government had little to offer due to perennial bankruptcy emanating from the poor performance of the economy. Not only was a considerable number of Zimbabweans at home reduced to beggars as a result of the inexorable socio-economic meltdown but also some of those who were abroad. In April 2019, for example, Zimbabwean students studying on state scholarship in Algeria were reportedly struggling to live decently without stipends as a result of government bankruptcy. This dire situation made some of the Zimbabwean students in Algeria to seek livelihoods through informal means such as begging and undertaking menial jobs (Mbanje, 13 April 2019). One of the concerned students outlined their plight as follows:

> Our government promised to give us annual stipends of US$3 000 every year to cater for our welfare. However, it turned out that no such money was disbursed since 2015. Our lives have become difficult and unbearable. We are halfway through the academic year and we have not received a penny (Ibid: 1).

Another student weighed in: "Some of us are working in construction sites where we are paid US$4 per day for nine hours and at times we are arrested after being perceived as immigrants" (Ibid: 1). "We are living from hand to mouth, begging from other nationalities, while some have had their gadgets confiscated for failing to pay off debts after borrowing from colleagues", said another (Ibid: 1).

Despite losing control of the economy, Mnangagwa's government was ever alert and very efficient when it came to the brutal suppression of popular protests against the ever-deteriorating living standards. The government's brutal response to protests against the hike in fuel prices in mid-January 2019 attests to this. On 13 January 2019, a day after the announcement of fuel price hikes, local civil society groups supported a call by the ZCTU for a three-day 'stay-away' or general strike (Ibid). Massive demonstrations ensued on 14 and 15 January 2018, mostly by young people, during which shops were looted while cars and buildings were burnt. The protests were concentrated in and around the main opposition strongholds, Harare and Bulawayo, but soon spread to other urban centres across the country (Ibid).

The government's response, which involved the deployment of the police and the army, was swift and vicious (Crisis in Zimbabwe Coalition, 7 February 2019; Pigou, 18 January 2019; Sguazzin, Latham and Bax, 24 January 2019). The government also blocked internet services in an effort to minimise networking among protestors (Pigou, 18 January 2019). The Zimbabwe Doctors for Human Rights (ZDHR) claimed that hundreds were shot while tens were killed. Soon after the demonstrations, the ZDHR was reportedly treating 107 patients for gunshot wounds and trauma (Ibid). According to the ZDHR, gunshot wounds accounted for 78 of the total number of people who were injured (Sguazzin, Latham and Bax, 24 January 2019).

On 18 January 2019, the Zimbabwe Human Rights NGO Forum published consolidated statistics of what transpired during the demonstrations of 14-15 January. The organisation reported that, as a result of the brutalities of the army and the police, 844 human rights violations were committed; 12 people died; 78 people were severely injured by gunshots; at least 242 cases of assault, inhumane and degrading treatment (including dog bites) were committed; and 466 arbitrary arrests and detentions were effected. Other violations included the invasion of privacy, obstruction of movement, and limitation of media freedoms and access to information (Pigou, 18 January 2019). The Crisis in Zimbabwe Coalition (7 February 2019) concurred that 12 civilians were shot dead but put the number of those who sustained gunshot wounds at only 80. It also reported that over 1 000 civilians were arrested "with the government giving the courts a directive to fast-track the trials of the arrested persons" (Ibid: 1). This directive irked many lawyers, some of whom took to the streets in protest against what they alleged to be the capture of the judiciary (Ibid).

Mnangagwa did not seem to show any regret to the state's heavy-handedness which had resulted in loss of lives and severe injuries during the January 2019 demonstrations. This was evidenced by a speech he delivered at a rally in the Mwenezi District of Masvingo Province on 16 February 2019 (Chitagu and Matiashe, 17 February 2019), part of which read: "Violent protestors burnt down buses and police stations and police cars. So, we said we do not want violence. So, we told soldiers to go and quell protests and the madness stopped. Now the country is at peace" (Muchenje, 1 March 2019: 1). Given the brute force that was used to quell the demonstrations, many Zimbabweans began to feel that Mnangagwa's administration was insensitive to their socio-economic plight.

As far as the severe socio-economic challenges that confronted many Zimbabweans during Mnangagwa's reign were concerned, the

United Nations' World Happiness Report summed it up all on 20 March 2019 by ranking Zimbabwe as the 146th unhappiest country out of 156 nations. The ranking used six indicators, most of which are socio-economic, to rank all countries in the world. The six variables are: a country's GDP per capita, social support, healthy life expectancy, freedom, generosity and absence of corruption (Munhendo, 22 March 2019; Zwinoira, 26 March 2019). Zimbabwe's poor ranking, besides being a strong indictment on the country's socio-economic and political environment under Mnangagwa, was not surprising given the prevalence of numerous challenges such as severe fuel shortages and long queues, liquidity crunch, high inflation, low productivity which constrains exports and employment opportunities, high fiscal and trade deficits, and grinding poverty (Zwinoira, 26 March 2019).

The theory of anomie, proposed by Robert Merton (1957) but largely borrowed from Emile Durkheim, is valuable in explaining how these conditions of torturous asperities, qualified by horrendous poverty, generated attitudes of despair among the many Zimbabweans prompting some of them to eke livelihoods through informal means. Anomie, according to Merton, is a psychological condition of stress or instability often signalled by a sense of futility, helplessness and pessimism, resulting from one's failure to meet personal needs and societal expectations. People caught up in this predicament, he argued, often attempt to meet such goals through illegitimate means; to them what matters most are the ends rather than the means. In applying Merton's theory to the Zimbabwean situation, begging was one of the means explored by some poverty-ridden people to cater for their needs and those of their dependants owing to the limited range of livelihood options in the crisis-ridden country.

So far, this chapter has explored Zimbabwe's rugged socio-economic and political terrain from 2000 which impoverished the generality of the population. It has also articulated how informal livelihood pursuits such as panhandling became widespread amid grinding conditions of poverty as formal survival options increasingly dwindled. People living with disability and children were the most vulnerable groups in this livelihood-wrecking environment and indeed they were the most visible section of the begging community. This chapter now focuses on their vulnerability and specific circumstances of deprivation and marginalisation which account for their relative predominance in panhandling pursuits of survival.

The Zimbabwean crisis and the predominance of disabled persons and children in beggary

Children and disabled persons have always been the most conspicuous section of the begging community in Zimbabwe. In 2014, for example, people with physical disabilities constituted 57% of beggars in Harare (Rugoho and Siziba, 2014). This is not surprising given the relative vulnerability of disabled persons as compared to other groups during the Zimbabwean crisis. This section explores the particular circumstances of vulnerability which largely account for the predominance of disabled persons, mostly the blind, and children in panhandling pursuits of survival in Zimbabwe during the new millennium.

Some scholars have castigated disabled beggars for lacking initiative and wanting to live cheaply by exploiting the mercy of others. Silape (1994), for example, argues that some disabled people, particularly the visually-impaired, have a low self-esteem about their capacity to engage in productive work on their own. This leads some of them to want everyone to be sympathetic to them and rarely put meaningful effort to seek employment. These perceptions are opposed by the findings of this book. This study, basing on its findings, notes that disabled persons were very vulnerable during the Zimbabwean crisis largely because their livelihood options were limited owing to their condition of disability. Some informal survival strategies such as smuggling and panning for gold and diamonds could not easily be executed by disabled persons, particularly the blind and crippled, since great mobility was required to negotiate rugged terrains, transport contraband over long distances while avoiding the authorities, and fleeing after being intercepted by the law-enforcement agents (Chigango, Samakande and Vheremu, Separate Interviews, 2014). As Simpson Gona, a visually-challenged beggar who operated in the town of Rusape in Manicaland Province since 2004, stated during an interview:

> The informal options of survival for a visually-impaired person like me are very limited. The sighted can try out all sorts of things and we cannot. They can even steal but I cannot identify what and where to steal, neither can I see that the police are coming to arrest me. The panners of gold and diamonds go up and down steep slopes and run away when soldiers and the police approach them. So we resort to begging since it is less criminal than stealing and the police often sympathise with us (Gona, Interview, 2014).

These sentiments were reiterated by a physically-handicapped man in a wheelchair who was surviving through begging in Masvingo City on Christmas Eve in 2010: "I would have loved to work if I was born like others. It is not my wish to be in the streets getting very little especially on times like these where we expect to be remembered; to me, Christmas is just like any other day" (*Radio VOP*, 24 December 2010). It should be noted, therefore, that the informal options of survival for people living with disability were very limited considering that some pursuits could not easily be undertaken by the physically-challenged, the deaf and the dumb. This partly explains the prevalence of disabled beggars in various parts of Zimbabwe from 2000 as conditions of living began to deteriorate at an alarming rate.

Aggravating the situation was the government's failure to fulfil its constitutional obligation to adequately cater for the needs of the disabled people. In most cases, serious financial problems limited the state's ability to adequately address the needs of the disabled people (Kwenda, 10 April 2010). Since Zimbabwe's independence in 1980, the Ministry of Labour and Social Welfare was responsible for the welfare of the disabled. The Zimbabwe Disabled Persons Act of 1992, for example, provided for the welfare and rehabilitation of disabled people and sought to achieve equal opportunities to make sure that they had access to all services enjoyed by the general community. The statute established a Director for Disabled Persons' Affairs to coordinate with government departments and local authorities and ensure that the needs of the disabled were catered for.

The Act also constituted the National Disability Board whose mandate involved, among other issues, ensuring equal opportunities for disabled people in areas such as education, employment, recreation and self-help projects (*Women News Network*, 29 May 2013). Until the 1990s, the government worked closely with the National Council of Disabled Persons of Zimbabwe (NCDPZ) over issues to do with the welfare of disabled people. From the 1980s, the council gave various forms of support and advice to disabled persons. Its Education Officer worked closely with the Ministry of Education to ensure the provision of favourable learning environments for disabled pupils in schools. Before 2000, the Council issued scholarships for the education of some disabled pupils. It also successfully lobbied the government to introduce degree programmes in universities and courses in teachers' colleges that focused on special education (Disability Awareness in Action, 1995).

Due to the collapse of the Zimbabwean economy, the government's social spending on people with disabilities fell drastically. The hyperinflationary environment significantly eroded the government's disability grant of ZW$20 a month which virtually became worthless after 2000 (*Irin News*, 13 June 2011). In November 2004, for example, this monthly allowance could hardly buy two loaves of bread (*Irin News*, 21 November 2004). As the Zimbabwean economy went on a free fall from 2000, the NCDPZ also faced serious financial constraints that hindered its efforts to meaningfully improve the material lives of the disabled (Disability Awareness in Action, 1995). In addition, the government's Department of Social Welfare failed to justify its continued existence. In July 2012 Peter Makoni, a visually-impaired beggar at Mutare's Meikles Park, blamed the government for neglecting the disabled people and forcing them to beg in order to earn livelihoods:

> We cannot have people going to the Department of Social Welfare every time to be given letters so that they can access health services but they never receive anything. I have witnessed cases where disabled people are being forced from one government department to another to have certain issues attended to... (Saxon, 11 July 2012: 1).

Most welfare institutions where some people living with disability

58

were sheltered had closed during the mid-2000s due to lack of government support. Most of the disabled beggars were previously housed at institutions such as Copota School for the Blind in Masvingo, Chinyaradzo Children's Home in Harare, Danhiko and Jairos Jiri Centres across the country. These institutions used to get financial assistance from the government and private companies but the country's economic downfall from 2000 made life in the care homes unbearable, forcing most residents to seek livelihoods in the streets (Kwenda, 16 April 2010). From 2004, for example, Copota School for the Blind faced severe financial constraints resulting in many visually-disadvantaged people deserting the institution and seeking livelihoods through begging (Tolsi, 30 September 2011). The bankrupt Zimbabwean government also stopped issuing cash grants to the estimated 14 000 disabled people in the country in 2011. In 2013, the government was forced to temporarily disburse the benefits after some people living with disabilities had taken to the streets to protest (Dube, 8 November 2014). In November 2014, Simon Mvindi, an official of the newly-formed Visually Impaired Strategic Trust of Zimbabwe People, moaned how the majority of handicapped Zimbabweans had become beggars due to lack of state support:

> People living with disabilities are suffering. They move from street to street, office to office and other places looking for money. In some cases, they are given a rand while the best outcome is a dollar. This is gross human rights abuse on the side of the government which is supposed to cater for our needs (Ibid: 1).

Thus, as Groce and others (2013) noted, the failure of official social welfare mechanisms to provide safety nets for vulnerable people is one of the chief causes of panhandling by disabled people (Groce and others, 2013). What also spurred begging by disabled Zimbabweans was the general reluctance by employers to engage them due to the stereotyped misconception that they are less productive. This discrimination was not peculiar to Zimbabwe alone but has a long history in various parts of the world. Hasazi and others (1985) noted that employers generally shun visually-impaired job-seekers and prefer their sighted counterparts. The Disability Awareness in Action (1995: 18) also noted: "In the developing world, the extremely high percentage of unemployment among disabled people means that they are forced to beg to survive. The few who do obtain jobs must accept very low levels of pay unrelated to their productivity". In their study of the socio-economic adversities of street beggars in Addis Ababa in Ethiopia, Groce and others (2013: 1) also observed how the marginalisation of disabled people tends to perpetuate their vulnerability:

> People with disabilities…are at increased risk of becoming poor through restricted access to education, health care, job training and employment opportunities. These factors, in combination with the effects of stigma and social isolation, limit the ability of people with disabilities to be full participants in their societies and to find employment that will support themselves and their families.

In Zimbabwe, Zvobgo (1990) noted that out of more than 200 visually-challenged graduates from Copota Secondary School since 1980, only eight were employed as teachers by 1989 while the rest were still unemployed forcing some of them to resort to begging in order to survive. In 1995, less than 1% of disabled Zimbabwean people were in formal employment (Beresford, 1996). The situation became worse for disabled people during the debilitating socio-economic crisis from 2000. A study conducted by the National Association of Societies for the Care noted that only 7% of disabled Zimbabweans were formally employed in 2002 (*Women News Network*, 29 May 2013). According to the Zimbabwe National Statistical Agency, only 2% out of a total population of 1.5 million disabled persons in the country were formally employed in 2012; 64% were reported to be earning livelihoods from the informal sector while many among the remaining 34% survived on begging (Moyo, 5 May 2014). As Munemo and Tom (2013: 203) observed in 2013, "It appears that the rate of unemployment for people with visual impairments in Zimbabwe has reached alarming proportions. This is evidenced by the rising number of beggars on the streets as well as other people with visual impairments roaming the streets or just seated at home". In July 2012, Simon Chipere, the then Executive Director of the Zimbabwe Handicapped Association, lamented the influx of disabled beggars in various parts of the country as a result of excruciating socio-economic tribulations:

> The increased advent of these vulnerable groups is a cause for concern to us. It clearly reflects the great tragedy that is in Zimbabwe today. There should be humanitarian mechanisms in place to assist the disabled. The government should know that disability is as old as creation, but what really has been done to improve the lives of people living with disability? (Saxon, 11 July 2012: 1).

The disabled employees in Zimbabwe's formal sector were usually the first to lose their jobs as inflation skyrocketed and the local currency went on a free-fall. Jethro Gonese, a visually-challenged man, for example, was employed as a schoolteacher in Zimbabwe during the early 2000s. Since he was blind, an assistant paid by the government helped him with the marking and chalkboard work. Around 2004, as Zimbabwe's economic woes worsened, the government stated that it could no longer afford to pay assistants. In an attempt to save his job with the hope that the economy would normalise soon, he started off by sharing his Z$1 000-monthly salary with the assistant. The situation became unsustainable when hyperinflation reduced his monthly salary to less than the price of a loaf of bread prompting him to cross into South Africa and survive from begging in Johannesburg (Tolsi, 30 September 2011).

With the number of potential alms-givers nose-diving by the day owing to crippling socio-economic problems, and with the government overwhelmed by the crisis and increasingly incapacitated to effect significant interventions, most disabled Zimbabweans became more vulnerable with no panacea seemingly in sight, thereby forcing many of them into begging. In January 2009, for example, a South African analyst commented on the conditions of neglect and the seemingly insurmountable challenges experienced by disabled people in Zimbabwe, most of who survived from panhandling:

> No one needs to be told of the suffering that Zimbabweans are

enduring in that country…Some of us may be even getting tired of hearing or reading about yet another Zimbabwean issue. But, there is a part of that country's population whose hardships are not splashed on the news headlines. Disabled people in Zimbabwe are suffering in muted silence and in the dark with nowhere to go and no one to turn to (*Press Reader*, 19 January 2009: 1).

It should be noted that people with disabilities have always been one of the most predominant sections of Zimbabwe's begging community in view of the limited livelihood options at their disposal. As Groce and others (2013: 13) rightly argued: "Begging may be a rational economic decision, no matter what the social and psychological toll the individual incurs. Thus, people with disabilities may turn to begging simply because they have no other options open to them or they may choose to beg given the limited range of options they face".

Children under the age of 16 years were another very visible constituency in Zimbabwe's panhandling community from 2000 as socio-economic calamities besieged the country. During the first decade of the 21st century the presence of beggars, mostly children, in Bulawayo became more visible as each year passed by to the extent that they were found not only along streets in the city centre, but even in the residential areas such as Luveve and Emakhandeni (Bulawayo Progressive Residents Association, 30 July 2014). In the cities of Harare, Bulawayo, Mutare, Gweru and Kadoma in 2000, UNICEF discovered that nearly 45.7% of street children were beggars while the rest engaged in other tasks such as vending and cleaning cars (UNICEF, 2001). A survey conducted by the Department of Social Welfare towards the end of 2000 revealed that there were about 5 000 children along the streets of Harare alone (Rurevo and Bourdillon, 2003). According to Futures International, a Harare-based NGO, there were at least 12 000 children salvaging livelihoods along Zimbabwe's streets and highways in May 2004 (*Eye Net*, 8 July 2004). In February 2013, Streets Ahead, a human rights group that worked to rehabilitate children, estimated that close to 3 000 children were begging or residing in the streets of Harare (Ncube, 3 February 2013).

In terms of the gender dimensions of child-begging, the general trend was that boys were more conspicuous. In late 2002, for example, Streets Ahead had 1 500 recorded cases of street children from Harare who had approached them for assistance of which only 200 were girls and the rest boys. The predominance of males was partly because many girls on the streets were often snatched up by elder women who hired them out to "use" them in their brothels as commercial sex workers. In addition, significant numbers of girls dreaded the streets as a livelihood option because they were more vulnerable than boys to various forms of abuse such as rape (Bourdillon and Rurevo, 2003). Oral interviews with some child-beggars revealed that it was also common practice in most child-headed families for girls to remain at home doing domestic chores such as laundry, cooking, taking care of the younger children and general upkeep while the boys went out to beg (Chara, Manekeni, Mushanda and Zangata, FGD: 2014).

The distressingly high figures of child-panhandlers provoke an interrogation into some of the particular circumstances behind the upsurge in begging by children from the year 2000 in Zimbabwe. According to Kopoka (2000), children are in most cases forced into the streets due to poverty, abuse, neglect, diseases and various forms of socio-economic deprivation. This is a very accurate explanation of the prevalence of begging by children in Zimbabwe during the first decade of the 21st century especially considering their vulnerability, frustration and despair in a decimated socio-economic landscape and violent political dispensation in which their supposed bread-winners were unemployed, poverty-ridden, famished, caught up in political violence, and dying of HIV/AIDS, COVID-19, and other diseases.

The HIV/AIDS pandemic, whose drugs were always scarce in the country owing to government bankruptcy and the shortage of foreign currency to import them, also contributed towards the prevalence of begging by children in Zimbabwe. The deaths of parents from AIDS left many child-headed families eking livelihoods through begging. By 2002, it was estimated that over 30 000 Zimbabwean households were headed by children under the age of 21 years and another 3 000 headed by children under 15 years. About

600 children were estimated to have lost their mothers (Civil Society Forum for East and Southern Africa, 11-13 February 2002). There were about 1.3 million HIV/AIDS orphans countrywide by the end of 2005 (US Government, 2005). In June 2009, 500 000 Zimbabweans were in need of ARV therapy and more than 300 000 were dying of AIDS-related diseases every week (Fournier, June 2009). "While other children of their age are in school", wrote Justice Mbiva, the Director of Vision HIV/AIDS, an organisation that monitored the welfare of children in Zimbabwe's slum communities in 2014, "children, especially from vulnerable communities, are spending most of their time in the streets, begging for a living. At a tender age, they have assumed responsibilities of bringing food to the table and this affects the wellbeing of a child" (Chifamba, 3 May 2014: 1).

The number of child-headed families also rose significantly owing to the high rate of unemployment and spiralling inflation which drove many parents across national borders to seek livelihoods. In the absence of breadwinners, some families sank into abject poverty forcing many children to beg for basic necessities. As the ZCTU noted in 2013: "With the prevailing economic conditions in which more than 80% of the population is unemployed, there is reason to believe that the future of children has been compromised as many are being left by their parents who are flooding neighbouring countries in search of employment. Many are left at a high risk of dropping out of school and eventually begging in the streets as they would assume the duties of being breadwinners" (Chifamba, 3 May 2014).

The experiences of twin brothers Jackson and Thomas Chatikobo are clearly illustrative of this scenario. They began begging for alms at Machipisa Shopping Centre in Harare in 2010 at the age of 14 after they had been abandoned by their parents who had gone to South Africa. Their father had left his job as an electrician with a Harare company early in 2008 when they were doing Form One to seek greener pastures in South Africa. They remained with their mother and throughout 2008, their father sent them money and groceries. It was in 2009 that their father stopped supporting them in any way. Their mother made a follow up to Cape Town where he was working.

They never saw their parents again but got word that their father had married another woman and divorced their mother while in South Africa. They were evicted from the two-rooms which their parents used to rent and were expelled from school due to non-payment of fees. They began begging for food and money at Machipisa Shopping Centre during the day and slept in an open space behind Machipisa Service Station for the greater part of 2010. It was only in early 2011 that they became touts who solicited for passengers on behalf of commuter omnibus operators at Machipisa Shopping Centre, an informal occupation that managed to sustain them over the years and enabled them to rent one room in the nearby Highfields Residential Area (Chatikobo and Chatikobo, Interview: 2014). This example illustrates how some children became beggars after being abandoned by their parents who had crossed into neighbouring countries in search of greener pastures.

Since 2000, the exodus of unaccompanied children, that is, those who travelled without parents or an adult relative, to seek livelihoods across national borders, sometimes through begging, is conspicuously illustrative of the tragic consequences of the Zimbabwean crisis and the failure of the government to mitigate their plight. As Chiweshe (12 October 2017: 1) sadly noted:

In Zimbabwe, the migration process has long been understood as an adult phenomenon with little attention to children. This is mainly because migration has long been assumed to be a dangerous endeavour for children on their own. Childhood, by all accounts, should be an exciting time of growth and personal development. It is a time to explore without worrying about all the challenges facing this world. Yet in Zimbabwe, there is an ever-growing tragedy of unaccompanied and undocumented child migrants. Their heart-breaking stories and experiences point to a child protection problem that the Zimbabwean government has largely ignored...The state of a government and a people is seen in how it treats its children. The growing number of children who are deciding that it is better to brave the unknown dangers of illegal migration than it is to stay in their home country starkly demonstrates the failures of the Zimbabwean state. The socio-economic and political crises post-2000 in Zimbabwe has led to children migrating on their own using illegal means, mainly to South Africa and Botswana. Most leave Zimbabwe because of diverse challenges at home and opportunities available in the destination, yet they are often unaware of the difficulties of migration. Illegal migration exposes these children - especially vulnerable due to their age - to a myriad of problems.

During the first five months of 2006, for example, statistics from humanitarian agencies indicated that more than 2 100 unaccompanied Zimbabwean children, a daily average of 14, were deported from South Africa to the border town of Beitbridge in southern Zimbabwe. In the last six months of 2006, according to the International Organisation for Migration (IOM), about 950 unaccompanied Zimbabwean children passed through a reception and support centre in Beitbridge which accommodated deported children pending family reunification. The centre was jointly run by the IOM, Save the Children (Norway), UNICEF and Zimbabwe's Ministry of Public Service, Labour and Social Welfare (New Humanitarian, 8 March 2007). In March 2007, James Elder, the then UNICEF Spokesman in Zimbabwe, explained why many unaccompanied Zimbabwean children were in South Africa: "These young people are doing it (crossing the border illegally), perhaps because they feel there is a lack of opportunities at home. Some of the 15-to-16-year-olds will be looking for financial opportunities to look after their siblings back home" (Ibid: 1).

In March 2007, the South Africa Women's Institute of Migration Affairs (SAWIMA), an NGO that provides assistance to refugees and displaced people, reported a rising number of unaccompanied Zimbabwean children entering South Africa (New Humanitarian, 8 March 2007). The organisation reported that most of the children were aged between 10 and 14 years (Ibid). By early November 2009, many unaccompanied children were reportedly fleeing Zimbabwe "in growing numbers" (Scott, 2 November 2009: 1). During the period June 2006-2010, an estimated 8 408 unaccompanied children aged between 12 and 17 years, mostly from districts in Chipinge, Masvingo, Mberengwa, Bulawayo and Chiredzi went to South Africa, with the majority citing economic opportunities as the major reason for migrating. Of the children who crossed, 41% used the legal border post, while 40% used the illegal Limpopo River route (Chiweshe, 12 October 2017). In early January 2014, South African authorities claimed that out of the 2 000 undocumented Zimbabweans deported each week, 20% were unaccompanied children (Dzimwasha, 13 January 2014). At this time, Save the Children estimated that 350-400 unaccompanied Zimbabwean children crossed the border into South Africa each day without passing through official checkpoints (Ibid). In August 2019, Bornman (13 August 2019: 1) noted that "although the number of (Zimbabwean) children crossing the border into South Africa on their own has dropped recently, there are still many unaccompanied minors at risk of becoming stateless".

Figure 1: Unaccompanied Zimbabwean child beggars in Musina, South Africa, 2009

Source: Bearak (23 January 2009)

Dambudzo Zijena, a boy from Mutoko District in north-eastern Zimbabwe, is an example of an unaccompanied minor who crossed illegally into South Africa at the age of 14 years to survive from begging owing to the country's socio-economic abyss and ill-treatment by his aunt. He had become an orphan at the age of six years after the death of his parents from AIDS. He was taken into the custody of his aunt who mistreated him by, among other things, denying him food forcing him to flee to South Africa (Moyo, 18 August 2014).

The rate of begging by children also increased as a result of rising numbers of school dropouts owing to the inability to pay school fees by parents and guardians, most of who had been rendered insolvent by anguishing socio-economic vicissitudes typified by unemployment, hyperinflation, price hikes and gnawing poverty. It was estimated that school costs for low-income families rose by 900% from November to December 2004 largely as a result of the escalating inflation (US Government, 2005).

Tecla, Dadiso and Privilege, young sisters with the surname Rusiro, were forced to drop out of primary school in Mutare's Sakubva Suburb after their parents, who were both visually-challenged and survived from the proceeds of panhandling at specific points in the city centre, failed to raise their school fees in mid-2007. After dropping out of school, they joined their parents on begging expeditions in various parts of Mutare's Central Business District such as the Meikles Park, bars, restaurants, fuel service stations and car parks. As inflation continued to skyrocket and prices of basic commodities escalated, they failed to save any revenue for them to go back to school. In 2009, Tecla died after being run over by a car along the Main Street in Mutare's city centre. A relative in Harare took over the custody of Dadiso while Privilege continued to beg with her parents until 2010 when she returned to school being funded by the Basic Education Assistance Module (BEAM), a programme funded by international NGOs to assist in the payment of school fees for poor children (Rusiro, Interview: 2013).

For most school-going children, begging was a means to an end and not an end in itself. For such children, panhandling was a temporary engagement meant to meet their educational requirements owing to the inability of their impoverished parents or guardians (Abebe, 2008). It was common for some children to beg during holidays or daily after school hours in order to raise money for fees and other educational materials such as books, pens and uniforms. In mid-June 2013, for example, some children in school uniform begged for money at Dangamvura Shopping Centre in Mutare's Dangamvura Suburb after being expelled from a local school for failing to pay fees. A Reverend at a local church said it was the tendency of most poor children expelled from local schools after failing to pay fees and levies to beg for money while in uniform to appeal to the mercy of potential donors. He stated that most of the expelled children were being sponsored by BEAM which deposited their fees into state coffers but the cash-strapped government always delayed to disburse the money, most likely after diverting it for other uses, resulting in innocent pupils being expelled (Mugwengwendere, Interview: 2013). As Marima, Jordan and Cormie (1995) noted, the presence of children in Zimbabwean streets was largely symptomatic of broader social and economic challenges haunting the nation.

Conclusion

After utilising a broad range of sources which include print and electronic media articles, reports of non-governmental organisations, government documents, eye-witness accounts from the general public and personal testimonies from the beggars themselves, the present chapter identified poverty as the underlying factor in the upsurge in panhandling activities in Zimbabwe from 2000. The land seizures from February 2000 triggered a multiplicity of crises. These included international isolation, unemployment, hyperinflation, food shortages, hunger and starvation. Ecological disasters, particularly droughts, exacerbated the situation. As poverty rates escalated, the generality of the population increasingly became disillusioned by the government's failure to alleviate their plight. Instead of addressing issues of poverty, the government institutionalised terror to suppress public concerns. Political violence in various brutal forms such as beatings, torture, intimidation, killings and displacements aggravated the plight of the ordinary people. As the formal means of earning livelihoods virtually disappeared, many downtrodden Zimbabweans devised several irregular mechanisms of survival such as panhandling. Zimbabwe literally became "a nation of beggars" (Mutenga, 3 July 2014: 1) because of the "force of circumstances" (Bourdillon, 1991:

98). Given the socio-economic and political problems in Zimbabwe from 2000, the unprecedented prevalence of begging should therefore be viewed in terms of the emergence of "a distress industry" (Abebe, 2008: 272) in which some downtrodden sections of the society displayed agency to avert adversity.

Chapter 2

Desperate Situations Demand Desperate Tricks: Begging Dynamics In Zimbabwe

Introduction

This chapter unravels the diverse livelihood initiatives of beggars in Zimbabwe. The country's begging landscape became an arena of fierce contestation among the beggars themselves on one hand, and between the beggars and the authorities on the other hand owing to the mounting socio-economic challenges from 2000. It increasingly became a highly competitive engagement as beggars congested the city centres in search of livelihoods at a time when the numbers of potential well-wishers were nose-diving as a result of the economic meltdown epitomised by deindustrialisation, unemployment, hyperinflation, escalating prices of basic commodities and services, and grinding poverty. Conflicts among beggars became a common feature as begging space in the major city centres increasingly ran out. The record hyperinflationary situation drastically reduced the monetary value of earnings for beggars as the Zimbabwean dollar became virtually worthless during a period when prices of basic commodities and services shot up by the day. As the numbers of panhandlers soared, state and municipal authorities increasingly became concerned resulting in several brutal clampdowns.

In view of the limited survival options in crisis-ridden Zimbabwe, begging was a highly contested undertaking with its own fascinating dynamics. It developed into "a fine art" involving a broad range of ingenious strategies to earn livelihoods (Bentwick, 1894: 125). In the words of Owusu-Sekyere, Jengre and Alhassan (2018: 4): "At the heart of the business is the beggar's ability to court public sympathy. This is because courting more public attention and, more importantly, courting the attention of the right sympathiser often translate into good business". The various mechanisms employed by beggars constituted "a talent for life" which reflected resilience by vulnerable

71

people to survive in times of crisis (Scheper-Hughes, 2008: 25). As will be noted in this chapter, begging skills basically involved managing space and time, and the ability to communicate effectively with potential alms-givers in order to induce their benevolence.

The creativity of beggars is clearly demonstrated by the various modes of communication which they employed. These forms of communication can be classified in terms of the extent of covertness or overtness in their request for alms. Osa-Edoh and Ayano (2012) came up with three categories of begging. These are passive, active and aggressive. Passive begging is when a person either sits or stands in one place with a banner or container anticipating donations. It also involves indirectly soliciting for gifts sometimes using deceptive means. On the other hand, active begging involves moving from one place to another asking for donations, while aggressive begging makes use of intimidation, threats and harsh words in soliciting for assistance. According to Burke (1999), passive beggars win more sympathisers than aggressive ones. The active and aggressive categories fit into Ottey's "direct approach" of begging in which panhandlers openly request for donations (Ottey, 16 May 2013: 1). It should be noted, however, that circumstances sometimes force beggars to use a combination of techniques in order to earn livelihoods. Thus, for example, beggars can initially request for donations politely from fixed positions but sometimes end up following well-wishers and harassing them under circumstances of chronic hunger. This chapter winds up by looking at the lived experiences of beggars, most of which were largely evidenced by tribulation.

Spatial dimensions of begging

Panhandling, particularly in urban and peri-urban centres, is a preoccupation that primarily involves critical skills of identifying spaces where the greatest possible numbers of potential donors either reside, frequent or pass through. The beggars have to be in such catchment areas at the most appropriate of times and possibly shift to alternative ones depending on the prevailing circumstances. The spatial mobility of beggars, however, tend to be determined by other variables. These include the suitability of climatic conditions for travel, availability of transport, the physical and health condition of beggars, the intensity of competition among fellow beggars, and frequency of anti-begging campaigns by law-enforcement agents. The ability to be at the most suitable place and at the most appropriate time is a vital survival skill for beggars. As Mihalache and others (2013: 70) noted, the decision by beggars to be at particular places where they are likely to get relatively more donations during specific times shows that they are "well oriented in space and time, so as to get the most profit of their activity".

Retail outlets in urban centres are examples of the spatially strategic settings for many beggars (Kariati, 21 May 2014; Mutandwa, 16 July 2012). What attract many beggars to places such as supermarket entrances are shoppers who have disposable incomes to buy some commodities and on their way out from shops, possibly spare some money-change for them (Dube, Kaonde and Masapa, Nengomasha and Rangwanda, Separate Interviews: 2013). Hotels and restaurants were, and are also still frequented by beggars in anticipation of food left-overs and money (Kasamba, Nedzoyi and Sande, FGD: 2013). Others frequent beer-halls and bottle stores hoping to capitalise on the presence of sympathetic drinkers. Since 2000, visually-impaired adult beggars in the company of small children were a common sight in Mutare's city centre beer-halls such as Manyati, Nightshift, Flavour Town, Potters, Mandisa, Bulldogs Pub, Soul City and Chidzere (Kanongo, Kativhu, Mhiko and Shato, Separate Interviews: 2013).

Banks and Automated Teller Machines (ATMs) are other strategic locations where some beggars are known to have positioned themselves, anticipating donations from people who would have withdrawn money. Ruwimbo Dara, a visually-challenged female beggar who was seated close to the entrance of Mutare's Barclays Bank (16 September 2013) alleged that "I have been operating here since 2003", "I have got a lot of assistance from people who come to deposit or withdraw money from the bank. I get a lot during pay days but very little on Sundays and public holidays when banks are closed and most people are away" (Dara, Interview: 2013). In Bulawayo, a female beggar and her wheelchair-bound daughter were a well-known permanent feature outside Stanbic Bank throughout 2013 (*Bulawayo 24 News*, 22 December 2013).

The streets, particularly at traffic-light and stop-sign intersections, have always been hives of activity for many beggars. This is largely because of the public perception that motorists are relatively wealthy people who can spare some alms for the poor (Ranga, Sesedzayi and Taremba, Separate Interviews: 2013). In February 2005, a Harare motorist complained about the congestion caused by beggars along the streets in the city centre: "The government must do something about these street beggars because they interfere with traffic and cause accidents if they do not get run down themselves" (SAMP, 5 February 2005). In September 2009, for instance, beggars were found at every traffic-light intersection in Harare (Kriel, 22 September 2009). In 2012, Elizabeth Takawira, a visually-challenged woman, was a permanent feature at a busy intersection close to OK Supermarket in Mutare's city centre while her two children, Tatenda (12) and Tavonga (9), dashed from one vehicle to another that had been stopped by red traffic lights, begging for alms (Saxon, 11 July 2012). Panhandlers were also very visible in city-centre car-parking bays where they directly sought alms from motorists or indirectly by offering services such as car-washing and car-minding in anticipation of monetary and other forms of tokens (Saxon, 11 July 2012; Mhiko, Sesedzayi, Shato and Taremba, Separate Interviews: 2013).

Figure 2: Begging from motorists at Harare's traffic light intersections, 2011
Source: Makoni-Muchemwa (7 April 2011)

Considerable numbers of beggars also target railway stations as well as urban and peri-urban bus termini. This is largely because of the generally held assumption among most beggars that travellers move with some cash or food items some of which they can spare for, the needy (Chinenge, Kusena and Marapa, Separate Interviews: 2014). Apart from those who take positions in shop verandas at public transport termini, some beggars seek alms from travellers in waiting rooms while others enter parked buses and trains (Goronga, Muranduko, Sengere and Wanga, Separate Interviews: 2013). Since the mid-2000s, for example, a visually-impaired woman took semi-permanent residence at the Birchenough Bridge bus terminus where she begged from passengers in parked long-distance buses (Mlambo and Sithole, Separate Interviews: 2014).

Tourist destinations in Zimbabwe have also been popular hunting grounds of some panhandlers. These include resort areas such as the Victoria Falls (Bloch, 5 April 2013). Such places are popular with beggars because of the presence of tourists, mostly from developed countries, some of whom sympathise with the plight of the poor in less-developed countries such as Zimbabwe (Chingu and Jombe,

Separate Interviews: 2013). As the Zimbabwean dollar became virtually worthless during the hyperinflationary period before 2009, foreign tourists became magnets of many beggars because of their possession of foreign currency. Even in other parts of the country outside tourist resort centres, a foreign-registered vehicle that parked during this period was often swarmed by beggars who asked for alms (Sesedzayi and Taremba, Separate Interviews: 2013). On 10 September 2009, Gordon Addams, a foreign tourist, complained of harassment by Zimbabwean beggars in need of money at Forbes and Beitbridge Border Posts (Addams, 10 September 2009). In 2013, Zimbabwe was regarded as one of the world's most unsafe tourist destinations partly owing to "endless harassment of tourists by beggars desperately seeking donations and unceasingly badgering the tourists with appeals for money" (Bloch, 5 April 2013: 1).

Border posts are also frequented by many beggars who solicit for cash and food from travellers and tourists. At Beitbridge Border Post in 2005, for example, beggars from various parts of the country converged to beg during the afternoons after which they slept at an open space in Dulibadzimu Stadium during the night. When the authorities threatened to evict them, they besieged the border post on 7 September 2005 disrupting traffic and inconveniencing travellers (SAMP, 8 September 2005). By the end of 2013, the proliferation of beggars at border posts had reached alarming proportions prompting Tambudzai Mohadi, the then Senator of Beitbridge, to raise the issue in the Senate in June 2014. She reported that in recent years, beggars from various parts of the country, most of who were visually-disadvantaged, had converged at the Beitbridge Border Post where some of them ended up stranded. She noted that since the border post does not close, the beggars operated round the clock (*Harare 24 News*, 20 August 2014).

Church premises are also gold mines for beggars during days and times when members of particular religious denominations congregate for sermons and festivals. This demonstrates the skill and imagination of some downtrodden groups to capitalise on the virtues of altruism and largesse generally associated with religious people. Indeed, it is a fact that religious people are well reputed in the public domain for being more generous to the needy (Chingu and Jombe,

Separate Interviews: 2013). In the case of Christians, some of the common Biblical verses which advocate for bountifulness are: "Whoever has a bountiful eye will be blessed, for he shares his bread with the poor" (Proverbs 22: 9); "Rescue the weak and the needy, deliver them from the hand of the wicked" (Psalms 82: 4); "Do not neglect to do good and to share what you have, for such sacrifices are pleasing to God" (Hebrews 13: 16); and "You shall love your neighbour as yourself" (Mark 12: 31).

Along Zimbabwe's highways, some beggars also station themselves at toll gates in an effort to seek alms from motorists. In October 2016, for example, the country's worsening socio-economic crisis was reportedly "forcing visually-impaired beggars to ditch city centres and travel several kilometres to try their luck at some of the country's toll gates. The Esigodini toll gate, located some 60 kilometres from Bulawayo along the Beitbridge Highway, has seen an increase in the number of blind beggars in recent months" (*New Zimbabwe*, 16 October 2016: 1).

Even though most beggars have precise locations of operation, they are known to have sometimes shifted either temporarily or permanently depending on prevailing circumstances. Spatio-temporary mobility can be determined by climatic conditions. Harsh weather conditions, for example, can restrict the spatial mobility of beggars. It is also common for beggars to change geographical locations during certain periods of time in view of stiff competition from their counterparts who sometimes threaten them with physical harm. In addition, the police sometimes dispersed beggars from their zones of operation but they usually returned after the law-enforcement agents had left (Matikinye, 21 September 2007).

The innovativeness of beggars can also be noted in the manner in which they skilfully negotiate time and space by being present at certain places at particular instances. During pay days, for example, they normally station themselves at places of employment or banks during lunch-break anticipating donations from sympathetic workers (Dara, Interview: 2013). Some are always up to date about the days of the week and particular times of the day when members of some religious denominations congregate (Chingu and Jombe, Separate Interviews: 2013). During lunch-breaks, beggars are a common sight

77

at hotels, restaurants and fast-food outlets, most having come with the hope of getting donations from workers and other people from various parts of the town who were having lunch (Kasamba, Nedzoyi and Sande, FGD: 2013). These examples illustrate the dynamism of some beggars, particularly their choice and timing of where to regularly operate from, and where to be at given times. This is in synch with Ogunkan and Jelili's (2010: 78) observation that, begging is significantly "a function of land use activities" as some impecunious sections of the society negotiate time and space in pursuit of survival.

The ingenuity of some beggars in negotiating space for survival is also reflected by their use of the house-to-house or door-to-door approach. This strategy involves moving around certain neighbourhoods begging for alms from prospective sympathisers (Muchairi, 22 November 2013). In Mutare's Dangamvura Suburb in 2012 and 2013, for example, an old woman used to beg for food, money and clothes from house to house in the company of three bare-footed children aged between three and five years who wore tattered clothes. She claimed that the three infants were her grandchildren, both of whose parents had died from AIDS. Two of the children belonged to her late son while the other one had been left by her deceased daughter (Mafarachisi and Mayaya, Separate Interviews: 2013).

In most cases, this itinerant or peripatetic approach was employed by poor people who could not easily convince passers-by in city centres about their plight because they had no visible disabilities or ailments that would immediately arouse the benevolence of a stranger (Mafarachisi, Interview: 2013). In view of the fierce competition for alms from conspicuously vulnerable people such as children and the physically-handicapped along the streets and other public spheres, this category of beggars approach potential well-wishers at their offices at workplaces or homesteads, usually in the middle-class and upmarket suburbs where they devote some time to explain their predicament in detail. Such an approach is inappropriate in Central Business Districts and congested marketplaces and bus termini where prospective benefactors are usually busy with various errands. In the house-to-house approach, visits are therefore timed to coincide with times such as after-work hours, weekends and public holidays when targeted benefactors are relatively less-preoccupied. In addition, this innovative timing has the potential to yield considerable material benefits such as used clothes, utensils and food items which well-wishers have at their premises (Mafarachisi and Mayaya, Separate Interviews: 2013).

Another fascinating spatial dimension of panhandling involves boarding long-distance buses along the country's highways seeking donations from passengers. This approach is premised on the assumption that the travelling public have something to spare. Itinerant begging on buses, mostly by disabled persons, has always been prevalent along Zimbabwe's highways linking major cities. The beggars take advantage of the fact that public transporters do not charge them bus-fare out of sympathy (Mugoti, Samson and Wakota, FGD: 2014). This form of begging is usually undertaken by pairs or groups of three. They usually operate within a specific distance along the highway before disembarking in a town or at a business centre from where another group take over. The group that disembarks boards other buses travelling in the opposite direction and they would spend the day shuttling up and down begging within their zone of operation (Kazore and Pachije, Joint Interview: 2014). There, however, does not seem to be any coordination in terms of the zoning. It appears that this is a function of the need to remain within reasonable distance from one's area of residence.

Along the highway linking the cities of Mutare and Masvingo during the period 2009-2013, for example, a lone visually-challenged male beggar aged about 65 years regularly operated between Mupamaonde and Nyika Business Centres. From Nyika to Roy Business Centre, two sets of visually-retarded women who operated in twos or threes operated in opposite directions. Other groups also operated in the same manner between Roy and Masvingo City (Mugoti, Samson and Wakota, FGD: 2014). The innovativeness of the visually-challenged beggars is reflected by the manner in which they organised themselves into groups and allocated each other operational zones and rarely encroached into each other's territory. Thus, as Groce and others (2013: 13) noted, beggars often improvise "unified social support mechanisms" in an attempt to earn a living, an innovation that can be likened to beggar brotherhoods in India (Kumarappa, 2007).

The begging routine on buses usually began with a group of beggars getting onto a bus that had parked to pick up passengers. The visually-disadvantaged panhandlers immediately told the bus conductor to drop them at a specific bus stop they would have chosen to disembark along the way. They would take a seat, usually at the back. After the bus has travelled for a few kilometres, the beggars moved up and down the bus pleading for donations in cash or kind. The process was usually accompanied by songs, poems and other recitations highlighting their plight in order to instil a sense of sympathy among passengers (Chikondo, Dhokoze and Kodogwe, FGD: 2014). One of the popular verses recited by most blind beggars went as follows:

Help us people of God. It is not our fault that we are blind but it is the wish of God. We cannot do self-help jobs as you because we are disabled. Please help us. Some people curse us for not bathing or washing our clothes, so please help us with money to buy soap. Even a piece of soap itself will do. We also have children. Help us maintain their livelihoods by donating towards their education and general upkeep. Without your help, we will not survive (Kazore and Pachije, Joint Interview: 2014).

The dropping of a coin in the begging bowl often triggered clapping of hands and thanksgiving verses in praise of the donor. An example of such verses of appreciation is: "May God bless you forever. We urge the Almighty to bless your journey. We wish that you and your family live in prosperity. Thank you very much" (Mugoti, Samson and Wakota, FGD: 2014; Tondi, Interview: 2013).

Space utilisation and timing have always been critical resources in begging pursuits of survival by Zimbabwe's poor. The innovativeness of beggars is reflected by their efforts to be at places where most alms could be obtained and during times when significant numbers of potential well-wishers were likely to have something to spare. The dynamism of begging is also evident in the opening up of alternative spaces owing to various considerations such as periodic state and municipal clampdowns, and competition from impoverished counterparts whose physical condition and appearance draw the attention of more donors.

Audio-improvisations of panhandling

For many panhandlers, oral communication skills are critical in drawing the attention of alms-givers. Most beggars verbally sought assistance using polite and highly persuasive language. By February 2019, 'Sicel uncedo' in the Ndebele language, 'Tinokumbira rubatsiro' in Shona, and 'We beg for help' had become "the beggars' anthem" in Zimbabwe (Chikiwa, 17 February 2019: 1). In addition, a significant number of beggars deliberately requested for small donations in cash or kind in order to avoid scaring away potential donors. The common statements used to articulate such requests included: "Help me in whatever way you can", "A piece of soap will enable me to bath and do my laundry", "A pencil will help my child at school", and "Even a coin will do"(Gomba, Mhike and Mudzonga, Separate Interviews: 2013).

The persuasive terminology employed by panhandlers sometimes included verses from the Bible that urge people to assist those who are in need. The common biblical verses derived from religious poetry include: "It is more blessed to give than to receive" (Acts 20: 35); "Whoever is generous to the poor lends to the Lord, and he will repay him for his deed" (Proverbs 19: 17); "Bear one another's burdens, and so fulfil the law of Christ" (Galatians 6: 2); and "Give and it will be given to you" (Luke 6: 38) (Gomba, Mhike and Mudzonga, Separate Interviews: 2013).

Some beggars crafted false but highly convincing stories to obtain alms from well-wishers. As Mihalache and others (2013: 71) observed elsewhere in the Rumanian capital of Bucharest, some beggars applied "empiric marketing knowledge" by fabricating stories to "touch the soul and…psychologically manipulate the people". A common strategy used by some beggars in Harare was approaching a prospective donor and pretending that they wanted to attend to a sick wife at Harare Hospital but did not have money for transport. Other statements included that they wanted some money for transport back to their rural home after failing to find a relative or friend in town who was supposed to meet the costs (Kariati, 21 May 2014). While such misrepresentations make some sections of the public to be sceptical about the authenticity and moral uprightness of some beggars, the issue remains that poverty drives some of its victims to devise an array of mechanisms to salvage livelihoods. On utilitarian grounds, such deceptive strategies are a manifestation of a moral economy involving innovativeness by some downtrodden people to survive in harsh socio-economic environments.

Informal audio-improvisations involving various sound alerts are an important mode of communication used by beggars to draw the attention of potential donors. Tichaona Kahwema, Choice Kurewa, Mildred Kashaya and Noble Chaza, both deaf and dumb beggars who operated outside supermarkets in the town of Chipinge since the mid-2000s, for example, shook rattles at regular intervals in order to attract passers-by (Chaza, Kahwema, Kashaya and Kurewa, Separate Interviews: 2014). Outside TM Supermarket in Mutare, Edna Kaonde and Ruth Masapa, both dumb women who began panhandling in 2008, shook empty metal plates with a few coins or stones to produce a sound in order to be noticed by pedestrians (Kaonde and Masapa, Separate Interviews: 2014). Tatenda Kativhu and Joel Shato, both deaf and dumb men, knocked an empty tin using a stick at regular intervals. The resultant pitched sound signalled their presence in a shed of big trees at the Meikles Park in Mutare's city centre where they panhandled since early 2009 (Kativhu and Shato, Separate Interviews: 2013). At Machipisa Shopping Centre in Harare since 2007, Shadreck Gonzo, Lameck Nhova and Theresa Senzeni who were both deaf and dumb blew a trumpet made from cattle horns to alert pedestrians of their presence close to a disused public telephone booth near the bus terminus (Gonzo, Nhova and Senzeni, FGD: 2014).

Another audio-improvisation employed mostly by disabled beggars to lure passers-by was clapping hands loudly at regular intervals. This strategy, according to Thomas Chinyere, a visually-impaired panhandler from Masvingo town since 2005, was useful in busy city centres where beggars seated along pavements could easily escape the notice of passers-by. Besides drawing the attention of pedestrians, the clapping of hands was also a symbolic way of thanking potential donors in advance (Chinyere, Interview: 2014).

Music is a notable resource utilised as bait to attract donors during begging pursuits. "Playing musical instruments or singing", as Groce (2013: 12) also observed in Addis Ababa, the Ethiopian capital, "is a trade widely reported in the historic literature as being a speciality of blind people". Some disabled beggars play musical instruments to attract passers-by with the optimism that they would sympathise with them and donate alms. The concertina was perhaps the most popular instrument played mostly by visually-disadvantaged beggars along Zimbabwean streets from the early 2000s. Box guitars are also a prized possession for many beggars. Most of them are home-made with their boxes improvised from empty cooking-oil metal gallon-containers (Gomba, Mhike and Mudzonga, Separate Interviews: 2013). Since they began begging on the pavements along Julius Nyerere Street in Harare from 2002, Luckson Chenje, Joel Mupatsa and Susan Nyati, both deaf and dumb, for example, played thumb pianos together in order to lure potential well-wishers (Chenje, Mupatsa and Nyati, FGD: 2014).

Along the streets of Zimbabwean cities in December 2010, many beggars sang songs of sorrow in pavements and staged roadside musical performances where they played instruments such as drums, rattles and guitars (*Radio VOP*, 24 December 2010). In the city of Mutare in 2012, Peter Makoni, a visually-impaired beggar, sang gospel tunes and played a box guitar at the Meikles Park in order to lure well-wishers (Saxon, 11 July 2012). Along Cameroon Street near Copacabana Bus Terminus in Harare in late September 2017, Limbson Mambiyo and his wife, Gladys Chirabgwa, both visually-impaired beggars, used music as "a luring tool" with the husband on the guitar and the wife on the vocals and rattles (Chekai, 28 September 2017: 1). Some interviewees from the begging community acknowledged that they actually rehearsed some of the songs and poems they recited to potential well-wishers. The rehearsals were usually conducted by peers and family members at home during the evenings after taking stock of the day's earnings (Gomba, Mhike and Mudzonga, Separate Interviews: 2013).

Figure 3: Visually-impaired beggars and their musical instruments: Harare, November 2019

Source: Gwaze (24 November 2019)

Beggars sometimes changed their communicative modes especially during times of police raids in city centres. The dynamism of some beggars was shown by their ability to temporarily change their begging techniques from overt to covert forms in order to camouflage their activities during police clampdowns. In Harare, as Matikinye reported on such shifting dynamics in September 2013:

> Police have been snapping on the heels of vendors, hawkers, touts, the blind, beggars and street kids who are constantly on the move to avoid arrest. The blind no longer rattle begging bowls at street corners, nor sing hymns along pavements to capture public attention and arouse their benevolence (Matikinye, 21 September 2013: 1).

The innovativeness of beggars, as evidenced by the deployment of various vocal communicative skills, has been explored in this section. These skills included employing highly persuasive language,

84

clapping hands, singing and playing musical instruments in an effort to capture the benevolence of well-wishers. The ingenuity of some beggars in surviving against the odds was shown by the manner in which they varied their vocal communicative strategies depending on the prevailing circumstances.

Visual techniques of begging

The creativity of panhandlers in general and disabled beggars in particular is reflected by a surfeit of visual mechanisms skilfully devised to draw the attention of passers-by and provoke their sympathies. In the case of disabled beggars, these strategies tended to depend on the nature of their disability which sometimes made it impossible for them to communicate verbally with potential donors. Deaf and dumb beggars, for example, usually made use of non-oral and visual means of communication to capture the attention and benevolence of potential donors. The visual communicative conduct of significant numbers of beggars included, among other things, putting up physical appearances that highlighted their downtrodden condition, displaying their disability or health ailments to the public, and availing various forms of documentation to explain and authenticate their plight.

One's physical appearance, whether improvised or genuine, that reflects conditions of abject poverty and destitution has proved to be a vital resource for many beggars as they seek to survive by exploiting the mercy of passers-by. The mere sight of a severely handicapped beggar or a malnourished child, for example, usually draws the sympathy of many. Thus, as Kwenda observed in most pavements in Zimbabwean cities in April 2010, some less-fortunate disabled persons without wheelchairs and crutches regularly moved up and down dragging themselves on their hands and knees in order to catch the notice of potential donors and arouse their sympathies (Kwenda, 10 April 2010).

Some beggars exposed wounds, injuries, deformities or diseases that they, or their dependents, had in order to elicit the sympathy of well-wishers (Kaushil, 2014; Tripathi and Arora, 2010). Other critically-ill beggars displayed to well-wishers, their body organs that required urgent medical attention. The common organs which they indicated included the heart, kidneys, breasts, bladders, limbs ravaged by cancer and other parts where they had been surgically operated (Chikondo, Dhokoze and Kodogwe, FGD: 2014). Yet others, whose urinary systems were dysfunctional, moved around soliciting for alms by exposing the medically-improvised equipment inserted into their bodies which enabled them to urinate without much difficulty. This surgical set-up involved piercing the bladder and inserting a tube which drained urine directly into an external plastic container fastened around the waist but concealed by a long blouse or shirt they would be putting on. These beggars often pleaded for money or food and many argued that they were incapable of performing laborious tasks because they would disturb and aggravate their delicate medical condition (Kazore and Pachije, Joint Interview: 2014).

From the foregoing discussion, a fascinating paradox emerges from the manner in which some beggars capitalise on their vulnerabilities such as deprivation and disability to their advantage. It is a fact that poverty and disability can be important indicators of marginalisation, vulnerability and victimhood. These indices of downtroddenness are, however, often mobilised and deployed by beggars to captivate public sympathies and bolster their bargaining position for more alms, hence reflecting agency on the part of that section of the population that is, or appears to be, underprivileged, marginalised and vulnerable. This is an interesting scenario in which victimhood and marginalisation generate agency while weaknesses give way to strengths. These circumstances demonstrate how victimhood can be both a strength and a weakness as beggars manipulate circumstances to salvage livelihoods (Dancus 2020).

As in other parts of the developing world, feigning illness or disability became a critical livelihood improvisation for some beggars as socio-economic impecuniosity worsened and the competition for alms-givers escalated (Balarabe, Mahmoud and Ayanniyi, 2014). In various Nigerian cities during the post-colonial period, for example, strategies of portraying themselves as sick, visually-challenged, deaf, or crippled were very common among beggars (Namwata, Mgabo and Dimoso, 2012). In December 2018, for example, Ada Nwachukwu, a desperate woman who faked blindness and had been roaming the streets of Nigeria to beg for alms, "hilariously regained her eyesight after police had threatened to unleash tear-gas on her" (Kamasah, 14 December 2018: 1). The con woman, who had been using a little girl believed to be her daughter as her 'guide girl', revealed to the police officers who apprehended her that she had already made 3 270 Naira from faking blindness at the time of her arrest (Ibid).

Kariati (21 May 2014) noted the prevalence of such practices in most Zimbabwean urban centres during the first decade of the 21st century. In various parts of the country, as some informants confirmed during interviews, some downtrodden people reportedly smeared body creams and liquid oils around their eyes to make them appear tearful and give an impression that they were visually-impaired (Chingoro, Madhuveko and Nhongonya, Separate Interviews, 2013). Some vendors who operated at Sakubva Bus Terminus in Mutare since the early 2000s recounted how at around this time, some beggars who feigned blindness betrayed themselves to journalists from the *Manica Post* newspaper. Acting on a tip off from some members of the public that a group of four beggars who operated at the terminus was not visually-deprived as they claimed and appeared to be, the journalists attempted to photograph them from a distance. Upon noticing that they were being photographed, the four gave the newsmen a chase! They caught up with them after which they confiscated their cameras and smashed them to the ground before disappearing in the sprawling Sakubva Suburb (Chingoro and Madhuveko, Separate Interviews, 2013). Indeed, feigning illness or disability was a deceptive way of earning a living but the improvisation of such strategies can best be appreciated when contextualised in the Zimbabwean crisis. Such innovations were a result of heightened competition for alms-givers in an environment portrayed by grinding poverty. As McFadden noted in Harare, some people pretended to be visually-challenged as an economic strategy to earn livelihoods through begging (McFadden, 30 July 2014).

Symbolic gesturing, mostly by disabled persons, is another important visual appeal to the mercy of well-wishers. As a mode of communication, sign language is not a monopoly of the deaf and dumb alone, but has been widely employed by other beggars to indicate need. These mercy-provoking gestures include extending a hat, cap or open palm (Separate Interviews: Arimenda, 2013; Charirwe, 2014; Chaza, 2014; Kaonde, 2013). Appreciation for a donation that had been made was sometimes expressed through smiles or other gestures of gratitude (Kassah, 2008).

The extent of some people's poverty can be indexed by the condition of their attire. Some beggars wore rags as a genuine expression of their impoverishment because they could not afford decent clothing (Matereke, Mukonda and Sibindi, Separate Interviews: 2014). Such genuinely-unfortunate appearances tended to work positively for some poor people by captivating the benevolence of donors. As Cosmas Okoli, a Nigerian national, told Disability Awareness in Action (1995: 33): "Seeing the ragged disabled people begging on the streets of Lagos elicits sympathy from the passers-by so that they go as far as dipping their hands into their lean pockets to give alms to the beggars".

There were, however, instances when some beggars were "ragged from choice" (Bentwick, 1894: 126). They deliberately donned tattered and dirty clothes as a matter of strategy to lure potential sympathisers. Informants who lived in the same neighbourhood with such improvising beggars stated that some of them had decent clothing but often sought donations while putting on torn clothes in order to induce the sympathies of passers-by (Matereke, Mukonda and Sibindi, Separate Interviews: 2014). It was also common practice for some beggars to walk bare-footed or with shoes without laces in order to appear helplessly in need. It was also alleged that some beggars intentionally put up scruffy or unsightly appearances by avoiding to bath and neglecting their hair for the same reason (Chako, Mukonda and Sibindi, Separate Interviews: 2014). Writing on beggars in New York during the late 19th century, Bentwick (1894: 126) complained:

> The professional beggar makes New York his happy hunting-ground, and dresses for his character like any other actor. "He is a Lazarus by day", says a writer, "but at night he puts off his rags and fares sumptuously. He is an artist, and his art is lying". In the poorer quarters

of the city on a Saturday night, when the poor man and his hard-working wife have received their pittance the professional beggar is sure to be on hand, with his detestable whine, his lies, his rags, his professional face, ready to coax the money from these poor people…

Significant numbers of beggars received similar public condemnation in Zimbabwe for employing such deceptive means to earn livelihoods. It should be appreciated that such fabrications were necessitated by conditions of chronic poverty in an environment where competition for scarce resources increasingly became fierce. In such circumstances, well-wishers tended to empathise more with those who were visibly vulnerable such as children, the visually-impaired and other physically-handicapped people. Begging through false representations became an important innovation by downtrodden people to eke an existence in a highly competitive dispensation where their conspicuously younger and disabled counterparts tended to win the sympathies of the majority of potential donors. From an empirical perspective, therefore, such deceptive improvisations can best be appreciated when studied within the context of the Zimbabwean crisis from 2000.

Some innovative beggars are on record for dressing themselves smartly and then crafting stories such as: having lost some valuable items or falling victim to thieves in an effort to convince passers-by to assist them with money. According to Esan (2009: 5), this category is 'high sense' begging which involves "telling important or unimportant lies to obtain people's help". In Nigeria in 2011, for example, it was "not surprising to see well dressed, able-bodied men and women… [along] the streets and public places using different styles to beg for alms" (Fawole, Ogunkan and Omoruan, 2011: 11). Marcus Munodawafa, an Insurance Salesman, narrated how, in mid-May 2014, he met a certain man in Kwame Nkrumah Avenue in Harare and gave him ZW$2 after he believed his story that he wanted to attend to his sick wife at Harare Hospital but did not have money for transport. Two hours later, Munodawafa came across the same man, this time in Julius Nyerere Avenue, who once again approached him and repeated the same old story. Munodawafa told him that he had already given him ZW$2 before but he replied that it was mistaken identity and then vanished into the crowd of pedestrians (Kariati, 19 May 2014). Such a "new crop of money beggars", as the *Africa News* (10 May 2016: 1) reported, "hit the streets of Harare" from mid-2016. Some of them approached well-wishers seeking money for bus-fare to go back home after claiming to have lost their wallets, either by accident or to thieves (Bamu, 21 October 2019). These examples show how dire situations during the Zimbabwean crisis saw the emergence of a constituency of extremely innovative and sometimes cunning beggars with the ability to outwit the relatively well-to-do in order to address their condition of poverty.

Various types of documentation constituted part of an assortment of other visual mechanisms used by beggars to solicit for help. This communicative innovation was mostly used by disabled beggars, particularly the deaf, dumb and visually-challenged to explain their plight to passers-by. Posters, for instance, were widely used in Zimbabwe's city centres particularly in pavements and along the streets. At every traffic light intersection in Harare, reported Margaret Kriel in September 2009, there was a beggar with a banner explaining his or her circumstances of deprivation (Kriel, 22 September 2009). The common statements written on such banners in most of Zimbabwean urban centres included: "I am deaf and dumb. I am asking for help"; "Please help me with food"; "I am disabled and my children are starving"; "I am unemployed, disabled and hungry"; "Please help the suffering"; and "If you help the disabled, God will bless you" (Personal Observations in Harare, Masvingo, Mutare and Rusape: 2000-2014). Other posters read: "Tomorrow it can be you" (Muchairi, 22 November 2013); and "I am begging for assistance" (Kwaramba, 23 November 2013). Some posters were written in print that was bold and big enough to draw the attention of passing motorists. Some informants from the general public, however, complained that such a strategy of soliciting for alms could distract drivers and cause traffic accidents (Chaza and Murwira, Separate Interviews: 2014).

Reference letters were another important visual communicative mechanism used by some panhandlers. The communicative conduct of some beggars, particularly the deaf and the visually-impaired, sometimes involved moving around with reference letters from various institutions authenticating their plight as a way of convincing members of the public that they were in great need of help. Some moved around with medical referral papers confirming their needy health condition (Namwata, Mgabo and Dimoso, 2012). Some of the institutions which issued such letters were the government's Department of Social Welfare, church organisations and welfare homes for disabled persons. In its recommendation for assistance, the letter usually stated the name of the vulnerable person and the nature of his or her vulnerability. Some officials from the Department of Social Welfare in Harare stated that they issued recommendation letters to genuinely impoverished people who approached them for help. They stated that they had little option but to issue such letters appealing for public support since the government was financially-crippled to assist them (Chizanza, Rwenze and Shawa, FGD: 2014). This was confirmed by Elizabeth Takawira, a visually-disadvantaged mother-of-two, who begged along Mutare's streets in 2012: "Life in Zimbabwe is worsening by the day and there is no one to look after my children. I tried to get help from the Ministry of Public Service and Social Welfare but to no avail" (Saxon, 11 July 2012: 1).

Officials at the Jairos Jiri Centre for the Disabled in Mutare insisted that they did not tolerate begging by people who had graduated in various crafts at their institution. Instead, they issued them with reference letters appealing to employees to engage them. It was unfortunate, however, that those who failed to secure employment used the reference documents to solicit for alms in order to survive (Magumbo, Rwasunda and Sigogo, FGD: 2014). A head of a religious organisation in Mutare also expressed similar sentiments. He argued that they never encouraged their impoverished and vulnerable members to beg but sometimes gave them reference letters outlining their plight with the hope that employers would be sympathetic and offer them jobs. He acknowledged that those who failed to secure jobs often abused the reference letters by using them to beg (Mugwengwendere, Interview: 2013).

The use of documents such as posters and reference letters to publicise their plight to passers-by was an important innovation devised mostly by those beggars who could not communicate orally.

There were, however, instances when some individuals connived to misrepresent one or more of them as deaf, blind or dumb to the Department of Social Welfare offices so as to be given a reference letter to facilitate begging pursuits (Benson, Kabonde and Murawo, FGD: 2014). In other parts of the world such as Nigeria, as Osa-Edoh and Ayano (2012) observed, beggars used envelopes or banners with images of very ill people to attract donations for their own use. Though deceptive, such strategies illustrate the creativity and resilience of poor people in combatting adversity.

Disability as an asset rather than a liability in begging pursuits

It is a fact that beggars with varying kinds of disability tend to attract the attention of passers-by than those who are not. Indeed, most beggars themselves often display their disabilities in an effort to provoke the sympathies of potential helpers. More often than not, the critically-handicapped beggars "allow their condition to speak for itself, using fewer or no words at all" (Esan, 2009: 2). In actual fact, as Zimbabwe's socio-economic woes persisted, some poverty-stricken people capitalised on the disability of their family members and relatives by stationing them at various points in towns for purposes of begging. The paradox of this strategy is that while it afforded some families with some source of livelihood, it was premised on the exploitation of disabled persons. This scenario was aptly explained at length by Watson Khupe, a Zimbabwean disability activist and researcher, in April 2010:

> There is a general misconception that for one to qualify to be a slave, one has to be an able-bodied person, strong enough so that he/she must be able to provide hard labour to the slave master. According to this logic, disabled people regardless of the nature of their disability, are incapable of being turned into slaves. Yet the painful truth is that some people with disabilities in Zimbabwe have been turned into what is referred to as cash-cow products through slavery. Slavery comes in different forms and it is non-discriminatory.

In Zimbabwe, an unprecedented poverty mainly caused by the

political and economic problems during the past decade, taught people to be innovative to such an extent that even the disabled people have been turned into money-spinner slaves. Slavery now comes in different forms. It is now common in Zimbabwe to find very severely disabled people strategically planted by their relatives at the corners of buildings in the city centre for the purpose of raising funds. Some of these disabled people are incapable of holding a plate or a tin or to stand on their legs. Some are not able to speak a single word as a result of speech disability.

One thing is certain though; these unfortunate disabled persons are not difficult to transform into productive slaves. Therefore, the plate or tin is placed very close to the poor (and) severely disabled person so that sympathetic passers-by may drop some coins in the tin or plate. These disabled people are left at these strategic places by their relatives every morning and then picked every evening. However, the disabled persons need to be hungry so that their appearance properly projects suffering so as to attract sympathy from the public. At times they, the disabled slaves, are made to resemble tourist attractions. This is done by exposing the most severely disabled part of their limbs so that members of the public flock to look at them in awe and sympathy.

The question often asked by some concerned citizens is: who is the direct beneficiary of funds raised through this method? Is it the poor and disabled person or the master, a relative who would have placed that disabled person at that corner of a busy street who gets the lion's share? It is obvious that the poor and disabled person is never privy to the total amount he/she would have raised? In fact, the amount so raised does not belong to that disabled person. This brutal abuse of innocent citizens has been taking place.... (Khupe, 19 April 2010: 1).

The practice of abusing people with disability for purposes of personal aggrandisement was also notable in other parts of the world. In Nigeria, in April 2010, for example, some panhandlers "(were) actually planted by able-bodied people who go to remote villages and lure disabled people to Lagos on the pretext that they want to help them" (Ibid: 1). These unsuspecting disabled people were kept at various strategic points on the streets in the most pathetic conditions to draw out the greatest amount of sympathy from passers-by. Their managers, who lived in comfort in posh houses, organised vendors to supply food to their money-making beggars. At the end of each day, the beggars surrendered their proceeds to the managers (Ibid).

Child begging

Child beggars, according to Hawkson (2015), are people below the age of 18 years who beg for alms. The involvement of children has always been one of the most controversial aspects of begging dynamics in various parts of the world in general and Zimbabwe in particular. Children have been involved in various capacities during begging pursuits since time immemorial but in most cases, they would have been roped in by adults. Some adult beggars have used their babies, some of them suckling, to illustrate the gravity of their plight and provoke the sympathies of passers-by. Some adults are known to have fronted children during begging pursuits as guides, usually in situations where the beggars were their disabled parents, guardians or relatives. In such circumstances, the children pushed the wheelchairs of their disabled parents, and also persuaded passers-by to donate alms (Chikiwa, 17 February 2019). This can be referred to as 'advocacy begging' whereby "one person begged in the name of or as an advocate or spokesperson for others. This type of begging mostly occurred where…children…presented themselves as advocates for their sick mother, father, or profiteer" (Owusu-Sekyere, Jengre and Alhassan, 2018: 6).

Another category of involvement included children themselves embarking on begging pursuits either because of poverty or after being forced by their parents to do so. The last category pertains to cases where children were hired out by their parents to beg on behalf of individuals or syndicates (Chikiwa, 17 February 2019). This brings to the picture what can be called 'begging entrepreneurs' who "are older folks who have recruited…children to beg in the city and paid them for the service rendered. How much a beggar is paid depended on the sales they made" (Owusu-Sekyere, Jengre and Alhassan, 2018: 6). It can be noted, therefore, that in this exploitative begging arrangement, the "unscrupulous and ruthless operators [use] the

94

destitute and the helpless as commodities" (Wijesiri, 9 December 2018: 1).

Children have often been used by adult beggars as bait to elicit sympathy from potential donors (Ord, 2010). In many cases, some disabled mothers have taken suckling babies on their arms or backs on begging pursuits in an attempt to arouse the mercy of onlookers. In his study of panhandling in Quito, Ecuador, Swanson (2007: 705) noted that "the presence of children has become integral to women's begging tactics". Similarly, along Harare's streets in August 2012, the presence of many visually-impaired mothers with children on their backs, begging from motorists was a common sight (Moyo, 9 August 2012).

Some adult beggars also found it expedient to move around in the company of children who they fronted as guides, escorts and agents who persuaded passers-by to donate alms. As Kaushik (2014: 14) noted on how this improvisation worked in various urban centres in India: "People feel bad by seeing a child in distress and need and hence they give alms to such children". The fronting of children by adults in begging pursuits was also rampant in Zimbabwe as economic wretchedness worsened. In 2000, UNICEF noted that 4.1% of the street children in the cities of Harare, Bulawayo, Mutare, Gweru and Kadoma escorted visually-challenged beggars (UNICEF, 2001). Sekai Marongwe, a visually-challenged woman who operated at Charge Office Bus Terminus in Harare in August 2011 with the assistance of Taurai, her 11-year-old son, told *Newsday* (21 August 2011: 1): "They have to help us because they will also eat from the money. People are able to see how desperate my case is when they look at my son". In November 2013, Pretty Chivango, a news correspondent, noted in awe:

Wandering children in Zimbabwe's capital's CBD of Harare is slowly becoming a norm. From as young as eight years old to teenagers, these children roam the streets from the early hours of dawn till late at night, mastering the 'art' of begging at a tender age. The popular cause for this growing trend is financial strain culminating in more and more children being forced onto the streets seeking the basics of life, food, clothes and shelter... (Chivango, 1 November 2013: 1).

In February 2017, Walter Mzembi, the then Zimbabwe's Minister of Tourism, expressed concern at the increasing number of children living and working in the streets of the country's urban areas. He noted that, "children as young as one year or above in the country were being used as bait by adults to solicit for money in the streets. The children solicit for cash from motorists and tourists and most of them are now relegated to street work" (Mawire, 7 February 2017: 1). In August 2019, Scott Panashe Mamimine, a human rights lawyer, lamented on the situation in many Zimbabwean urban centres:

> It has now become an acceptable norm in our society, seeing grandparents, parents or siblings using these children as pawns or baits for coins on the streets. Children have effectively been turned to be worms on the hooks in order for the adults to catch fish. The use of children in this manner is strategic to cut a deep electric sense of empathy and pity from passers-by who are easily persuaded and moved to draw out something from their pockets or dashboards. This instance speaks eloquently of the quagmire we are in as a nation, notwithstanding international and regional laws which castigate any forms of abuses or exploitation of children in this manner (Mamimine, 12 August 2019: 1).

The use of children to beg in order to provoke the sympathies of donors has been condemned by the general public and various official domains such as national governments, civil society organisations and the United Nations. Despite the moral concerns over such practices, it needs to be understood, however, that conditions of dire poverty drive marginalised people to craft a broad range of strategies in order to survive. The paradox of such cunning improvisations is that they represent "a badness that is also a kind of strength" (Scheper-Hughes, 2008: 47).

Some parents sometimes sent or forced their children to embark on solitary begging pursuits, owing to the ever-deteriorating socio-economic conditions. In particular, some parents who were unable to pay school fees are known to have instructed their children to roam the streets in school uniform to beg for money (Moyo, 9 August 2012). In February 2002, for example, it was estimated that most of the 12 000 Zimbabwean street children, 5 000 of whom were in Harare, increased in number during weekends and school holidays when they [school children] were sent out by their parents into the streets to beg in order to supplement family incomes and raise money for school fees (Civil Society Forum for East and Southern Africa, 11-13 February 2002). In May 2002, Tendai Mangoma, a Zimbabwean journalist, noted that the number of child beggars on Harare's streets was increasing as grinding socio-economic maladies forced many parents and guardians to send their children on begging errands (Mangoma, 29 May 2002).

In mid-2011, the *Daily News* (21 August 2011: 1) rang alarm bells over the increasing number of adult female panhandlers who were enlisting the services of their children to beg in Zimbabwe's urban areas, particularly Harare:

> Many beggars in Harare have roped in their children as a way of getting to generous people who may be moved by the children's pitiful sight to part with a few dollars. Young boys and girls, many of them barely into their teens, now prowl Harare's streets while their parents sit in the shadows away from the public's questioning gaze. While some of the children seem to enjoy it, darting from street to street, sometimes almost tripling passers-by, theirs is a sorry tale of a lost childhood as they are initiated into the begging system early on in life. Some of the beggars said they had no choice but to make their children beg because that was the only way they could feed them.

In December 2011, a survey by Child Aid Zimbabwe (CAZ), a local children's rights organisation, revealed that more than 300 children below the age of seven years were being forced by their parents to beg from strangers in Harare's Central Business District. The survey also showed that most of the children were of school-going age (*Bulawayo24 News*, 10 December 2011). Another research carried out in Harare in November 2013 by CAZ noted that more than 200 children below the age of seven years were being exploited by adults to beg from passers-by, including motorists and patrons in take-away shops and restaurants (Munanavire, 8 November 2013). Some parents actually set daily minimum amounts of money which their children had to beg, failure of which unspecified action would be taken. Alice Matare, a 13-year-old girl who roamed the streets of Harare's CBD in March 2015, for example, reported that her mother forced her to beg and set a daily target of at least US$3: "I have to collect at least $3, which is my daily benchmark. Failure to raise this amount will land me in trouble" (Takawira, 26 March 2015: 1). The Defence for Children International Zimbabwe (2014: 1) noted with concern that even though Zimbabwe's Children's Protection and Adoption Act prohibits the use of children in "hazardous and harmful conditions, and using them for begging purposes", this practice, among other informal livelihood pursuits, was "rife and often went on with the knowledge, encouragement or instruction of the parents".

In 2014, data provided by a government survey revealed that 4 701 children were living and working in the streets in Zimbabwe, including 2 050 in Harare, the capital city, with begging being one of their major preoccupations (Masiyiwa, 10 November 2016). In June 2015, Charity Sibanda, a Harare lawyer, noted that cases of child begging were becoming rampant in Zimbabwe (Matikinye, 10 June 2015). Between January and August 2016, the government removed 78 children from Harare's streets (Ibid).

Child begging remained visible as a critical survival pursuit in Zimbabwe's urban centres after the downfall of Robert Mugabe. "In Zimbabwe", as Kudzai Chikiwa, a journalist, observed in February 2019, "it has become a norm to see children as young as six asking for alms from Good Samaritans while their parents will be singing gospel songs to entertain and draw sympathy from well-wishers" (Chikiwa, 17 February 2019: 1). Judith Ncube, the Provincial Affairs Minister for Bulawayo Metropolitan Province, weighed in and lamented the influx of child beggars in Bulawayo's Central Business District: "We need to engage the Social Welfare [Department] and find out what can be done to solve the issue of child beggars' increase in Bulawayo. What is touching is that they are of school-going age and many are girls" (Ibid: 1).

The use of children to beg became so rampant that the Zimbabwe Republic Police (ZRP) and municipal authorities often launched operations to clear children from the streets and at the same time arrested their parents or guardians for violating children's rights. On 6 February 2013, for example, three women from Harare's Epworth Suburb were arrested at the intersection of Samora Machel Avenue and Leopold Takawira Street in the city's Central Business District while begging together with their children. The three women were Agnes Mandaza (30), Nyasha Simango (22) and Revai Bhatisani (38). Agnes Mandaza was arrested while begging in the company of her three children aged 14, 10 and 8. Revai Bhatisani was in the company of her four children aged 15, 9, 5 years and 9 months while Nyasha Simango was with her 2-year-old child. The children were immediately taken to the Department of Social Welfare. On 7 February 2013, the three female beggars were brought before the Harare Magistrate's Court to answer charges of contravening the Child Protection Act by using their children to beg for money and food in the streets. They were each sentenced to a wholly suspended term of 30 days in prison (*Bulawayo 24 News*, 8 February 2013).

The efforts by the Zimbabwean authorities to curb the use of children to beg were largely unsuccessful because of the government's failure to put in place effective poverty-alleviation mechanisms and schemes. In early 2016, Zimbabwe's Ministry of Public Service, Labour and Social Welfare set up multi-sectoral taskforces to monitor the situation of children living and working on the streets. In May 2016, the taskforces in Harare facilitated the arrest of 20 mothers who were using their children to beg on the streets (Masiyiwa, 10 November 2016). Despite these efforts, as Masiyiwa (10 November 2016: 1) observed in late 2016, "…thousands of children are on the streets, and the number is increasing. Government programs have been reuniting a few with their families, and some mothers have been arrested in the capital, Harare, for using kids to beg".

The strategy of fronting children to beg was also well executed by Ganuka, a visually-impaired man, together with one of his four disabled wives and two of his 20 children in Harare's CBD, as Veronica Gwaze, a *Sunday Mail* reporter observed in November 2019. Gwaze noted:

Like most blind beggars, he is always accompanied by one of his children - a young boy who appears streetwise. A few yards away from him, his second wife, Feria, is also begging and is accompanied by a young girl, their daughter. For any passer-by, it is hard to tell that the two are husband and wife (Gwaze, 24 November 2019: 1).

Some children made the decision to seek livelihoods through begging either on their own or after being influenced by peers with whom they shared the same predicament of absolute poverty. In most cases, such children were orphans while others had been abandoned by their parents. Thomas Sangati, a 14-year-old boy, reported during an interview in the Gweru Central Business District in 2016 that he was forced to resort to begging after his mother and single parent was nearly always away from home on commercial sex work without leaving him anything to eat (Interview with Thomas Sangati, 12 March 2016). Some orphans revealed during interviews that they ended up seeking livelihoods through panhandling after failing to make ends meet owing to the death of their parents from HIV/AIDS (Separate Interviews with Sotwa, Sundai and Zvofa, August to September 2015). This study noted that many child-headed families in Zimbabwe's urban areas earned livelihoods from begging, initially from the immediate environment among sympathetic neighbours and relatives and later, far afield from among strangers and charitable organisations. The spatial shift was necessitated by the fact that neighbours and relatives in the immediate environment, having been the first port of call, soon developed donor fatigue, forcing the desperately needy children to seek alms further away from their homes (Ibid).

Consequently, in July 2017, as Zimbabwe's economy continued "to bite the dust", according to Kadirire (9 July 2017: 1), "more and more children in and around Harare [were] being forced to beg from motorists at road intersections". He added: "Some of the children will be carrying family siblings on their back as they dangerously move, bowel in hand, between moving vehicles. At the traffic lights by Simon Mazorodze and Remembrance Drive [in Harare], small boys take turns to beg for loose change from kombi drivers" (Ibid: 1). These sentiments were immediately echoed by Taylor Nyanhete, the then National Director of the Zimbabwe National Council for the Welfare of Children, who lamented "the increase of child beggars on the street" and added that the main reason why their numbers continued to rise was because "there [was] no source of income to sustain their families and on the other side, government [had] no budget to meet the needs of these children" (Kadirire, 9 July 2017: 1).

Child begging also became widespread in Zimbabwe's rural areas during the reign of Emmerson Mnangagwa as harrowing socio-economic experiences, epitomised by chronic hunger and absolute poverty, among other things, became part of life for many citizens. An example can be drawn from the Gokwe Kaguta area under Chief Nemangwe in April 2019 where "impoverished children…resorted to begging by way of sleeping across busy roads. This [was] done as a way to force motorists to stop so they can listen to the children's plight and give them something to hold on to" (Chirisa, 25 April 2019: 1).

Elsewhere, in the developing world, some children are known to have been hired out to individuals or syndicates who deployed them to beg for alms after which a commission was paid to their parents or guardians (UNICEF, 2001). Swanson (2007: 205) noted that this form of "child renting" was widespread among beggars in most urban centres of Ecuador. By December 2019, Zimbabwe's socio-economic penury was forcing some impoverished parents to hire out their children to handlers under whom they begged for a 'commission.' In Harare, for example, most of these begging children, some of whom were as young as six years old, were drawn from the high-density suburbs such as Epworth and Hopley, among others. The new breed of beggars was transported into the city centre each day before being allocated places to beg from. At the end of the day, the person who brought them collected his share from the youngsters before giving the parents or guardians their share of the spoils. The child was often given a token for his or her toils. The majority of the people who hired the youngsters were vendors, who monitored the young beggars' movements from a distance. Most of the youngsters were reportedly coached to lie that their handlers were their biological parents (Mashinya and Gwaze, 15 December 2019; *Pindula News*, 15 December 2019).

In cases that clearly illustrate the cruelty of poverty, some desperate parents even sold their young children to syndicates that were notorious for using children to beg along the streets in urban centres of neighbouring countries, particularly South Africa. In January 2019, for example, a 27-year-old woman from Zimbabwe's Masvingo Province allegedly sold her three-year-old daughter to a South African-based syndicate that was known to use children as beggars at busy traffic intersections. The woman, Grana Chiondegwa, of Village 11A, Mushandike Resettlement Area, allegedly struck a deal to receive 300 Rands every month from the syndicate in return for having her daughter exploited in the neighbouring country. Chiondegwa confessed in court that she was forced to give the child away after her husband, Tinashe Mutombeni, had deserted her together with their five children. Chiondegwa reportedly approached Olinda Munodawafa, her church mate who came from the neighbouring Mashava area and revealed that she could not fend for her children and had no means to get food and school fees for them. Munodawafa is believed to have advised her to link up with a woman known as Chepiri from the Shurugwi District who would take the minor to South Africa for the purpose of begging along the streets in return for some money every month. Munodawafa took the girl to Chepiri's village in Shurugwi District but a tip-off from the villagers resulted in the arrest of the accomplices and saved the minor from being trafficked to South Africa (Mswazie, 7 March 2019). This abominable practice of parents allegedly forcing their children to South Africa to beg was also reported to be prevalent at the Bere Compound in the Mashava area of Chivi District in Masvingo Province (Ibid).

Figure 4: Child beggars for hire: Harare, 2019
Source: Mashinya and Gwaze (15 December 2019)

As this section has demonstrated, child begging has been on the rise in Zimbabwe since the onset of the new millennium owing to the debilitating socio-economic crisis. The influx of children of varying ages as informal street workers and the broad range of mechanisms which they devised to obtain alms illustrate the magnitude of the crisis. The use of children as a begging technique to arouse the mercy of passers-by illuminates how some downtrodden people sought to survive amid adversity. Even though the exploitation of children by adults in begging shows that survival struggles know no morals, there is need to contextualise such activities in the Zimbabwean crises from 2000 and analyse the situation in terms of the moral economy of child labour.

Media begging

Begging for financial resources to meet medical costs by people with critical health conditions became widespread particularly from 2002 as Zimbabwe's socio-economic maladies worsened. Medical costs skyrocketed due to hyperinflation in an environment where unemployment and poverty rates were escalating and the provision of government social welfare services to the sick and poor was deteriorating at an alarming pace. As a result, most patients could not afford the exorbitant medical fees since they were not on medical aid schemes owing to socio-economic challenges. In addition, many medical aid investments were eroded by inflation and medical aid societies failed to meet the costs of treatment. Many critical drugs were in short supply and medical equipment became obsolete as the government increasingly became bankrupt and its foreign currency reserves ran dry. In addition, the hyperinflationary environment resulted in a serious brain drain in which most medical specialists sought greener pastures abroad. At the beginning of 2003, for example, Zimbabwe had lost more than 2 100 medical doctors and 1 950 certified nurses to countries such as South Africa, Botswana, Namibia, Britain and Australia (*Financial Gazette*, 27 March 2009). By September 2006, more than 50% of the key medical professionals had left the country (*Agence France-Presse*, 24 September 2006). In 2008, the state-owned Parirenyatwa Hospital stopped performing surgical operations because of shortages of staff and equipment, underfunding and mismanagement (*Relief Web*, 25 February 2008). Consequently, medical costs shot up beyond the reach of the ordinary Zimbabweans since local doctors referred most people with chronic ailments abroad for specialist treatment.

The costs of treating various forms of cancer, for example, became very prohibitive in Zimbabwe. The most common cancers in the country were cervical, breast, prostate, Kaposi Sarcoma, non-Hodgkin's lymphomia, tongue and pituitary tumour extension (Chipunza, 27 November 2013; Zaba and Mazulu, 1 November 2013). The medical technology, for example chemotherapy and radiotherapy, used to contain cancers was very expensive and beyond the reach of ordinary people. At the beginning of 2013, for instance, chemotherapy required up to US$100 per cycle of treatment depending on the stage of the cancer and a patient could require a minimum of six cycles and a maximum of 12 (Zaba and Mazulu, 1 November 2013). In 2013, the cost of treating some cancers ranged between US$25 000 and US$30 000 while the same treatment cost US$10 000 in India (Chipunza, 27 November 2013). In view of these agonies, various strategies were devised by critically-ill people to beg for financial assistance to meet medical costs.

Some desperate patients suffering from chronic ailments embarked on media-begging which involved approaching the print and electronic media institutions such as newspaper houses as well as television and radio stations to publicise their appeals for medical assistance. They usually gave the media their physical addresses, phone numbers and bank account details for onward transmission to the donor community. As some examples below to illustrate, this strategy sometimes bore fruit. An 18-year-old Mutare girl successfully underwent life-saving surgery in London in early October 2009 after five years of begging for money in Zimbabwe to meet the medical costs. Since 2004, Nomatter Taremeredzwa Mapungwana had a facial tumour on the upper left jaw which made her lose weight and threatened to cover her face. Zimbabwean doctors referred her to a British specialist in London. Nomatter's mother approached the state electronic and print media for assistance to broadcast their plight in order to raise £10 000 which was required for payment. The fundraising effort, which was coordinated by the Girl Child Network, a local NGO, raised the amount from Zimbabweans across the whole world. Air Zimbabwe, the country's national airline, paid the airfare bill (Mathuthu, 10 October 2009).

Again, in October 2009, Nelson Kunyonga, a Harare man, approached the country's media institutions appealing for financial assistance to have his son treated for cancer in South Africa. The cancer was eating up the flesh of his skin on the face and head. Zimbabwean doctors advised him to seek specialist attention in South Africa since there was no medication in the country (Madzamba, 17 October 2009).

Similarly, Kudakwashe Chiwira, a 38-year-old Bulawayo man, approached the state-owned *Chronicle* newspaper in April 2011 appealing for publicity for his need of financial assistance to undergo specialist medical treatment in South Africa which local hospital facilities could not handle. He had experienced serious heart problems since 2007 which required a surgical operation to a damaged valve at Steve Biko Academic Hospital in South Africa. He could not afford the medical cost of US$80 000 demanded by the hospital (*Chronicle*, 24 April 2011).

In December 2011, Sinikiwe Sibanda, a Bulawayo widow, also appealed to the state-owned *Chronicle* newspaper to publicise the urgent financial need to have her daughter undergo surgery in South Africa for a heart disease. The girl needed R50 000 to undergo treatment for a rheumatic heart disease. She was informed by local doctors that two valves in her heart were damaged and needed to be replaced by specialists in South Africa (Mafu, 11 December 2011). In January 2012, World Remit, an online money transfer agency, managed to cater for all the medical expenses (Gunda, 5 January 2012).

Decent Mamvura-Mafukushe, a Mutare man, approached the state-owned *Herald* newspaper in May 2012 to publicise his urgent need of up to R170 000 to have his son, Advocate Mafukushe (13) undergo plastic surgery in South Africa. The boy was seriously burnt in January 2011 after the family's paraffin stove exploded while he was cooking. Even though he had spent seven months at Mutare General Hospital, the wounds failed to heal and doctors referred him for specialist treatment in South Africa. His poor family could not raise the costs and appealed to the state media to inform well-wishers of their plight (*Herald*, 8 May 2012).

In June 2013, Advance Mpofu, a 33-year-old man from Magedleni Village near the town of Plumtree in south-western Zimbabwe, presented an appeal in national newspapers and radio stations for financial assistance to undergo surgery in South Africa to remove a brain tumour. He had been treated before but the problem resurfaced. The Bulawayo United Hospitals, where he was admitted, did not have the medical equipment to carry out a scan of his brain. He required US$500 to undergo the scan in South Africa (*Bulawayo 24 News*, 24 June 2012).

The increasing incidence of media-begging shows how some critically-ill poor looked beyond their immediate communities in search of survival. The prevalence of such media appeals for assistance from the general public and international donors exposed the Zimbabwe government's failure to alleviate the plight of its desperate citizens. Ironically, some of the media houses such as the Zimbabwe Broadcasting Corporation (ZBC), Zimbabwe Television

106

(ZTV), *Chronicle* and *Herald* which publicised the appeals for assistance were state institutions. Interestingly, media-begging, among other things, illustrates how some impoverished citizens sometimes utilise the institutions of a failed state to survive.

Coercive begging strategies

The hostile reception from some sections of the public partly explains why some desperate beggars employed coercive strategies, what Rugoho and Siziba (1988: 54) refer to as "aggressive begging", to get alms. Strategies involving the pestering of people for donations constitute what Ahola (2011: 36) termed "aggressive and disturbing begging". As Fawole, Ogunkan and Omoruan (2011: 9) observed in Nigerian cities, beggars who sought donations through forceful means were "a social menace" to the public. "Not all beggars use supplicating words to beg... Some beggars use insults, profanity, or veiled threats in aggressive panhandling", noted Fawole, Ogunkan and Omoruan (2011: 10) in various parts of West Africa, "The Caucasian coloured beggars from Chad and Niger Republic also intimidated their targeted donors into giving alms by clinging unto them". According to the New York City bye-laws, aggressive begging involves "intentionally touching or causing physical contact with another person or an occupied vehicle" and "approaching or speaking to a person...if that conduct is intended or is likely to cause a reasonable person to...fear bodily harm..., otherwise be intimidated into giving money or other thing of value, or...suffer unreasonable inconvenience, annoyance or alarm" (Roblee-Hertzmark, 2012: 9). The molestation on potential well-wishers is most probably an indication of desperation and a lack of diplomacy or persuasive skills on the part of some beggars.

In their study of street life in Harare during the new millennium, Rugoho and Siziba (2014) found out that the majority of aggressive beggars were aged between 15 and 19 years. In Harare's streets and car parks in June 2007, some beggars were seen hustling motorists to guard their cars for a fee (Gwara, 5 June 2007). Michael Ottey (16 May 2013: 1), a tourist to Zimbabwe in early 2009, narrated a "downright aggressive" encounter he had with young beggars along

107

the streets of Harare:

> I gave some loose change to a child beggar. Before I knew it, I was surrounded by more than a half-dozen other kids tugging at me and demanding money as well. One young girl who was about seven or eight years old grabbed and latched on to my left arm and refused to let go. I raised my arm and lifted her off the ground and still would not release my arm. A local merchant, noticing what was happening, came out of his store and began to shove the kids away from me while screaming at them in their native language. I learnt my lessons: If you are going to give money to children on the street, make sure you know there are any others around or be prepared for a full assault. Even handing out candy or pencils to children can create a mob scene.

In November 2013, as some journalists observed in Harare, it was common for child street beggars to pester women until they gave them something (Muchairi, 22 November 2013). By mid-March 2020, the footbridge near Harare's Town House had become a haven of notorious boys who "gave women and girls a torrid time as they would demand, not ask for money" (Dhliwayo, 18 March 2020: 1).

As this section has illustrated, aggressive begging became common along the streets of Zimbabwe's urban centres as desperation manifested itself among some panhandlers who had been exasperated by unending socio-economic dire straits. The chapter has shown that women were in many cases vulnerable to the shenanigans of aggressive beggars. Despite aggressive panhandling being criminal according to the law, it was one of the several mechanisms adopted by some marginalised people as they sought livelihoods in an inhospitable socio-economic environment.

Begging: A means to an end and not an end in itself?

There were some indirect forms of begging in which poor people performed some tasks without being requested after which they asked for remuneration. These innovative tasks included guarding and washing cars parked by their owners in city centres, controlling traffic at busy intersections and filling up potholes in urban streets.

These services clearly illustrate that for many marginalised people, begging is a means to an end and not an end in itself. Indeed, if jobs and other support services are available, most downtrodden people would choose to be formally employed or embark in other more rewarding income-generating projects.

What can be termed service-begging is performing some tasks for people often without being requested, what Ahamdi (2010: 136) termed "false jobs," after which the beggar/s pleads for reciprocation, usually in monetary form. Such covert begging strategies include car-minding for motorists who would have parked in city centres to visit various places such as restaurants, cinemas, shopping and work centres. This preoccupation became so lucrative in view of the prevalence of car thefts across the country. Some car-minders were, however, reported to have deflated tyres or damaged vehicles whose owners had turned down their services (Bourdillon, 1991).

In several parking lots in Zimbabwe's urban centres, many motorists returned to their vehicles to find them washed and the tyres polished. When the unsuspecting vehicle owner returned, the cleaner requested for a fee as payment for the service. During interviews conducted in the city of Mutare in mid-2019, some beggars revealed that they normally targeted expensive cars for cleaning because they presumed that their owners were well-to-do and would give them more money for the service. There was unanimity among the participants that they never cleaned ramshackle vehicles as they expected little or nothing from their owners (Separate Interviews Jakado, Kesani, Nanga and Padya, November 2019).

Some innovative beggars controlled traffic at busy intersections when traffic lights were not functioning. As one Harare boy called Takunda who, together with three other peers, controlled traffic at the intersection of Bishop Gaul and Samora Machel Avenues stated in mid-January 2020:

> Together with my three friends we like to control traffic, especially when there is no power to calm the confusion which normally results in congestion and sometimes accidents. We all used to beg, but we normally meet the same people who are now fed up, and see us as grown-ups who can use their hands to put food on the table (Dhliwayo,

Takunda added that motorists gave them money, clothes or food for the service. He also revealed that Indians from Belvedere Suburb were very generous and often gave them food and United States dollars (Ibid).

In many urban areas, some beggars sought alms from passing motorists by filling in potholes that became characteristic of many streets in CBDs and residential areas. Given that the Zimbabwean government was critically bankrupt and urban councils severely cash-strapped, many urban roads deteriorated into a state of neglect and disrepair. Some innovative beggars took it upon themselves to fill pot-holes with sand, stones and mud after which they sought alms from passing motorists (Chipadze, Hunga and Puture, Separate Interviews: 2020). What emerges from these activities is a fascinating irony where marginalised people such as panhandlers provide a critical service where the local and central governments would have dismally failed.

Some touts at urban bus termini offered porterage services often without the consent of the owners of goods they ferried. Their modus operandi usually involved snatching luggage from pedestrians approaching a bus terminus on the pretext of assisting them after which they pleaded for money, sometimes forcefully (Duri, 2016). In similar arm-twisting fashion, others ferried luggage to and from bus termini and loaded or offloaded it from buses in anticipation of financial reciprocation (Bhuke, Cheneso, Chingoro, Gomba and Madhuveko, Separate Interviews: 2013).

It is indeed true that the provision of services without being invited sometimes inconvenienced members of the public in various ways. It is being argued, however, that such forms of begging should be viewed as a strategy commonly employed by the relatively-abled and middle-aged poor to eke livelihoods in a fiercely contested panhandling environment in which well-wishers tended to sympathise more with children and conspicuously disabled persons. In addition, the initiative of some impoverished people to offer services in anticipation of alms contradicts the view of scholars such as Namwata, Mgabo and Dimoso (2012) that begging is an easy way of earning livelihoods employed by some indolent people. Instead, what becomes apparent is that most people resort to begging due to deprivation and marginalisation; if employment opportunities and resources to start income-generating projects were available, they would realise their productive capabilities. Thus, as Fitzpatrick and Kennedy (2000) assert, most vulnerable people do not sit idly mourning their plight and anticipating charity but are desperate for support in the form of services and resources in order to move on.

In their pursuits of survival, some beggars exhibited entrepreneurial attributes by selling some items in order to get money, thus demonstrating that begging is a means to an end and not an end in itself. In addition, such activities illustrate that some beggars can be enterprising people if the necessary support is availed to them. The selling of items by some marginalised people sometimes constitutes a covert and at times forceful form of begging. It is a form of begging on grounds that it exploits and provokes the emotions or sympathies of people in order to have their goods bought. It is "disguised begging" in which panhandlers "[market] their poverty" in order to attract customers to purchase their goods (Swanson, 2007: 710).

In their study of beggars in Addis Ababa, Groce and others (2013) noted that 87% of informants were optimistic of a future beyond begging and were hoping to engage in other activities such as small-scale trading, or crafts like shoe repair and tailoring if resources for training and inputs were available. In Zimbabwe, the innovativeness of beggars who operated in buses plying the highways was also shown by the way in which some of them diversified into hawking. In 2013, for example, it was common with visually-challenged beggars on buses along the Masvingo-Bulawayo Highway to initially request for alms after which they made some rounds selling basic commodities. During the process, they pleaded with passengers to buy their goods in order for them to survive. The most common commodities they sold were body creams, cosmetics, soap and toothpaste (Personal Observation: 2013). Some of the commodities had been donated to them by manufacturers, wholesalers and retail shop-owners. In some cases, beggars actually bought the wares from shops (Chikondo, Dhokoze, and Kodogwe, FGD: 16 August 2014).

111

This reflection of micro-entrepreneurship epitomises the resourcefulness of some beggars to earn livelihoods in a hostile socio-economic dispensation. It also illustrates that given the necessary inputs and facilities, some disadvantaged people in society can engage in more productive livelihood-earning pursuits.

It should be noted that many beggars are prepared to abandon begging if opportunities to partake in other more rewarding income-generating activities become available. During interviews conducted by Quidiz (2005), none of the informants acknowledged resorting to begging on grounds that it was lucrative or brought easy money. As Roblee-Hertzmark (2012: 7) noted: "Despite what much of the popular press would have us believe, it is not lucrative and it is not something that many people would choose given other options. Begging is a desperate act".

It is wrong to assume that begging is always a last resort livelihood activity (Groce and others, 2013). This is evidenced by some beggars who undertake begging pursuits concurrently with other income-generating activities. In July 2012, for example, Tavonga (9) and Tatenda Takawira (12), two brothers who begged at busy street intersections in Mutare supplemented the income they got from well-wishers by cleaning cars and selling cigarettes (Saxon, 11 July 2012). In April 2013, Dube (15 April 2013) observed that scores of disabled people who used to survive solely from begging in Bulawayo had diversified into the vending business. Among them were the mute and deaf. This diversification was necessitated by the nationwide financial crisis which made donations from sympathisers hard to come by. Most of them sold airtime cards, cigarettes and sweets along the streets. Such initiatives by beggars demonstrated their alert engagement with changing times.

As a matter of fact, begging is a temporary livelihood option for many poor people, most of who are prepared to abandon it altogether in favour of other pursuits if opportunities arise. The temporary nature of begging can partly be explained in terms of psycho-generational developments. As some children grow old, their self-esteem develops to the extent of viewing begging as humiliating (Evans, 2006). Some may abandon begging and instead assume other roles as overseers and protectors of younger beggars (Abebe, 2008).

In June 2007, Chipo Sithole, a 16-year-old girl who begged in Harare's streets, stated that she would abandon begging for other income-generating projects at the end of the year because of her maturing age: "I cannot continue begging because of my age. What normally happens is that girls of my age graduate from begging to prostitution" (Gwara, 5 June 2007: 1). Other factors that determine the temporality of panhandling are the degree of poverty, the material circumstances and the emergence of more viable livelihood opportunities (Abebe, 2008). As Abebe (2008: 271) noted:

> ...beggars are not passive victims of their circumstances, but are aware of the fact that begging is not a perpetual predicament in their lives. Moreover, the activity of begging is complex and fluid, and is based on the changing nature of...livelihoods and socio-economic conditions. Age, gender, social maturity and availability (or lack) of alternative income-generating strategies are important variables shaping both their spatio-temporal participation in and withdrawal from the activity.

The experiences of Siphosethu Ndlovu, a disabled woman aged 28 years in 2013, vividly illustrate that begging is only a livelihood option which some people are prepared to abandon for other more productive income-generating projects. She was born in 1995 with multiple disabilities in the rural Lupane District of Matabeleland North Province in Zimbabwe. During her childhood, she was so physically challenged that she could neither feed herself, nor walk without being assisted. She grew up at her rural home and never went to school. As she grew up, she practised how to feed herself using her toes. At the age of 10 in 1995, she was taken to Bulawayo by her uncle who promised to enrol her at a special school for disabled persons. Upon arrival in Bulawayo, his uncle took her to the pavements every morning to beg for alms. During the late 2000s, she abandoned begging for knitting in order to generate income. On the pavement of a Bulawayo supermarket in May 2013, she knit toilet and bathroom sets such as cistern and toilet bowl covers as well as floor mats using empty maize-meal polythene bags. She knitted using her toes while holding the maize-meal sack between her teeth and the toes on her left foot. She then sewed with her toes on the right foot using a piece of thick wire as a needle. She managed to buy a wheelchair and sustained herself from the income she got after selling the wares (*Women News Network*, 29 May 2013). These experiences reiterate the observation made in this section that for most beggars, panhandling is a means to an end and not an end in itself. In actual fact, many people whom we interviewed for this book were prepared to abandon begging altogether if other options of survival become available.

Begging and social capital

Even though many of the people living in poverty regarded begging as a temporary livelihood option, some innovative beggars attempted to invest in social capital by pooling their resources together and forming institutions and structures that would save as safety nets in the struggle for sustenance. The Social Capital Theory asserts that relationships and social networks are an integral resource utilised by vulnerable people in order to make ends meet (Rantalaiho and Teije, 2006). Thus, beggars meet their counterparts in similar predicaments and create "bonding social capital" in order to eke livelihoods (Mtonga, 2011: 115).

Aptekar (1988) noted that friendship among street beggars afforded them social acceptance and security, and emotional and material support often denied to them by their families. As noted by Orme and Seipel (2007) in their study of street children in Accra, Ghana, beggars often form informal friendship associations in order to assist each other to meet basic survival needs. Some beggars forged close relationships, what Scheper-Hughes (2008: 48) calls "fictive kinship" that involved supporting each other on a daily basis such as looking after each other's children and providing financial and other forms of assistance in the event of illness and dire shortage of basic necessities. In some Nigerian cities, as Salami and Olugbayo (2013) noted, many immigrant beggars pooled their resources together and assisted each other during times of deprivation. In terms of organisation, therefore, some beggar societies, though largely informal, were not very different from professional and other organisations such as trade unions and burial associations in terms of their collective welfare endeavours (Hanchao, 1999).

In Zimbabwe, attempts to broaden and formalise networking among beggars were first made in 2004 through the formation of the Harare Street Beggars Association. It was headed by Kingstone Chisale who himself begged along the streets of Harare. It was born out of the need to find decent ways of begging among the country's visually-impaired beggars by among other things, finding ways of preventing competition and clashes among themselves. The association did not last long largely because as Zimbabwe's socio-economic crunches continued to worsen over the years, competition for alms among beggars became fiercer while others crossed the border to seek livelihoods in neighbouring countries (*Daily News*, 11 February 2005).

Conclusion

This chapter has illustrated that most beggars in Zimbabwe, particularly from the onset of the new millennium, were desperate people who had to employ unscrupulous strategies in order to survive. As a survivalist undertaking, panhandling involves numerous improvisations, most of which entail the careful management of time and space in order to capture the attention and sympathy of passers-by and the general public. True to the adage: 'poverty knows no morals', some strategies employed by beggars to obtain alms border on immorality, criminality and deception as evidenced, among other things, by aggressive begging, feigning disability and illness, formulating false stories of misfortune, as well as using and hiring out children. It should be emphasised that while such strategies leave a lot to be desired, they need to be understood and appreciated in the context of the inexorable Zimbabwean crisis during which many desperate people seek livelihoods at any cost. While a considerable section of the Zimbabwean population became beggars, many are prepared to abandon begging altogether if other more rewarding livelihood options become available.

Chapter 3

Survival of the Fittest:
The harsh realities of begging experiences in Zimbabwe

Introduction

This chapter considers some of the major challenges that confronted beggars in Zimbabwe, which necessitated some to adopt survivalist strategies in the harsh environment. This was largely because in addition to the general socio-economic and political woes that besieged the country from 2000, beggars experienced a surfeit of hurdles as they sought for alms in Zimbabwe. Worse still, some of the age-old problems faced by the begging community around the world, for example, negative societal attitudes and stereotyping, remained pervasive in 21st century Zimbabwe. To aggravate their plight, the beggars experienced serious challenges that specifically emanated from the Zimbabwean crisis since 2000. These included the rising poverty levels and the significant drop in the number of potential well-wishers, inflation, cash shortages, and a broad range of ruinous government policies and practices.

Negative societal attitudes towards beggars

In various parts of the world, many sections of the mainstream society tend to regard beggars with suspicion and condescension. Public and popular attitudes towards vulnerable people such as beggars are largely negative and emphasise on their inadequacies and failure. In the public domain, there is a general perception that most panhandlers are lazy and do not want to work, hence "a beggar's mentality" (Welthhagen, 2013: 12). Writing in the 19th century, Bentwick (1894: 125) expressed similar sentiments, arguing that for most beggars, the "means are so ample there and...charity is so free". They have also been castigated as indolent no-hopers who cannot survive without charity (Owolabi, 2012). In addition, beggars have often been negatively stereotyped as liabilities, social outcasts and lunatics whose appearance is scruffy, unkempt, dirty and repulsive (SAMP, 8 September 2005). Among the Yoruba people of Nigeria, begging is "as mortifying as stealing", and beggars are resented to the extent that "one of the…daily prayers is that God should 'not make begging their means of livelihood'" (Esan, 2009: 3).

The language used to characterise them is largely unsympathetic, exclusionary and dominated by defamatory rhetoric (Daly, 1996). In official and public discourses, references to beggars are often pervaded by exclusionary terminology as "delinquency, false manipulation of public sympathies, ignorance, laziness and filth" (Swanson, 2007: 705). In many parts of the world, derogatory labels have been used to castigate or incarcerate vulnerable people as villains. In Peru and Bangladesh, for example, street children and beggars are commonly referred to as thieves and illegitimate people (Tipple and Speak, 2004). Among the Shona, the majority ethnic group in Zimbabwe, panhandling in general is known as *kupemha* while begging specifically for grain and other non-monetary items is referred to as *kusunza* (Hannan, 1959). During the period of socio-economic hardships in Zimbabwe from 2000, these terms assumed derogatory dimensions in the public discourse to refer to the activities of lazy and parasitic people who seek livelihoods at the expense of other suffering sections of the society (Jena, Kwase and Wozemwa, Separate Interviews, June-July 2019).

These negative perceptions largely explain the hostile reactions from some members of the public when approached by beggars. In their study of panhandling in Bucharest, Rumania, Mihalache and others (2013) noted that one out of 20 drivers approached by beggars at traffic intersections was impressed while one out of 100 pedestrians requested for help along the streets responded positively. In Zimbabwe's rural areas during the period 2007-2008 when the country experienced severe shortages of food and other basic commodities, some relatively well-to-do people devised a surfeit of strategies to disguise foodstuffs, particularly maize meal, in order to ward off beggars. As testified by a number of informants, such strategies were both diverse and prevalent. Tofanei Mutambu of

118

Zvidzai Village in Chimombe Communal Lands, for example, observed:

> The people are now in the habit of buying maize or maize meal at night. You have to go with a big suitcase to hide it so that you do not attract unnecessary attention from other villagers because they will swarm your home begging for food for their families (Kwaramba and Mtimba, 31 October 2013).

Chenai Mukombo from Munyikwa Village in Buhera district also reported on other strategies:

> Besides going to the grinding mill at night, some people no longer carry the whole 25-litre buckets or the 20-kilogram bag of maize for grinding. You have to go there with small quantities like five kilograms so that people will think that you are also struggling (Ibid: 1).

It now becomes apparent that the agony of enduring indifferent reactions from the mainstream society and potential donors is one of the chief features of a beggar's life. Such negative perceptions fail to take into account the needs of the poor and the context in which their vulnerability emanates from (Tipple and Speak, 2004). Religious and philanthropic organisations are, however, more inclusive and sympathetic towards vulnerable people by viewing them with pity and compassion. However, such attitudes may underestimate the potential of many vulnerable people by portraying them as passive and helpless victims who are always in need of charity (Ibid).

Criminalisation of beggars by central and local government authorities

In many countries around the world, the authorities regard beggars as a public nuisance and liken their presence in Central Business Districts to an invasion (SAMP, 8 September 2005). Thus, central and local government authorities regard them as "out of place in the city" (Swanson, 2007: 710). These attitudes, together with attempts by central and local government authorities to remove poor people from the streets, have severely jeopardised the livelihoods of many beggars.

Various countries around the world have put in place laws that criminalise begging. In India, for example, the Bombay Prevention of Begging Act of 1959 made vagrancy or begging illegal (Tipple and Speak, 2004). In addition, the Bombay Prevention of Beggary Act outlawed begging and made it punishable by up to 12 months in prison. This law defined beggars to include those "having no visible means of sustenance and wandering about or remaining in any public place in such conditions or manner, and makes it likely that the person doing so exists from soliciting or receiving alms" (Roblee-Hertzmark, 2012: 9). In Morocco, begging is punishable by up to six months in prison (Ibid). In Ghana, begging is outlawed and punishable under the National Liberation Decree of 1969 (Kassah, 2008).

Even though there are no anti-begging laws in Zimbabwe, central government and municipal authorities regard begging as a menace to orderliness especially in city centres. Zimbabwean authorities have routinely carried out operations to wipe out beggars from the streets in an effort to sanitise the urban areas. In July 2006, for example, the government launched an operation to clear all urban centres of street children and beggars. By mid-August, the government claimed that it had rounded up more than 10 000 street children and beggars in Harare alone (Blair, 19 August 2011). The exercise was not successful in the long term as streets were soon flooded again by the street children and beggars (Nyatsanza, 22 April 2009).

In mid-September 2007, more than 300 people were arrested by the Zimbabwe Republic Police and the Harare Municipal Police in Harare's Central Business District for various offenses such as vending, touting, loitering, begging and gambling. In an effort to avoid being apprehended, many vendors, hawkers, touts, the visually-impaired, beggars and streets kids were constantly on the move as they played cat-and-mouse with the police. During the blitz, some beggars avoided exposing themselves by suspending some of the strategies they routinely used to capture public attention and arouse people's benevolence such as rattling begging bowls at street corners and singing hymns along pavements (Matikinye, 21 September 2007:

1).

From late January into early February 2013, the police in Harare launched Operation *Usagare Mumugwagwa* (Do not stay on the streets) to round up street beggars and arrest parents who forced their children to beg (Ncube, 3 February 2013). Tadious Chibanda, the then Harare Provincial Police Spokesman, said the children who were rounded up would be taken to the government's social welfare institutions for rehabilitation while their parents would be apprehended: "It is an offence under the Child Protection Act to allow a minor to beg in the street. These children are being abused by their parents and end up as street kids" (Ibid: 1).

Physical mobility was an important attribute during anti-begging campaigns by the police and municipal authorities when beggars could be arrested, detained, ordered to pay fines for loitering or selling items without a license, or relocated to distant areas. Usually, those beggars who had no critical physical disabilities had to run away to avoid being arrested and having whatever commodities they could have been selling confiscated because they were the major targets of the police while the conspicuously disabled were in most cases left alone (Jena, Kwase and Wozemwa, Separate Interviews: 2019).

On 27 August 2015, police details from Harare's Central Police Station launched a blitz on street children, the majority of who were beggars. They rounded up 74 street children at various points in the capital before dumping them in some of the most remote parts of Zimbabwe during the night. They were reportedly dumped one by one in remote rural areas, namely Muzarabani, Mount Darwin and Mavhuradonha. In particular, the Mavhuradonha area was known to be lion-infested. Interviews carried out with a number of the street children, some of whom managed to return to Harare, revealed ruthlessness and gross abuse of human rights on the part of the police (Chaunza, 14 December 2015: 1).

Mike Tafirenyika, one of the victims who was picked up by uniformed police officers on 27 August 2015 at around 2200 hours near the Monomotapa Crown Plaza Hotel, narrated his ordeal:

> We were kept in police cells for four days while waiting for the number to accumulate to at least over 50 people. They then drove us to

Mavhuradonha Mountain, near Mount Darwin. The area is lion infested. Getting back from there was not easy as we did not have any cash with us (Ibid: 1).

Another victim also explained his terrifying experience at the hands of the police:

I was picked up at midnight while sleeping in Harare Gardens on charges of obstruction. We were about 40. A lorry came to collect and take us to Muzarabani where they dropped us one by one along the road, telling us that we should stay there. It took me six days to return to Harare because I was begging for transport throughout the road. I was lucky to be given $5 by a well-wisher, which I paid to Tauya Coach as bus fare. While in the bus, I was given another $3 by a well-wisher after lamenting my ordeal (Ibid: 1).

Willard Tambo, another boy who was raided together with others at a place where they scavenged for their supper in the Harare CBD, added:

The police told us they were taking us to a place where we were going to get registered for census. We were kept at Harare Central Police Station for three days. We were vetted for criminal records and cleared by members of the Criminal Investigation Department who found us innocent, but we were told that they were going to release us. On the third day, when we were supposed to be released, we ended up in a lorry. We were dropped at Muzarabani and ordered not to return to Harare (Ibid: 1).

Commenting on the August 2015 blitz, a street child who was now working as a peer educator under the Streets Ahead, a local NGO, reported that the incident was only the tip of an iceberg as homeless children were always exposed to a broad range of human rights abuses by the state's law-enforcement agents. He explained:

Soldiers and the members of the police in the night visit our makeshift houses harassing us. They ask us the reasons why we are on the streets and pretend to ask us about our identity documents. Young girls in the process are raped within the vicinity of our bases, while defenceless boys are often sodomised. As a result, a number of street children contract sexually transmitted diseases like gonorrhoea, genital herpes and syphilis (Ibid: 1).

In the immediate aftermath of the rounding up of the children and their subsequent dumping outside Harare, Street Exit Strategies, an NGO that rehabilitated street children, engaged the Zimbabwe Human Rights NGO Forum for assistance to sue the government. Respect Mugodhi, an official of Street Exit Strategies, outlined their case against the state as follows:

> What is happening to these young girls and boys is inhumane. It is against human rights. It goes against our mandate of reintegrating street children into mainstream society. Upon hearing such sad and inhuman developments happening to our constituency, we engaged human rights lawyers who are looking into the cases. We understand at times these children misbehave. They sometimes commit crimes around town, but we believe that this is not the way to deal with them. We want the public to know this is happening. What we have done is taking up the case against the…Home Affairs (Ministry) and the Commissioner General of the Police for torturing our clients. We are still quantifying the amounts for which they are to be sued. We believe it is a serious human rights abuse. Everyone has rights whether he lives in the street, shack or anywhere (Ibid: 1).

Despite attempts to disperse beggars from city centres, government clampdowns have not been successful in most parts of the world in general and Zimbabwe in particular because they fail to address the fundamental causes of begging (Crisis UK, 2003). As Wijesiri (9 December 2018: 1) succinctly put it: "Every social problem we encounter demands a solution, but a practical solution can be arrived at only through an intelligent understanding of the nature, extent and root cause of the problem. The beggar problem is no exception to this rule". At this point in time, the Zimbabwean government is best advised to "get used to beggars, because until we deal with the very root causes of poverty and injustice, they are not going anywhere" (Phillips and Shah, 26 January 2016: 1). Even though anti-begging operations had limited successes, they severely jeopardised the livelihoods of many beggars by depriving them of their hard-earned cash through payment of fines while others were temporarily removed from their catchment areas of alms.

Zimbabwe's economic malaise and the worsening plight of beggars

The major target of any panhandler is money even though other alms such as clothes and food are also sought after. It follows, therefore, that any development that disturbs the flow and value of money constitutes a severe crisis for most beggars. As discussed in considerable detail in Chapter 1, a debilitating socio-economic crisis of unprecedented proportions besieged Zimbabwe from 2000 and caused untold suffering for the majority of its citizens, most of who were plunged into a sea of chronic poverty. Among other things, unemployment levels soared while the standards of living deteriorated substantially. The effects of these developments on the welfare of beggars were catastrophic as the number of potential alms-givers plummeted while the capability of those who could squeeze something was significantly watered down. Worse still, hyperinflation wreaked havoc and rendered worthless the little donations in local currency that trickled in.

The cumulative effect of Zimbabwe's socio-economic meltdown from 2000 was abject poverty for the majority of citizens. It became an issue of bare survival from beggars as they sought alms from passers-by and the general public most of whose members were also wallowing in poverty. In April 2015, for example, Elliot Ncube, a beggar living with disability from Tshabalala Suburb in Bulawayo, stated that street begging became problematic from 2000 as potential donors were hard hit by socio-economic challenges. He explained:

> Since 2000, I have been begging in the street, but I could spend the whole day without getting a dollar, so last year I decided to start vending. I sell airtime cards, cigarettes and sweets. Selling is better than begging

because due to the economic crisis in the city, no one can just give anyone anything for nothing (Dube, 15 April 2013: 1).

To exacerbate the situation, the Zimbabwean economy was ravaged by inflation during the first decade of the new millennium and the country's currency became virtually worthless. These developments made life unbearable for beggars in two ways. First, potential alms-givers had little to offer since they themselves had been impoverished by the prevailing socio-economic challenges. Second, whatever money the beggars got from those who could afford to part with something was valueless. As Stephen Chan, a Professor of International Relations at the School of Oriental and African Studies University of London, stated: "You could not offer beggars anything in the street, because they would just throw it away. It was meaningless. You would have entire alleyways just full of worthless notes" (Perryer, 7 October 2019: 1).

Coins became a liability rather than an asset for Zimbabweans in general and beggars in particular as inflation continued to gnaw the local currency. In December 2014, the government had introduced 'bond coins' -so named because of the US$50 million bond that made them possible. Some beggars ended up rejecting bond coins as the currency continued to depreciate. In January 2015, for example, a news correspondent who handed bond coins to a beggar in Harare "received a burst of laughter and a 'no thanks'" (Dier, 9 January 2015: 1).

Zimbabwe's socio-economic crisis and fierce clashes among beggars

As noted earlier in this chapter, Zimbabwe's socio-economic degeneration from 2000 severely jeopardised the livelihoods of many beggars since the number of potential alms-givers dwindled significantly while inflation eroded the daily collections that came in local currency. Consequently, it became common for the older beggars to bully the youngsters and confiscate their alms while fierce clashes often erupted as competition for potential well-wishers heightened.

Young beggars became more vulnerable as their marauding elders sometimes robbed them of their daily collections. In early July 2000, for example, Diti, a nine-year-old orphan who begged at the junction of Second Street and Tongogara Avenue in central Harare, stated that one of her major challenges was harassment by boys of the street who often took away her daily collections. She lamented: "There are many boys here - more and more. They beat us until we give them everything. I am always hungry" (Blair, 10 July 2000: 1). Similarly, in March 2015, Tapiwa Nhare, a 15-year-old boy who begged in Harare's CBD narrated his daily ordeal: "I depend on begging for survival. I usually collect money just enough to buy daily food and also give part of it to the 'street tycoons'. If you do not bring a dollar to the big guys, you do not have a place to sleep" (Takawira, 26 March 2015: 1). In July 2017, some young beggars in Harare's streets complained of being harassed by their older counterparts during which the money they had collected was seized (Kadirire, 9 July 2017). There were also reports that some older boys in Harare's Central Business District demanded a portion of alms collected by young beggars on a daily basis akin to some kind of tax (Ibid).

Clashes among street beggars as they competed to get alms from donors became common and sometimes degenerated into verbal and physical assaults. Scuffles were common at traffic-light intersections as panhandlers crowded and elbowed each other at the windows of motor vehicles that had stopped in an attempt to get donations from drivers (Charirwe, Kahwema, Mukondiwa and Ruwende, Separate Interviews: 2014). If a note or coin happened to accidentally drop to the ground, a brawl often ensued as all beggars claimed it (Kahwema, Nungu and Vheremu, Separate Interviews: 2014). Some young beggars who operated in groups sometimes scrambled over a portion of food that would have been given to one of them by a well-wisher (Mukondiwa, Nungu and Zirongo, Separate Interviews: 2014).

Fierce clashes sometimes erupted after beggars in city centres encroached into each other's zones of operation (Kaushik, 2014). This often happened when newcomers who were not familiar to an area occupied spaces where established beggars were operating (Chawasarira, Marapa, Shato and Zirongo, Separate Interviews: 2014). Commenting on how some beggars collectively guarded their zones of operation in the Harare city centre in June 2007, Gwara (5 June

2007: 1) stated: "They form a class of their own and have well-defined territories, which they fiercely guard". In most cases, the females, children and the critically disabled lost out in such physical contests (Chawasarira, Ruwende and Vheremu, Separate Interviews: 2014).

Begging contestations that erupted in many urban spaces across the country clearly illustrate how the struggle against poverty sometimes generated a multiplicity of struggles among beggars as they sought livelihoods. It is beyond doubt that begging was not an easy way of earning a living. It was sometimes characterised by fierce competition in which survival was often earned by the fittest.

Liquidity crunch and the beggars' deepening sorrows

The nationwide shortage of hard currency during the second decade of the new millennium compounded the suffering of most beggars. The scarcity of cash and the increased uptake of plastic money made life unbearable for beggars who relied on street handouts. Since the cash crunch began, many Zimbabweans resorted to point-of-sale machines and mobile money services such as Ecocash, Telecash and One Money for their daily needs leaving no change-money to hand out to the needy.

By late 2018, as a result of the cash crisis, more than 80% of all transactions in the country were being conducted through mobile money transfer platforms, according to the Reserve Bank of Zimbabwe. A 2018 World Bank report ranked Zimbabwe as a country with one of the highest numbers of people in sub-Saharan Africa using cell phone money transfers (*Zimbabwean*, 26 August 2019). As the shortage of hard currency continued, the whole country was awash with a new breed of beggars soliciting for cash in exchange for plastic money. As a report in August 2019 put it:

The frantic hunt for cash often turns into begging. At the long lines to buy gasoline or diesel and in supermarkets, women, men and children move from person to person asking for cash. "Can I use my phone to pay for your goods, if you pay me cash?" they plead (Ibid: 1).

Many cash barons who sprouted across the country charged up to 60% interest for those who had mobile money and wanted cash (Dzarowa and Simati, Separate Interviews: 2020). What this meant was that most potential well-wishers had limited amounts of notes and coins, a situation that made them very reluctant to donate the hard-earned cash to beggars. During an interview in September 2017 along Cameroon Street in Harare, Limson Mambiyo, a visually-impaired man who begged in the company of his wife, moaned:

> Since people started relying on Ecocash and bank cards, the amount of money we receive from well-wishers has significantly dropped. Before, we could roughly get up to $15 a day but now on a day of serious hard work $5 is what we get. We used to get $20 every month from the Social Welfare but now whenever we go there, they always say there is no money (Chekai, 28 September 2017: 1).

By late August 2018, many beggars in urban centres across the country, for example, Bulawayo, possessed mobile phones in an effort to receive monetary donations electronically "after enduring months of walking up to 15 kilometres to their homes…with little or no coins as the cash crisis in the country had affected their benefactors" (Chikiwa, 25 August 2018: 1). Melusi Nyoni, a 35-year-old man who begged by the Ross Camp gate along Basch Street in Bulawayo, said he now struggled to pay rent and buy food because people who used to help him no longer had cash. He lamented:

> I live in Lobengula (Suburb) and I pay $65 rent monthly. Recently, I have been struggling to pay because most days I go back home without even a coin. My friend advised me to write my Ecocash number on a piece of paper so that people may know that I accept Ecocash. This has worked wonders. I can get up to $20 in three days. Some people who have my number sometimes make transfers in the middle of the night (Ibid: 1).

Similarly, Ntombizodwa Mabika, a visually-challenged female beggar who sat at the corner of Jason Moyo Street and Third Avenue in Bulawayo in September 2018, pointed out that she ended up moving around with her mobile phone and that her neighbour had installed a message tone specifically for Ecocash transfer confirmation messages on the cell phone. She would then go to supermarkets where they told her the balance in the electronic wallet after which she purchased food for her children (Ibid). On the same note, Tafi Dube, a 49-year-old visually-impaired male beggar who sat outside Pioneer House along Fife Street in Bulawayo during the same period, said he now used Ecocash: "There is a cash crisis and it is hard for people to get even a coin to pay for a kombi but if you have an Ecocash account, they can transfer something into your account. I started using Ecocash recently" (Ibid: 1).

It can be seen that Zimbabwe's monetary crisis negatively affected the operations of beggars, most of who survived from donations that came in the form of hard currency. Despite being marginalised, impoverished and desperate, many beggars did not lose sight of the need to cope with the challenge of cash shortages by acquiring mobile phones to enable them to receive alms electronically. This goes to show that subaltern struggles for survival involve, among other things, being alert and adoptive to changing times and the dictates of the moment.

The Coronavirus (Covid-19) and the national lockdown from March 2020

The number of potential alms-givers nosedived while begging options dwindled considerably as a result of the Zimbabwe government's declaration of a national lockdown. In an effort to contain and curb the spread of the Coronavirus (Covid-19) which was wreaking havoc worldwide, the government initially imposed a 21-day nationwide lockdown from 30 March 2020. During the three-week lockdown, all citizens were obliged to remain within their homes and could only venture outside when it became very necessary, most workers were ordered to stay at home except those in sectors that offered essential services, and public transport was banned with the exception of the state-owned Zimbabwe United Passenger Company (ZUPCO) that serviced only local intra-urban routes. The lockdown was extended by two more weeks up to 3 May 2020. Whilst some of the restrictions were revised and/ or were reduced, those curtailing the movement of Zimbabweans remained in place until the last quarter of 2020 (Mudahondo, 29 March 2020).

Given the restrictions to the movement of people imposed by the lockdown, many beggars became desperate as they were required to stay at home. In addition, the streets of Zimbabwe's urban centres were virtually empty as potential alms-givers were obliged to stay at home. In Harare during late March 2020, for example, many visually-impaired street beggars felt that the virus was "better than what they [were] going to experience for 21 days of lockdown" (Ibid: 1). Londani Mupapa, one Harare visually-handicapped male beggar, lamented:

> We are going to die of hunger and stress before even the virus reaches to us. Corona virus is not our main worry but how we are going to sustain our families. Myself, l am a father of five and we cannot beg along empty streets. It was better if the government had given us food hampers so that we would stay home with no problem (Ibid: 1).

In addition, the ban on public transport services severely threatened the livelihoods of itinerant beggars who had previously sought alms from long-distance buses. Chipo Chimba, a visually-challenged Harare woman who survived through begging in buses, vowed that she would rather die of the virus fending for her children than staying home: "Our lives are from hand to mouth. We do not have any savings, henceforth l will continue begging in the streets since buses are now limited" (Ibid: 1).

On 1 April 2020, Tymon Rukuni, a visually-disadvantaged beggar from the town of Rusape, lamented that the public transport ban had left him with very limited spaces to beg making it difficult to feed his six children (Moyo, 1 April 2020). Rejoice Chinembiri, another visually-deprived beggar from the same town, expressed similar sentiments:

> We are used to boarding buses for purposes of begging. From the proceeds, we bought maize meal and other groceries to feed our families. Now that public transport services have been suspended, we are in

trouble. We have just been to our Member of Parliament and the Department of Social Welfare seeking assistance but came back empty-handed (Ibid: 1).

Nhamo Makusha, another visually-impaired Rusape man, weighed in: "The nationwide lockdown has greatly disadvantaged people like us who survive through begging from buses. Since 30 March 2020 when the lockdown took effect, I have not had a decent meal and I am starving" (Ibid: 1). On 1 April 2020, David Tekeshe, the Member of Parliament for Makoni Central Constituency in which the town of Rusape is located, added weight to the lockdown-related concerns raised by the visually-challenged beggars:

Right now, I have just brought vegetables for relish and hope this may alleviate their plight. They had been told to seek assistance from the police and the Department of Social Welfare but nothing came out besides having their names registered. These people say the last day they were able to beg was Sunday (29 March 2020) on the eve of the lockdown and since then, they have not eaten anything. These people are suffering and urgently need assistance (Ibid: 1).

On 14 April 2020, Higher Life Foundation, a local charitable organisation, donated 362 food hampers to people living with disabilities, most of who survived on begging and had been negatively affected by lockdown interventions. The donation was confirmed by Ishmael Zhou, who doubled up as the Executive Director of the Zimbabwe National League of the Blind and the Chairperson of the National Association of Societies for the Care of the Handicapped:

We received generous donations comprising packets of 10 kilograms Parlenta mealie-meal, 10 kilograms chunks, 2 kilograms beans, 2 litres cooking oil and 500 grams salt. This will go a long way in alleviating the hunger affecting people with disabilities at a time the country is on lockdown. Most people with disabilities depend on begging, especially those that are blind, and some depend on street vending, channels which have been closed (*Pindula News*, 15 April 2020: 1).

131

As part of interventions to assist Harare street children, most of who survived on begging, the government relocated them to safe houses in the outskirts of Harare at Mount Hampden, Ruwa Rehabilitation Centre and Jamaica Inn Training Centre for Rural Women where they were to be accommodated and catered for during the lockdown period. In less than a week after being relocated, most of the children had escaped and were back on the streets of Harare to beg. One of the youths who had been accommodated at the safe houses explained why he fled:

> I feel I am better off in the streets where I can make a little money to buy myself food. Besides, we are not sure what the government plans to do with us once the lockdown period is done. Maybe, they intend to send us back to the very homes that we escaped from. The food rations we were getting at the safe houses were too little. It is better when we fend for ourselves out here in the streets. I want to be a motor mechanic and be able to fend for my family. My wish is for us to be given such skills at these safe houses (*Pindula News*, 17 April 2020: 1).

These sentiments from the child beggar expose the hollowness of the Zimbabwean government's usually piecemeal, myopic and short-term strategies of addressing the challenges encountered by vulnerable groups in the country. The youthful panhandler yearned for a permanent solution to his condition of poverty and deprivation and not having time being wasted in some shelter where they were not engaged in any meaningful activities that prepared them for a bright future. What emanates from the aforesaid is that, it is not the wish of many poor people to be permanently stationed along the streets as beggars. If opportunities and resources are availed to them, they are prepared to abandon begging for other livelihood options.

Though noble, the restrictions imposed by the Zimbabwean government to curb the spread of the Coronavirus severely disrupted the *modus operandi* of many beggars and left most of them on the brink of starvation. Many beggars were stranded as Zimbabwean streets were virtually empty because many motorists and pedestrians stayed at home in compliance with the lockdown regulations. The banning of most forms of public transport also poured more misery on those panhandlers who sought alms on buses along Zimbabwe's highways.

Conclusion

This chapter examined some of the numerous challenges experienced by beggars as they sought livelihoods in Zimbabwe from the onset of the new millennium. It has noted that beggars are generally viewed negatively by many sections of the public around the world in general and Zimbabwe in particular. Worse still, the Zimbabwean government and municipal authorities have always regarded beggars as a menace and launched many operations to clear them from the streets. As if these problems were not enough, the nationwide socio-economic travails from 2000, together with the lockdown restrictions imposed by the government to curb the spread of the Coronavirus, added misery to the downtrodden beggars. Given these challenges, it is the central contention of this chapter that begging is not an easy way of earning a living.

Chapter 4

Home Is Not Always Best!
Begging across national borders

Introduction

Zimbabwe's socio-economic discombobulation and political turbulence from 2000 saw millions of its citizens scattered across the world as beggars. The flooding of famished Zimbabweans, including beggars, most of who were living with disability, into neighbouring countries assumed torrential proportions as the clutter worsened. This chapter looks at begging by vulnerable Zimbabweans across national borders, paying particular attention to South Africa, Botswana and Mozambique. Most Zimbabwean beggars were found in South Africa and Botswana largely because they were Southern Africa's two most economically-successful nations (Nyamnjoh, 2006). South Africa is one of Africa's largest economies while Botswana is one of Africa's wealthiest countries (Plentive, 26 October 2007). Being Africa's biggest economy during the 21ˢᵗ century, South African streets became "a magnet for immigrant beggars who [saw] the country as a step out of poverty" (*Zimbabwe Black Book*, 18 May 2010: 1). In November 2019, long after the downfall of Robert Mugabe, for example, scores of economic refugees, who included "the disabled, the frail, the old and youths with some carrying infants on their backs", were reportedly pouring into South Africa where some ended up begging (Gurusa, 3 November 2019: 1). In Botswana and South Africa, Zimbabwean beggars were commonly known as *makwerekwere*, a contemptuous slang word referring to foreigners, particularly illegal immigrants who were often viewed with contempt as dangerous strangers (Hungwe, 2012; Nyamnjoh, 2006; *Word Press*, 23 May 2008).

Mozambique also attracted many Zimbabwean beggars due to the relatively long and porous border that it shares with Zimbabwe. Furthermore, the presence of Zimbabwean beggars in Mozambique illustrates the depth of the Zimbabwean crisis in that while Mozambique's economy had traditionally been weak compared to that of Zimbabwe, it was rebounding and was proving more attractive to Zimbabweans indicating that it offered better chances for picking alms (Duri, 2012a).

This chapter briefly looks at the presence of Zimbabwean beggars in Botswana and Mozambique before conducting a detailed study of their activities and experiences in South Africa. South Africa is being given more detailed coverage because, being the biggest economy in Southern Africa, the country became the destination for many Zimbabwean beggars than was the case with other neighbouring countries. That said, this chapter argues that home is not always the best for citizens if their livelihoods are perpetually threatened by a surfeit of insecurities such as socio-economic deprivation and political oppression. For some impoverished and downtrodden but innovative Zimbabweans, begging in diasporan spaces became a realistic option worth risking than sitting idly and moaning their predicament on home soil. Thus, begging across national borders by some marginalised sections of the Zimbabwean population demonstrates agency and competence on the part of the subaltern to negotiate the world in times of severe crises.

Accounting for the presence of Zimbabwean beggars in neighbouring countries

The ever-increasing presence of Zimbabwean beggars in neighbouring countries, particularly South Africa, during the new millennium is clearly traceable to the socio-economic and political crisis from 2000 which Chapter 1 explored in considerable detail. As the crisis persisted over the years, poverty levels skyrocketed, forcing many Zimbabweans to become beggars abroad. It should be noted that while some Zimbabweans left the country as beggars the others who were not, had initially hoped to find employment abroad but later resorted to begging after their hopes had been dashed.

As dealt with pithily in Chapter 3, while Zimbabwe's socio-economic challenges from 2000 forced many citizens to become panhandlers in an effort to earn livelihoods, begging within the country became unsustainable as the crisis unfolded. Unemployment, rising cost of living and escalating poverty levels reduced the number of potential alms-givers and plunged many beggars into despair. Besides eroding the disposable incomes of many potential well-wishers, hyperinflation reduced whatever money that had been collected from begging to pittance. To aggravate the situation, the bankrupt Zimbabwean government was incapacitated to bail out the beggars, most of who were disabled.

The socio-economic meltdown, together with ecological disasters such as droughts, left many Zimbabweans with hardly anything to donate to beggars. Kennedy Nyoni, a 29-year-old visually-deprived beggar who came to Johannesburg in 2004, told the *Mail and Guardian* that he left Zimbabwe because there was very little money in circulation due to the harsh economic environment:

> Our main reason for being here in South Africa is not to make something. It is just to make a living here. It is a hard living, but it is still a living - something we cannot do in Zimbabwe because even if the economy is slowly recovering, people do not have a lot of money to give us. In South Africa or in Zimbabwe, our jobs are the same- we are beggars (Tolsi, 30 September 2011: 1).

Kingstone Chisale, the then coordinator of the Harare Street Beggars Association, said in February 2005 that escalating poverty rates in Zimbabwe resulted in stiff competition among beggars at a time when the number of potential donors from the mainstream public was dwindling. "Begging is one of the last things a person would do", he said in February 2005, "but here in Zimbabwe there are now many beggars on the streets resulting in serious competition for a few dollars which they will be chasing after" (*Daily News*, 11 February 2005: 1). This forced considerable numbers of beggars to cross into neighbouring countries, especially South Africa, particularly after the Zimbabwean government scrapped the support programme for people living with disability in 2004. Chisale also explained why Johannesburg was the most popular destination in South Africa for the majority of Zimbabwean beggars:

Johannesburg is the economic hub of the region, and everyone tends to trek there in search of a living. We had no more than 130 members [of the Harare Street Beggars Association] who left the streets of Harare [in 2005] because they were not getting much to look after their families (Ibid: 1).

Gift Mupambiki, a 32-year-old man who became visually-challenged because of measles at the age of three years, also decided to leave his home in northern Zimbabwe in 2007 because of starvation resulting from a severe drought. At that time, many Zimbabweans hardly had anything to donate owing to the severely agonising socio-economic adversities. He said: "There was drought. We were surviving by begging, but people did not have anything to give" (*Irin News*, 13 June 2011: 1).

In view of the hyperinflationary environment in Zimbabwe that severely eroded their collections, a considerable number of Zimbabwean beggars relocated to neighbouring countries where the currencies, for example, the South African Rand, the Botswana Pula and the Mozambican Metical, were relatively much more stable. Lucy Ndebele of the Zimbabwe Council for the Blind reiterated that many people living with disability realised that they could earn more from begging in neighbouring countries owing to the unprecedented rates of inflation in the country (*Irin News*, 13 June 2011). As Joseph Ruzvidzo, a visually-challenged Zimbabwean panhandler in Johannesburg said in March 2007: "Begging here pays us a lot more than when we beg at home. We cannot do any other kind of job and begging is our only way out of the economic blues that are biting Zimbabwe" (Marufu, 21 March 2007: 1). In September 2007, Shylet Madhabuya, a 38-year-old visually-challenged beggar in Johannesburg stated that due to extremely agonising socio-economic challenges marked by unemployment and hyperinflation in Zimbabwe, she had to leave for South Africa where she could get more:

Begging in South Africa pays us a lot more than when we beg at home where one hardly makes enough money to buy food which is another reason why I decided to come here. Leaving my family behind

138

was the hardest thing, but I had no choice. If I continued begging in Zimbabwe I would have died of hunger (Mapumulo, 25 September 2007: 1).

The exodus of Zimbabwean beggars, most of who were disabled, to neighbouring countries could have been minimised if the government had cushioned them in various ways from the prevailing socio-economic miseries. Lamentably, as discussed in Chapter 1, the Zimbabwean government was in a state of perennial bankruptcy from 2000 owing to the dismal performance of the economy and international isolation, among other things. In 2004, for example, the bankrupt Zimbabwean government stopped funding self-help projects for the visually-disadvantaged people. This forced Kennedy Nyoni (29), Maphios Chimbwereshe (32) and Nicholas Maponde (33), both visually-impaired men who had graduated from Copota School for the Blind, to leave the country for Johannesburg where they eked livelihoods through begging (Tolsi, 30 September 2011). The monetary assistance which the government gave to vulnerable people, particularly people living with disability, was grossly inadequate, given the hyperinflationary environment that was prevailing in the country. In early 2005, for instance, the Zimbabwean government gave each registered disabled person a monthly social grant of ZW$7 000 [about nine Rands] at a time when a loaf of bread cost $ZW5 000 [about six Rands] (Peta, 4 February 2005).

The Zimbabwean government also failed to provide job security to its disabled employees. Prior to 2009, the visually-challenged employees in Zimbabwe's formal sector were usually the first to lose their jobs as inflation skyrocketed and the local currency went on a free-fall. Jethro Gonese, a visually-handicapped man, for example, was employed as a schoolteacher in Zimbabwe during the early 2000s. Since he was visually-impaired, an assistant paid by the government helped him with the marking and chalkboard work. Around 2004, as Zimbabwe's economic woes worsened, the government stated that it could no longer afford to pay assistants. In a desperate effort to retain his job, he initially shared his Z$1 000-monthly salary with the assistant. When hyperinflation reduced his monthly salary to less than the price of a loaf of bread, he was left with no option but to cross into South Africa and survive from begging in Johannesburg (Tolsi, 30 September 2011).

There were, however, cases of Zimbabweans who entered neighbouring countries, mostly South Africa, without the intention to beg but ended up doing so after experiencing unexpected misfortunes. In several of such cases, a person went to South Africa either to visit or to seek opportunities in various ways after making arrangements with colleagues who were already there. They then failed to locate their acquaintances, some of whom either switched off their phones or vanished upon their arrival in order to avoid them. This left them stranded with no food, shelter or bus-fare to go back home, thereby forcing them to beg for alms in order to survive (Hakutangwi, Mashizha, Matanga, FGD: 14 August 2010).

In other instances, some Zimbabweans entered South Africa to seek asylum as economic and political refugees but turned to street begging in order to survive after their applications had been turned down by the Ministry of Home Affairs in that country. According to procedure, the unsuccessful applicants were taken to Lindela Repatriation Camp to await deportation (Sibanda, 1 May 2006). It was while they were awaiting deportation that "many ran away from the authorities and ended up playing cat-and-mouse games with the police in the streets of Johannesburg" (Ibid: 1).

Other examples of how some Zimbabweans embarked on beggary without previously planning to do so can be drawn from the early months of 2020 when the whole world was hit by the Coronavirus (Covid-19). In mid-April 2020, many countries around the world were on lockdown to minimise the spread of the Coronavirus (Covid-19). In South Africa, President Cyril Ramaphosa declared a 21-day lockdown from 27 March to 16 April 2020 (Brown, 27 March 2020). The lockdown was extended by two weeks until the end of April 2020 and indefinitely from then on (Savides, 9 April 2020). During the lockdown period, all people were obliged to stay at home unless they were to attend to health services, buy groceries or collect social welfare grants. Unnecessary movements were forbidden. The services that were allowed to continue operating include: health, security (including police and army), production, commodity distribution and supply, banking, electric power generation, grocery retail and pharmacies (Mahlangu *et.al*, 24 March 2020).

These lockdown regulations threatened the livelihoods of many Zimbabwean diasporans, forcing some of them to survive through begging. In South Africa, many Zimbabwean immigrants who had been surviving through informal means, for example, self-jobs like vending, found themselves stranded after the government suspended their operations. In line with the lockdown regulations, many companies were closed, leaving only essential staff operating. Many workers, with the exception of those employed by the government, were not paid for the period they were not at work. In mid-April 2020, a number of Zimbabweans in South Africa lamented how they had become destitute as a result of the lockdown. Claude, a Zimbabwean man from Durban, for instance, said:

> The lockdown has affected us especially on money since most of us are self-employed meaning that if you do not go to work, there is no money. Those who work outside the Civil Service, for example, in Indian shops, are not paid for the period those businesses are closed. We are starving and when the month comes to an end, landlords want their rentals (Goba, 14 April 2020: 1).

Pastor Ronnie Bere, a Zimbabwean clergyman in Pretoria, added:

> The lockdown has affected most of those in my sphere of influence…Most foreigners do menial jobs, vending or work in restaurants. The lockdown…means we have no income for a period of five weeks. Unlike our South African brothers and sisters employed by government and those receiving aid from the recently unveiled Unemployment Insurance Fund (UIF), most foreigners have nothing. They are not sure how they will last until the end of the lockdown, and a number have taken to begging inside supermarkets; they pretend to be shopping but asking for donations from shoppers. Most highlight the need for food and are worried about where to get money for rentals this month-end as landlords need that money too for sustenance (Ibid: 1).

Samantha Mukombwe, another Zimbabwean in South Africa,

weighed in:

> As an illegal immigrant based in South Africa, this lockdown has badly affected me. I earn less than the South African minimum wage and I cannot even save it since I survive from hand to mouth. And the South African government is only assisting its citizens during this period, so I do not know how I am going to pay my bills, buy food and I cannot come home because the border is already closed (Ibid: 1).

This section has explained why the number of Zimbabwean beggars in the diaspora, particularly in neighbouring countries, continued to rise since the onset of the new millennium. Among other things, the section noted that many Zimbabwean who panhandled to survive abroad had fled the country as socio-economic hardships worsened. The outbreak of the Corona Virus in early 2020 and the subsequent imposition of lockdown regulations by governments in the region and beyond in an effort to contain the spread of the disease threatened the livelihoods of a considerable number of Zimbabwean diasporans and relegated many of them to beggars.

Zimbabwean beggars in Botswana and Mozambique

The presence of Zimbabwean beggars in other neighbouring countries should not be overlooked even though they were far fewer as compared to those who sought livelihoods in South Africa. Despite the figures being relatively low, the presence of Zimbabwean beggars in neighbouring countries such as Mozambique and Botswana deserves attention in order demonstrate the ability and capability of vulnerable people to navigate diasporan spaces in pursuit of sustenance during times of crises. By doing so, this chapter also unravels some of the regional and global ramifications of the Zimbabwean crisis from 2000.

From 2000, Botswana experienced significant inflows of vulnerable Zimbabweans fleeing socio-economic tribulations. In May 2003, there were about 40 000 illegal Zimbabwean immigrants in the country (Mukumbira, 1 May 2003), a significant inflow indeed given that the country's population at this time was 1.8 million (Mukumbira, 20 May 2003). In July 2003, government estimates indicated the presence of 60 000 undocumented Zimbabweans in the country (Butcher, 11 July 2003). In 2009, the number shot up to approximately 100 000 (Betts and Kaytaz, 2010). Among the undocumented migrants were beggars, most of who were from the provinces of Matabeleland and urban centres such as Bulawayo and Gwanda because of their proximity to the border (Butcher, 11 July 2003). In July 2004, however, there were reports of visually-challenged and other disabled Zimbabweans from as far as Harare, 760 kilometres away, entering Botswana's urban areas to beg (Mafingenyi, 15 July 2004; Sokwanele, 20 July 2007).

The government of Botswana employed various strategies to curb the influx of illegal immigrants into the country. In 2003, it erected a 300-mile electric fence along its border with Zimbabwe (Munnion, 3 July 2008). During late October 2006, a military-style operation against illegal immigrants, mostly Zimbabweans, was launched in Gaborone. Soldiers and policemen went door-to-door at night in suburbs such as Ledumadumane smashing down doors, demanding identity documents and arresting illegal immigrants (SAMP, 8 November 2006). In July 2008, the government also deployed army units with heavy artillery along the border with Zimbabwe as more Zimbabweans fled the country due to escalating socio-economic exiguity and political violence (Munnion, 3 July 2008).

In most cases, the Botswana government deported undocumented migrants. In 2002, for example, Botswana authorities claimed to have deported 26 717 illegal Zimbabweans (*Associated Press*, 16 July 2003). In January 2008, 683 Zimbabweans were deported. The number of deportees stood at 8 314 in December 2009; 2 600 in December 2010; 2 423 in December 2011; and 2 180 in December 2012. In 2012, Botswana deported 17 402 illegal Zimbabweans while in 2013, 22 675 were deported during the first 10 months (Kitsepele, 25 November 2013). Despite these efforts, many undocumented Zimbabwean immigrants continued to register a strong presence in Botswana as they sought livelihoods, with a considerable number preoccupied with various forms of begging.

In July 2003, thousands of hungry Zimbabweans were reportedly begging for work in various parts of Gaborone's city centre. It was common for them to whisper: "Piece work, piece work" to any passer-by. Some of them brandished their Ordinary Level certificates as proof to potential employers that they had passed secondary school education in Zimbabwe and were therefore employable. Some immigrants showed retrenchment letters from Zimbabwean companies that had long since closed as reference. Others produced membership cards of the opposition MDC to show that they were not tainted by association with Robert Mugabe's ZANU-PF regime (Butcher, 11 July 2003).

In Gaborone's White City Suburb in June 2006, large numbers of Zimbabweans sat in groups at an open space and whenever a vehicle stopped, they rushed to beg for piece jobs. The area where they congregated became popularly known as Harare, thus named after Zimbabwe's capital city (Dube, 4 June 2006). Meanwhile, other Zimbabwean immigrants moved from door to door in Gaberone's affluent suburbs of Phakalane and Mokolodi begging for jobs which usually earned them between P400 and P600 per month (Ibid). Most of the piece jobs sought by Zimbabweans included plaiting hair as well as housekeeping duties such as washing clothes and plates, painting and washing cars (Interviews, 2019).

Some Zimbabwean beggars also tried their luck in Mozambique. In April 2010, for instance, news reporters witnessed several beggars along the streets of Beira. One of them was Elizabeth Takawira, a visually-disadvantaged mother of two children, Tatenda (12 years) and Tavonga (10 years). They eked livelihoods through begging at Beira's street intersections. In order to supplement their income, Tawanda and Tavonga washed cars and sold cigarettes. Elizabeth had left Zimbabwe's Chivi District in 2007 together with her two children as economic distress deepened. She had tried to seek help from Zimbabwe's Ministry of Public Service, Labour and Social Welfare to no avail. While at her rural home in Chivi District, she had been denied food handouts by the ZANU-PF government after being accused of supporting the opposition MDC. She crossed the border without travel documents and was given transport by a Good Samaritan to Beira where she begged and slept on the pavements

144

Peter Makoni was another visually-challenged Zimbabwean beggar operating in Beira in 2010. He spent most of his time at the Mira Mar Centre on the beaches singing gospel songs and playing a box guitar to lure tourists and solicit for gifts. He stated that besides luring and entertaining potential donors, he also played music to drown his sorrows of deprivation. Makoni teamed up with Elizabeth Takawira, a visually-challenged Zimbabwean woman discussed above, to beg and supplemented their income by selling boiled eggs along the streets (Ibid).

This section highlighted how some neighbouring countries such as Mozambique and Botswana played host to Zimbabwean beggars, particularly from the onset of the new millennium. Countries like Botswana instituted a number of measures to repel undocumented Zimbabweans, including panhandlers, without much success owing to the escalation of socio-economic maladies in their home country. As the remaining sections of this chapter will vivify, the influx of Zimbabwean beggars in South Africa was much more pronounced given the country's status as Southern Africa's industrial powerhouse.

Begging in South Africa: The perilous journey

Given its reputation as the regional economic giant, South Africa became the most attractive hunting ground for many vulnerable Zimbabweans, some of whom salvaged sustenance through panhandling. Since most of the impoverished migrants had no travel documents, the journey into South Africa was an uphill undertaking fraught with a multiplicity of life-threatening risks. For many suffering Zimbabweans, however, the risks were worth taking than dying from starvation and many other woes at home.

Map 1: The South Africa-Zimbabwe border
Source: *Economist* (9 August 2007)

Zimbabweans without official travel documents employed an array of strategies to illegally cross into South Africa to seek livelihoods in various ways such as begging. Entry into South Africa through the official border posts was sometimes secured by bribing the officials on both sides of the border such as soldiers, the police and immigration authorities (Bearak, 23 January 2009). Some visually-challenged and other disabled Zimbabwean beggars interviewed in Johannesburg in 2005 and 2006 stated that they successfully crossed the border into South Africa without travel documents after pleading with immigration officials that they were coming for medical treatment (SAMP, 26 February 2006).

Even though crossing the border into South Africa through undesignated points in the vicinity of Beitbridge Border Post was a precarious undertaking, it was by far the most popular means (Marongwe and Moyo, 2016). In 2015, for example, there were about 200 illegal crossing points along the border of South Africa and Zimbabwe (Muleya, 30 May 2015; Ncube, 19 February 2017). Several risks were involved, for example, being arrested or shot by state security agents while sneaking through the barbed razor-wire fence on the South African side of the border. The border fence is set a few hundred metres south of the international border, which runs down the centre of the Limpopo River (*Irin News*, 26 May 2010). In early January 2006, for example, a suspected clandestine migrant from Zimbabwe was shot dead by a South African soldier who was patrolling the border (*Independent Online*, 18 January 2006).

Undocumented migrants who were arrested while crossing into South Africa were usually deported back to Zimbabwe. In the first five months of 2008, for example, South African officials reported that 20 397 Zimbabweans were deported but the International Organisation for Migration argued that the real figure was close to 17 000 every month (Smith, 6 July 2008). Between 2006 and 2010, approximately 25% of Zimbabwean children attempting to cross the border to South Africa were arrested and subsequently detained by the South African law-enforcement agents (Chiweshe, 12 October 2017).

Figure 5: South African border fence vandalised by illegal migrants, 2012
Source: *New Humanitarian* (9 February 2012)

A series of three razor-wire fences, up to three metres high and spanning 268 kilometres on the South African side of the border, constituted a formidable barrier for many undocumented Zimbabwean migrants (*New Humanitarian*, 9 February 2012; Otoole, 9 July 2013; Smith, 6 July 2008; Solidarity Peace Trust, 21 November 2004). The border fence was constructed in phases by the Apartheid South African government in the mid-1980s (Otoole and Botes, 4 April 2011). The structure was once referred to as 'the snake of fire' because of its lethal electric charge (Otoole, 9 July 2013). It has three lines of razor wire with an electric fence between, and the voltage "can be calibrated from deadly to the uncomfortable electric tingle used for game fencing" (*Irin News*, 26 May 2010: 1). At 10-kilometre intervals along the fence, there are Echo stations, as well as brick and mortar camps that can accommodate up to 10 soldiers, with functional computer facilities that monitor and control the electricity range when the fence is switched on (Ibid). The electric fence reportedly killed 89 people between August 1986 and August 1989. In 2001, the Centre for the Study of Violence and Reconciliation proposed a figure of at least 100 deaths prior to February 1990 (Otoole and Botes, 4 April 2011). In 1993, owing to the human fatalities it had previously caused, the fence was switched to the non-lethal alarm-mode and is almost always entirely switched off (Otoole, 9 July 2013; Otoole and Botes, 4 April 2011). Over the years during the post-Apartheid era, the South African government has carried out massive renovation and repair works on the border fence. In March 2020, for example, the government began erecting 40 kilometres of 1.8-metre-high fencing along the border at a budgeted cost of R37 million (*African News Agency*, 19 March 2020).

Despite being a notable barrier to the free movement of people and goods, many undocumented migrants found their way through the border fence. Some migrants cut holes into the three barbed wire fences in order to secure passage across the border (Davies, 18 July 2008). The more agile migrants scaled the perimeter fence and disappeared into South Africa (Gurusa, 3 November 2019). In early May 2007, "even pregnant women or women with a baby on their backs [were reportedly] jumping a two-metre high razor-wire fence" (Guerin, 10 May 2007: 1). It is a lived reality, therefore, that "the border fence continues to be trampled, cut and burrowed beneath by smugglers, poachers and migrants illegally moving across the border, much as it has for years" (Otoole and Botes, 4 April 2011: 1).

For those who decided to swim across the Limpopo River, which is 200 metres wide at some points, the risk of being devoured by crocodiles was always great (Smith, 18 July 2018). On 29 May 2015, for instance, a group of 18 undocumented Zimbabwean migrants and a fisherman teamed up and killed a three-metre-long crocodile which had attacked them at an unofficial crossing point along the Limpopo River, 900 metres east of Alfred Beit Bridge. The group reportedly first trapped the crocodile in a fishing net as it was advancing towards them before stoning it to death. The migrants soon fled the scene when a member of the Police Neighbourhood Watch Committee arrived since it is a criminal offence to kill wild animals in Zimbabwe no matter how dangerous they may be to human life (Muleya, 2015). The undocumented migrants were, therefore, caught in between a rock and a hard place whereby they were in danger of being killed by crocodiles at a time when the state's anti-poaching laws criminalised the killing of the predatory reptiles.

Besides crocodiles, undocumented migrants were also in danger of being attacked by other wild animals that inhabited the densely-forested Limpopo River valley near Alfred Beit Bridge. In December 2016, three Zimbabweans, including a nine-year-old boy, were attacked and killed by a hippopotamus along the Limpopo River near Beitbridge while skipping the border into South Africa (Muleya, 17 April 2016). In early October 2017, a Zimbabwean border-jumper was attacked and killed by a hippo along an illegal footpath while crossing the Limpopo River into South Africa illegally. The man's body was found by a worker of the Beitbridge Town Council (Chipato, 13 October 2017). On 23 July 2018, the dead body of Nosiza Sibanda, a 43-year-old Zimbabwean woman from the town of Chitungwiza, was found by the police near an illegal crossing point along the Limpopo River near Beitbridge Border Post amid fears that she was killed by a hippopotamus (*Zimbabwe News Live*, 24 July 2018). On 24 July 2018, Inspector Philisani Ndebele, the then Matabeleland South Provincial Police Spokesperson, confirmed the incident:

I can confirm that a 43-year-old woman was found dead along the

Limpopo River yesterday morning. It is suspected that a hippopotamus killed her while she was trying to illegally cross over to neighbouring South Africa. Police officers discovered her body next to the bridge yesterday at around 4am while doing patrols and no foul play is suspected (Ibid: 1).

Figure 6: Squeezing beneath the South Africa border fence
Source: *Bulawayo 24 News* (19 March 2020)

Furthermore, on 22 August 2019, a group of border jumpers that attempted to cross into South Africa without using official points of entry was attacked by a hippopotamus. The attack left a 20-year-old woman dead and her three-year-old son seriously injured (*Zimbabwe Republic Police News*, 25 August 2019). On 25 October 2019, a Zimbabwean man suspected to be a border jumper was attacked by two hippopotamuses while trying to illegally cross into South Africa through the Limpopo River. After the attack, the fourth of its kind in 2019, the man was rushed to Beitbridge District Hospital where he died on admission. The two hippopotamuses were later shot dead by rangers from the Zimbabwe Parks and Wildlife Management Authority (Zimparks) (*Vantu News*, 29 October 2019). Part of a statement from the Beitbridge Town Council concerning the incident read as follows:

> Two hippos were gunned down in the Limpopo River [after] having injured an individual suspected to be a border jumper in the early hours of Friday [25 October 2019]. The injured individual is said to have passed on later at the Beitbridge District Hospital. This is the fourth such incident in the border town this year alone. As the Municipality of Beitbridge, we are really concerned about the loss of life as we continue to face this human-wildlife conflict (Ibid: 1).

Zimparks, through its Spokesperson, Tinashe Farawo, also confirmed the incident:

> It is common cause that when wildlife animals are overpopulated, it results in a conflict between humans and wildlife. Usually when such occurrences happen, we put down these animals and that is what happened to these two hippos which have been terrorising people along the Limpopo River. We also urge people to stay away from water bodies to avoid unnecessary deaths (Ibid: 1).

The thick forest along the border near Beitbridge Border Post is habitat to a large number of venomous snakes. Snake bites are also common during the 10-kilometre walk through the forests between Beitbridge town and the South African interior (Gurusa, 3 November 2019). Worse still, the journeys are undertaken at night and without torches or lights to avoid being noticed by the army, police or thugs (Ibid). The other dangerous wild animals encountered by undocumented migrants in the forested border zone included elephants and hyenas (Ncube, 19 February 2017).

Many undocumented migrants also drowned while crossing the Limpopo River (Bearak, 23 January 2009). In April 2004, for example, the South Africa Broadcasting Corporation (SABC) reported the death of five Zimbabweans who drowned while attempting to cross the Limpopo River into South Africa. Their bodies were recovered "badly eaten by crocodiles. Police had to fire shots to scare off the crocodiles" (Solidarity Peace Trust, 21 November 2004: 58). During the night of 13-14 January 2006, at least 10 undocumented Zimbabwean migrants from the Dite area, about 60 kilometres from the Beitbridge Border Post, were feared to have drowned while trying to cross the flooded Limpopo River into South Africa. South African media reports indicated that 15 would-be immigrants had died, but the Zimbabwe Support Action Group, a Johannesburg-based émigré organisation, claimed to have verified 10 deaths (*Independent Online*, 18 January 2006; *VOA*, 18 January 2006).

In the first week of April 2014, the Beitbridge police were busy investigating four cases of drowning in the Limpopo River by suspected Zimbabwean border jumpers. According to Chief Superintendent Patrick Majuta, the then Police Officer Commanding Beitbridge District, two bodies that had already been recovered at different points along the river during patrols were believed to have drowned during the weekend of 5-6 April 2014. According to Majuta, a third body, which was partially buried in sand, was located late on 7 April 2014 and was retrieved the following day. He said that another team was searching for the other man who was reported to have drowned on 4 April 2014 while crossing the Limpopo River near the Mawale area. Chief Superintendent Majuta added that all the three bodies were recovered from the eastern side of Beitbridge town (Muleya, 8 April 2014). Just a few days later, on 9 April 2014, Zimbabwean and South African police details patrolling the area close to Alfred Beit Bridge discovered the bodies of 17 suspected border jumpers who were believed to have drowned in the Limpopo River. Some of the bodies had missing limbs when they were recovered from a cave and there was a strong possibility that they had been hidden there by crocodiles (Bell, 11 April 2014).

In early January 2015, two suspected Zimbabwean border jumpers died from drowning and the other two were rescued following a failed attempt to cross the Limpopo River and illegally enter South Africa. Commenting on the incident, the Beitbridge police expressed concern that despite the crocodile-infested Limpopo River being flooded, undocumented migrants were still taking chances (Makuyana and Diale, 7 January 2015).

On 4 January 2017, four Zimbabwean men suspected to be illegal migrants died after they were swept away by the heavy currents of the massive Limpopo River while crossing to the Vhembe area of South Africa (Machamire, 9 January 2017). The incident prompted South Africa's Health Department to issue a warning to Zimbabweans, among other countries' nationals, against using the Limpopo River to cross in and out of the country, as they risked drowning (Ibid).

In mid-February 2020, the Beitbridge Zimbabwe Republic Police was reportedly investigating a case in which a Zimbabwean man was swept away while trying to cross the flooded Limpopo River from South Africa to Zimbabwe. According to the police, the unnamed man was swept away by the raging water in the presence of his friends who failed to rescue him. This case was rather rare, given that most Zimbabweans drowned in the Limpopo River on their way to, rather than from, South Africa (Mabhiza, 6 February 2020).

Despite these life-threatening challenges, many Zimbabweans continued to violate the border with South Africa in pursuit of livelihoods. Since 2007, dozens of visually-challenged Zimbabwean beggars were also reportedly crossing the crocodile-infested Limpopo River to try their luck in South Africa. An example is the 44-year-old Lorcadia Dewa, a well-known street beggar in Mwenezi town in Zimbabwe's Masvingo Province, who crossed into South Africa in 2008. She narrated how she entered South Africa illegally: "I had no passport so I paid some men who helped me cross the crocodile-infested Limpopo River to enter South Africa through holes in the fence separating the two countries" (Khumalo, 29 July 2014: 1).

From the early 2000s, some enterprising opportunists, mostly Zimbabwean men, capitalised on the prevalence of illegal border-crossers into South Africa to generate income by assisting them to cross the Limpopo River on foot (Bearak, 23 January 2009). In July 2008, for example, the standard 'escorting fee' for each migrant was 40 Rands (£2.50) (Smith, 6 July 2008). While crossing, the guides took the lead using sticks to measure the hidden depths of the river, which could be shoulder-high even during dry seasons, and "those eager to stay dry while crossing often [took] off most, if not all, of their clothes" (Tshabalala, 2017: 196). With the guide in the lead, the rest followed in a single file clutching the back part of each other's shirt, blouse or dress to avoid being swept away. In some cases, however, the guides robbed border-crossers of their possessions after assisting them to cross the Limpopo River (Bearak, 23 January 2009).

Figure 7: Zimbabwean undocumented migrants daring to cross the Limpopo River on foot

Source: *Zimbabwe Republic Police News* (25 August 2019)

By late 2014, some enterprising cross-border touts had designed makeshift boats to ferry illegal migrants across the Limpopo at a fee of around 350 Rands per head (Makuyana and Diale, 7 January 2015). This development prompted the Beitbridge ZRP to launch an operation to destroy the makeshift boats. What was particularly worrying, according to the then Police Spokesperson, Brigadier Hlangwani Mulaudzi, was that many boat-owners would "ferry illegal immigrants for an agreed fee and in the middle of the river, they hike the price which, if you fail to pay they throw you in the river" (Ibid: 1).

In mid-March 2018, some smuggling syndicates operating along the Zimbabwe-South Africa border had reportedly devised inflatable boats to cross the flooded Limpopo River. The syndicates, working in cahoots with villagers in the Makakavhule area, about 40 kilometres west of Beitbridge border town, smuggled undocumented migrants, mostly Zimbabweans, and a wide range of groceries (Netsianda, 18 March 2018). Some of the inflatable boats were allegedly owned by South African white commercial farmers who resided along the river (Ncube, 19 February 2017; Netsianda, 18 March 2018).

Crossing the border into South Africa illegally had a myriad of other risks. Illegal border crossers could be confronted by the *guma-guma*, a slang reference to criminals who committed a broad range of abuses such as extortion, robbery, and rape in the bushy area along the border close to Beitbridge Border Post (Bearak, 23 January 2009; Hungwe, 2012). In September 2011, a visually-challenged Zimbabwean beggar in Johannesburg told the *Mail and Guardian* that crossing the border into South Africa through illegal routes was a great risk owing to the predatory activities of robbers:

> The hardest part is hiding from the *Guma Guma* (the touts/ bandits) who prey on desperate Zimbabweans. I was afraid of them because they crack you, knife you and take everything from you. I remember running away from them down these steep slopes with three other blind people. I was very afraid (Tolsi, 30 September 2011: 1).

Figure 8: Inflatable boats used by smugglers along the Limpopo River, 2018
Source: Netsianda (18 March 2018)

Another example that illuminates the ruthlessness of the cross-border brigands can be derived from an incident of 23 May 2012 when, at around 6am, two Zimbabwean undocumented migrants went to the Limpopo River near Alfred Beit Bridge with the intention of crossing into South Africa through an undesignated entry point (*Limpopo Mirror*, 8 June 2012; Netsianda, 12 October 2012). They were spotted by a four-member gang of armed robbers who included Alfred Makaye, a 20-year-old man of Zaka Village in Masvingo Province, and Viosi Kapuru, his 21-year-old counterpart from Bepura Village outside Beitbridge town. The group of robbers, which was armed with machetes, knives and a pistol, confronted the two complainants and demanded money amid threats to kill them. One of the gang members fired a single shot with a pistol in the air to scare the victims. They then searched the victims and robbed them

156

of 720 Rands and a Nokia mobile phone before they fled into the bush. The victims reported the matter to the police, who assigned two plain-clothes detectives to accompany them to the scene. At the scene, Makaye and Kapuru, armed with machetes, unknowingly approached the plain-clothes detectives and demanded money. The officers were forced to retreat since they were not armed. They, however, returned to the scene after two days, armed with pistols and reinforcements from the Police Dog Section. They set a trap for the suspects and, upon realising that they had been trapped, Makaya attempted to slash one of the detectives with a machete. The officer opened fire, shot him on the left thigh and apprehended him. Kapuru escaped but was arrested after two days (*Limpopo Mirror*, 8 June 2012; Netsianda, 12 October 2012). The two gangsters were each sentenced to eight years in jail, of which three years were conditionally suspended for five years (Netsianda, 12 October 2012).

The *magumaguma* reign of terror along the South Africa-Zimbabwe border continued over the years and during the early months of 2016, for example, "hardly a week passed by without someone being reported to have been mugged or robbed by criminals, who operated along the…Limpopo River" (Muleya, 17 April 2016: 1). A few years later, on 29 September 2018, Never Sibanda and Godfrey Mbedzi, aged 23 and 29 years respectively, both of whom came from the Tshikwalakwala area under Chief Matibe, hatched a plan to rob border jumpers intending to cross into South Africa through an illegal crossing point along the Limpopo River in Tshikwalakwala. The two men went to the Limpopo riverside and hid in the reeds with Mbedzi wearing a Zimbabwe National Army (ZNA) uniform and armed with a toy pistol, while Sibanda was armed with a log. They emerged from the reeds and intercepted three suspected border jumpers and Mbedzi threatened to shoot them if they failed to comply with their orders. They then forced the migrants to each pay 400 Rands at 'gun point' to secure their release. They were then given 1 200 Rands after which they freed the three suspected border jumpers. The victims later reported the matter to law-enforcement agents who were on patrol leading to the arrest of Sibanda and Mbedzi at their homestead. A total of 900 Rands, the toy gun and the ZNA uniform were recovered from the accused persons (Muleya,

12 October 2018).

In mid-January 2019, four men who had gained notoriety for terrorising undocumented migrants crossing the Limpopo River near Beitbridge were foiled by some people they had attempted to rob at gunpoint. Witness Chauke, the 24-year-old gang leader, who was armed with a Smith Browning pistol loaded with two rounds and an okapi knife, was disarmed by migrants, severely assaulted and killed at the confluence of the Umzingwane and Limpopo Rivers while his three accomplices fled (Muleya, 24 January 2019).

Just six months later, on 16 June 2019, a four-man gang of armed robbers comprising Saymore Msipa, Brian Chitomu, Johannes Chikoore and Enest Chikozho waylaid and ambushed two undocumented migrants who were crossing the Limpopo River near Beitbridge Border Post into South Africa through an undesignated point. One of the gang members brandished a machete and threatened to attack the two men if they did not give them money and other valuables. The gang went off with 180 Rands and clothes. A report was made to ZNA soldiers who were patrolling the area. The soldiers later arrested Msipa who was already putting on the jacket robbed from one of the victims. Further checks led to the arrest of the other gang members (Madima, 21 August 2019).

Young undocumented female migrants were particularly vulnerable to various forms of abuse as they sought to cross the border. A 2007 study indicated that some girl migrants exchanged sex for transportation by truck drivers. Some girls who migrated to South Africa were reportedly forced to have sex with border guards to secure entry. At many unofficial border-crossing points, the *magumaguma* are known to also have sexually abused girl children (Chiweshe, 12 October 2017). In November 2009, for example, Ruvarashe Azangwe, a 16-year-old Zimbabwean girl who was surviving through panhandling in Musina, recalled a terrifying encounter with the *magumaguma* who attempted to rape her in the bushes near Beitbridge while she was crossing into South Africa together with her sister. She said: "I fought them. So, they said they wanted to cut me. They cut me and they ran because there were soldiers coming" (Scott, 2 November 2009: 1). Ruvarashe sustained serious injuries and needed 20 stitches to sew up a 10-centimetre-long cut in her arm. She also lost all her belongings, including a mobile phone, to the robbers (Ibid).

It is quite apparent that various forms of sexual abuse were a major challenge for Zimbabwean women in general and girl children in particular as they crossed the border into South Africa illegally. From the beginning of January to early May 2010, for example, the Médecins Sans Frontières (MSF), an international medical charity organisation, treated 103 survivors of sexual violence at the hands of cross-border robbers, of which 71 cases had taken place since 1 March (*Irin News*, 26 May 2010). In 2010, the MSF identified 242 cases of rape perpetrated on undocumented female migrants by criminals along the South Africa-Zimbabwe border (Otoole and Botes, 4 April 2011). By early 2016, an average of five women were raped quarterly by criminals on the banks of the Limpopo River, while crossing into South Africa (Muleya, 17 April 2016).

Not all Zimbabwean beggars entered South Africa without valid official travel documents; some actually had them in their possession. Shylet Madhabuya, a visually-challenged beggar from Mutare, for example, had a valid Zimbabwean passport when she entered South Africa in May 2007 on a 30-day visa. She engaged in begging pursuits in Johannesburg but went back home every month to see family members and renew her passport (Mapumulo, 25 September 2007). In August 2010, Kingston Chimenya, a 31-year-old visually-challenged beggar in Rustenburg, South Africa, stated that he had a valid passport when he left his home near the town of Nyanga in north-eastern Zimbabwe. He had come to South Africa by himself and was guided along the way by other sympathetic travellers (*Zimbabwean*, 14 August 2010). He did not return to Zimbabwe after the expiry of his 30 days visitor's visa. The case of Chimenya illustrates cases of Zimbabwean beggars in South Africa who entered the country on a 30-day visa and became illegal immigrants after their permits expired (Hakutangwi, Mashizha, Matanga, FGD: 14 August 2010).

From the border, Zimbabwean immigrants used various modes of transport to travel into South Africa. Some groups of beggars organised their own transport to take them further into the South African interior. On 2 October 2005, for example, a public taxi loaded with visually-disadvantaged Zimbabwean beggars who had entered South Africa illegally was stopped by the Johannesburg Metro Police on the M1 Highway near Glenhove. The 14 visually-challenged beggars aboard were arrested and taken to the local offices of the Department of Home Affairs from where they were detained at the Lindela Repatriation Camp (SAMP, 3 October 2005).

Some disabled Zimbabweans found their way into the South African interior after being given free rides by generous truck and bus drivers. In March 2007, for example, Joseph Ruzvidzo, a visually-impaired man originally from Chegutu town in Zimbabwe, who was begging in Johannesburg, stated that on their journey into South Africa, most people in his predicament got free rides from bus drivers who were sympathetic to their plight of disability, provided they were not too many per trip (Marufu, 21 March 2007).

Despite the life-threatening risks associated with crossing the border, the inflow of Zimbabweans, among them beggars, into South Africa mostly though irregular means continued to escalate as the Zimbabwean crisis worsened. From 2005, the exodus of visually-challenged beggars into South Africa became more conspicuous as Zimbabwe's socio-economic and political crisis deepened (*Irin News*, 13 June 2011). South African farmers along the border with Zimbabwe estimated that 4 000 Zimbabweans illegally crossed the border into the country in early 2007. This represented about 100 000 people every month, which far exceeded official 2007 statistics of approximately 20 000 per month (Sokwanele, 20 July 2007). Between 2000 and May 2008, 1-3 million Zimbabweans fled to South Africa (*Irin News*, 23 May 2008).

The exodus of Zimbabwean beggars into South Africa escalated, particularly from 2008 when the Zimbabwe dollar became virtually worthless (Khumalo, 29 July 2014). In September 2011, non-governmental social workers' organisations estimated that there were 600 visually- challenged and other disabled Zimbabwean beggars in Johannesburg's streets (Tolsi, 30 September 2011). In September 2016, Tito Mboweni, a South African businessman, former Reserve Bank governor and Minister of Finance of that country, expressed alarm at the ever-rising numbers of desperate Zimbabweans who were begging at street corners in South Africa: "It saddens me every day to see destitute Zimbabweans begging on our street corners. Let like-minded people help. Let us create a Zimbabwe Solidarity Movement to help our people. I volunteer to co-ordinate a solidarity program" (Zhou, 22 September 2016: 1).

Having successfully crossed into South Africa, most Zimbabwean beggars headed to the major cities such as Johannesburg, Pretoria, Cape Town and Durban as well as all the smaller towns across the country. Many disabled beggars in the major cities were foreigners, with Zimbabweans in the majority, because the South African government had a special pension fund for its disabled citizens (Bedfordview Residents Action Group, 19 October 2010). Of all South African cities, Johannesburg, the economic capital, hosted the majority of beggars (Immigrant for Social Justice, 31 August 2014). In January 2011, for example, an independent observer noted that there were "more Zimbabwean street beggars in Johannesburg than South African ones" (*Zimbabwe Independent*, 6 January 2011: 1). By July 2015, nearly all the disabled people begging for financial assistance at the street intersections in Johannesburg were Zimbabweans (*Zim-Eye*, 28 July 2015).

The socio-spatial dimensions of begging in South Africa

This section examines the manner in which beggars skilfully interacted with space and other social partners in an effort to promote and facilitate their livelihood activities. Beggars had to be conversant with the human geography of their environment in order to harness as many alms as they could. Thus, they had to strategically position themselves in particular settings that increased their visibility to passers-by and potential well-wishers. Social engineering by beggars involved partnering, or seeking the company of, certain groups of people or individuals in an effort to lure alms-givers and enhance their fortunes. These people included family members, relatives, acquaintances and even strangers, who could be children or adults. The skilful negotiation of space and the social milieu was, therefore, critical in the beggar's struggle for survival.

As in Zimbabwe and other parts of the world, Zimbabwean beggars in South Africa operated in those areas with a high concentration of human and vehicle traffic, mostly in urban areas, where there were greater chances of getting alms. In March 2007, for instance, there were several visually-challenged Zimbabwean beggars at strategic points in Johannesburg's upmarket suburbs such as Fourways and Sandton (Marufu, 21 March 2007). Most beggars positioned themselves along the streets, at traffic-light intersections, bus termini, shopping malls, outside banking halls and in passenger trains. In 2010, for example, visually-challenged Zimbabwean beggars accompanied by young children were a common sight on Metro-Rail trains; scores of visually-disadvantaged men being guided by their heavily-pregnant wives became permanent features on the pavements of Esselen Street in Sunnyside, Pretoria; panhandlers of all ages congested the Mobile Telephone Networks (MTN) rank in Johannesburg while their counterparts heavily congregated the premises of Greenstone Mall on the East Rand (Immigrant for Social Justice, 31 August 2014). Begging at traffic light intersections was full of drama. Whenever cars stopped at a traffic light, even visually-challenged beggars would rush into the road accompanied by guides and signal for assistance at every car window. They often clapped in appreciation whenever coins were dropped in their begging bowls (Khumalo, 29 July 2014).

Many disabled Zimbabwean beggars, mostly the visually-challenged, did not operate alone but always enlisted the services of people who accompanied them, usually in return for a fee. These aides could be children and adults. This was done for a number of reasons, one of which was the need to have assistants who would guide them through the urban milieu and its traffic jungles, among other things. The company of children also provoked the sympathy of many well-wishers while some guides actually persuaded passers-by to donate alms. The presence of assistants or guides also offered security to the beggars and their collections of alms. The assistants also took stock of daily collections and assisted the beggars with other daily chores (Ibid).

Some physically-handicapped beggars made use of grown-up family members and relatives as guides and assistants. In September 2011, for example, Jethro Gonese, a visually- challenged Zimbabwean man who begged in the town of Springs on the East

Rand, walked the white line under the guidance of his 20-year-old son who operated as his assistant (Tolsi, 30 September 2011). In 2011, Gift Mupambiki, a 32-year-old visually-deprived beggar from northern Zimbabwe, found his way to Johannesburg where he begged along the streets during the day and squatted together with other blind beggars near Ellis Park Stadium during the night. Together with other blind beggars, they usually enlisted young relatives as assistants to fetch water for them, cook and accompany them on begging pursuits in return for a share of the proceeds (*Irin News*, 13 June 2011). In April 2015, Tyson Augustine, a 45-year-old visually-handicapped man who had fled Zimbabwe in 2006, begged in Johannesburg's CBD with the assistance of his 35-year-old relative who acted as his guide as they navigated through the urban traffic (Isilow, 9 April 2015).

It was also common for visually-impaired married couples to accompany each other on begging missions in the city centres being ushered by assistants (Chiguvare, 16 April 2020; Peta, 4 February 2005). Albertina Mukanhiri and her husband Enock are an example of a visually-impaired Zimbabwean couple that begged together in the Johannesburg CBD in February 2011 (Tolsi, 30 September 2011). Such examples illustrate how family-kinship dynamics remained important determinants in struggles for sustenance by vulnerable Zimbabweans in post-Apartheid South Africa.

Figure 9: A visually-challenged couple begging in Johannesburg
Source: Peta (4 February 2005)

163

It was also common for some visually-challenged panhandlers to recruit their physically-able Zimbabwean acquaintances as aides during begging pursuits in South Africa, thus bringing out a fascinating paradox about struggles for survival in which the vulnerable ended up being the employers in diasporan enclaves. In September 2007, for example, Shylet Madhabuya, a 38-year-old visually-impaired Zimbabwean beggar in Johannesburg, paid Takudzwa Gapara, her helper and guide, an average of R30 to R50 per day depending on the takings (Mapumulo, 25 September 2007).

Considerable numbers of visually-handicapped beggars are known to have been escorted along the streets by South African assistants who charged them a fee (SAMP, 26 February 2006). An example can be derived from Ropafadzo Taruvinga, a visually-challenged Zimbabwean beggar in central Johannesburg in March 2007, who admitted paying her South African assistant an average of 50-100 Rands a day depending on the amount they would have raised (Marufu, 21 March 2007).

It also became a fairly widespread practice for some beggars to operate in pairs or groups after which they shared their daily collections, a strategy that cushioned those who would not have been as fortunate as their counterparts. In August 2010, in the city of Rustenburg in the North West Province, for instance, Kingston Chimenya, a 37-year-old visually-impaired Zimbabwean man, begged together with Pedro, his friend from Mozambique. They stayed next door to each other in the informal settlement of Yizo Yizo outside Rustenburg. Every morning, they embarked on a two-kilometre journey on foot from Rustenburg to the traffic lights at the corner of Klopper Street and Swartrugens Road close to the city centre. They usually split their daily takings equally between them (*Zimbabwean*, 14 August 2010).

Figure 10: A visually-challenged Zimbabwean couple panhandling in the streets of Louis Trichardt, 2020

Source: Chiguvare (16 April 2020)

It is a fact that women who beg with children are likely to get more money than other beggars, as passers-by pity the children that they will be travelling with. It is for this reason that many Zimbabwean beggars in South Africa fronted children of various ages in panhandling missions. Moving around with their children, some of whom were suckling babies, was a common strategy used by Zimbabwean female beggars to appeal to the sympathy of passers-by to their plight of deprivation. In March 2010, the *Mail and Guardian* identified several single mothers begging in the company of their very young children at various points in Johannesburg. Nyasha

Mapako (24) and her two-year-old child, for example, begged at the Corlett Drive intersection in Bramley while Melisa Mazhungu (17), together with her 15-month-old son, stationed themselves near the McDonalds Mall on Glenhove Road (Keepile, 18 March 2010).

In October 2010, the number of Zimbabwean roadside female beggars with suckling children in Johannesburg rose so sharply that the South African police seized the minors on grounds that their living conditions were not conducive for infants. The children were taken to welfare homes administered by the Displaced Persons Unit. Examples of such shelters in Johannesburg in 2011 were Governor's House in Hillbrow and Wembley Sanctuary in Turffontein. The children could only be returned if their mothers got jobs and decent accommodation in order to guarantee their well-being. Examples of Zimbabwean female beggars whose children were taken away during the blitz were Ruwarashe Chibura and Memory Konjiwa (Dixon, 16 August 2011). Among other things, the social workers at these institutions sought to assist towards the welfare of displaced people by tracing and contacting their families and ensuring that they did not live along the streets (Solidarity Helping Hand, 4 March 2013).

Let it be borne in mind that while the South African authorities viewed Zimbabwean beggars as a problem and their use of children to beg as grossly immoral, the panhandlers themselves saw their activities as a solution to their problems. In March 2013, Faith Mafa, a 22-year-old visually-challenged Zimbabwean mother who begged in Johannesburg, argued that panhandling together with children was a lucrative avenue of winning the pity of potential alms-givers: "It is better when you are sitting with a baby on the street. People feel sorry for you and give you money" (Solidarity Helping Hand, 4 March 2013: 1). Similarly, in August 2013, Irene Mahuni, a Zimbabwean beggar, sought alms together with her four-year-old son along Rivonia Road in Johannesburg (*Sandton Chronicle*, 25 August 2016). In early 2017, Mbuyiselo Botha (9 April 2017: 1), a gender activist, observed that "it (was) not unusual to see a woman with a child begging at an intersection in South African cities", and added:

It seems that everywhere you look, there is a woman with one or two children asking for hand-outs at robots. Some of these women are blind, but the majority are able-bodied. A snap poll published in a local daily newspaper recently shows that the majority of the women who beg alongside children on the streets are from Zimbabwe. A Zimbabwean official was quoted as saying that he was not aware of that fact. One would expect that the role of the Zimbabwean High Commissioner in South Africa would be to assist destitute Zimbabweans, including women and children, but they are clearly on their own.

Figure 11: Roadside begging by mothers with young children in Johannesburg
Source: Botha (24 April 2019)

Reports abound that some childless Zimbabwean adult beggars hired children from colleagues in an effort to get more alms from passers-by. During an interview with the *Zimbabwe Mail* (7 August 2016), a woman in Johannesburg only identified as Mercy revealed that many Zimbabwean women were hiring out their babies to other people who then used them as bait to attract well-wishers while they pretended to be genuine beggars. She elaborated: "I hire a baby for 100 Rands per day or less and I go along Empire Road or Byersnaude where I ask for help from motorists. Many drivers feel pity when they see the baby and give me money, not knowing I am not the mother of the baby" (Ibid: 1). A close friend of Mercy identified as Talent said at times they took turns to share one baby as they begged: "Here in South Africa, life has become difficult and sometimes we share one baby as long as the mother gets her money. I cannot go back to Zimbabwe right now for I know even prostitutes are suffering more than us there. It is better here" (Ibid: 1). One woman confirmed that she 'rented out' her one-year-old daughter to others in exchange for cash: "I love my child, but in order for me to feed her, I have to do that. I am not the only one doing this. We are so many..." she said, adding that she only gave out her baby to women she knew would not harm her (Ibid: 1).

It is indeed lamentable that, out of poverty, some adults made use of children of school-going age to beg. In December 2019, for example, Augustine Armando, a visually-impaired man originally from Epworth Suburb in Harare, was begging in Pretoria's CBD being guided by Nesbert, his 10-year-old grandson. Having left his wife in Zimbabwe and started begging in Pretoria in 2012, Armando invited his grandson to South Africa in 2018 for the purpose of escorting him on begging missions with the hope that they would raise enough money for him to return to school (Mutandiro, 19 December 2019).

Regarding child beggars, it should be noted, that not all Zimbabwean child beggars had the sanction of their parents or guardians to seek livelihoods in South Africa's urban centres. As discussed in Chapter 1, some Zimbabwean child beggars came into South Africa unaccompanied as a result of socio-economic indigence. A considerable number of these children embarked on service-begging in various South African urban centres. In late 2008 and early January 2009, for instance, there were numerous reports about scores of Zimbabwean children outside supermarkets in Musina who competed to carry groceries for shoppers in anticipation of tips (Bearak, 23 January 2009). An example was Prince Jelom, a 13-year-old orphan, who fled his poor grandmother in rural north-western Zimbabwe to earn a living through begging for alms after pushing trolleys full of groceries for shoppers outside Musina supermarkets (Gerardy, 11 January 2009).

It is without doubt, as this section has shown, that the tactful navigation of the physical and social landscape is one of the chief attributes of Zimbabwean beggars in neighbouring countries such as South Africa. In their daily struggles for a living, Zimbabwean beggars identified those areas where large numbers of potential alms-givers frequented or passed through. In these 'catchment' areas, the panhandlers strategically positioned themselves in order to be more conspicuous to passers-by. Social networking with persons of varying ages, depending on prevailing circumstances, was also a must for the poverty-ravaged beggars. Assistants had to be sought, especially by visually-challenged panhandlers, to operate as their guides, auditors and general hands, among other things. This section has also demonstrated how children, from suckling babies to those of school-going age, were sometimes instrumentalised by adult beggars in the pursuit of livelihoods, even though this practice has been widely condemned, demonised and criminalised by many stakeholders such as administrators and human rights defenders.

Challenges of Zimbabwean beggars in South Africa

The numerous hardships endured by Zimbabwean beggars in South Africa could have many to regret ever coming, were it not that the situation at home always became more and more hopeless with the passing of each day. Negative societal attitudes towards beggars which, at times, became closely linked to their identity as foreigners and sometimes culminated in xenophobic tendencies, constituted one of the most serious challenges faced by Zimbabwean panhanders in South Africa. They also had to endure the negative reception and perceptions by the South African government which often led to discrimination in the provision of social services, clampdowns, arrests and deportations. Poor living conditions epitomised by squalid accommodation and inadequate food, among other things, were other hurdles that confronted many Zimbabwean beggars. As if these problems were not enough, the Corona Virus pandemic from early 2020 worsened the plight of Zimbabwean beggars in South Africa.

The hostile reactions from some sections of the South African public constituted a notable challenge that frustrated many Zimbabwean beggars, in addition to negatively affecting their daily collections. It is a fact that begging across national borders is not an easy undertaking as it is always difficult to draw the attention of people of other nationalities who may also be having their own problems. In many instances, Zimbabwean beggars, most of them disabled, were often regarded as a menace by the generality of South African citizens. As Watson Khupe, a Zimbabwean disability activist, noted in 2010:

> Begging is an embarrassment even to the beggar himself/herself. It is more embarrassing if one becomes a professional beggar in a foreign country. For instance, the majority of disabled beggars that are seen in streets of South Africa are Zimbabweans. Some call them expatriate, *makwerekwere* or diaspora beggars. The xenophobic violence that has been continually taking place in that country has been claiming the lives of the disabled beggars as well (Khupe, 19 April 2010: 1).

The negative reactions by some sections of the South African public sometimes translated into xenophobic discourses and resulted in untold suffering for Zimbabwean beggars. In 2008, for instance, xenophobic attacks on foreigners in South Africa affected many Zimbabwean beggars. The attacks began in Alexandra Township in northern Johannesburg in May 2008 and soon spread to other parts of the country. By 23 May, 42 people had been killed and 17 000 displaced (*Irin News*, 23 May 2008). Gift Mupambiki, a 32-year-old visually-challenged Zimbabwean beggar, together with others who stayed in the dilapidated buildings in Johannesburg's city centre, for example, were evicted by South African assailants who wanted them to leave their country. They fled the premises and took refuge at a nearby police station. Having stayed there briefly, they went on to squat in a run-down building near Ellis Park Stadium. The building had 600 tenants, 176 of them visually-challenged. In February 2010, they were served with an eviction notice after most of them had failed to pay rent. The owner of the building disconnected water and electricity supplies forcing the visually-impaired beggars to rely on

170

relatives and hired assistants to fetch water for them from public water taps in the city (*Irin News*, 13 June 2011).

Generally speaking, the South African government has had very little sympathy towards the plight of Zimbabwean panhandlers. This official negative perception largely stems from the fact that begging is illegal in South Africa. The South African government has always viewed beggars as a menace and often launched clampdowns to eliminate them from the streets. During such operations, many Zimbabwean beggars were arrested, detained, fined and deported. For many Zimbabwean beggars, being deported was a great setback as it meant being taken back to Zimbabwe, a country they had fled because of its inexorable crises (Ibid).

On 27 January 2005, for example, the Johannesburg Metropolitan Police launched a two-hour operation to clear beggars from the city's streets. Code-named Operation Token Days, the blitz netted many blind beggars, including children mostly from Zimbabwe (SAMP, 5 February 2005). The exercise was part of the 500 Days Campaign Against Vice meant to clear Johannesburg of its image as the capital city of crime in southern Africa (*Daily News*, 11 February 2005; SAMP, 5 February 2005). The operation targeted street beggars at traffic light intersections in the city centre and Sandton. It was discovered that of the more than 300 beggars who were rounded up, the majority were Zimbabweans most of who did not have travel documents meaning that they had entered, or were living in, the country illegally. The illegal immigrants were sent to Lindela Repatriation Camp in Krugersdorp awaiting deportation (*Daily News*, 11 February 2005; SAMP, 26 February 2006). According to Wayne Minnar, the then Johannesburg Metro Police Spokesperson, the police "loaded a bus up with more than 300 blind beggars. Most were Zimbabweans who were here illegally, so we gave some to the Lindela Repatriation Camp, and then released the others because it was not such a serious crime and we did not know what to do with them. So we released them within 48 hours" (Smith, 26 February 2006: 1).

From 3 February 2005, hundreds of Metro Police officers were deployed around Johannesburg in a massive blitz to rid the city of beggars. This was also part of the 500-day Operation Token Days. The operation targeted greater Johannesburg, including Randburg,

171

Fourways, Sandton and Roodepoort. Edna Mamonyane, the then Johannesburg Metro Police Spokesperson, said municipal authorities were concerned with the number of beggars at intersections around the city (Feris and Cox, 3 February 2005). She said the decision to pick up beggars was in response to the fact that traffic officials had received many complaints from the public about traffic intersections where begging had mushroomed and "blown out of all proportion" (Ibid: 1). Motorists were reportedly disturbed by the increasing numbers of adults and children milling around between cars, hoping for donations. They complained of being verbally abused if they did not offer money. Others allegedly claimed that their vehicles had been damaged by window-washers who, without permission, proceeded to clean windows even if told not to. At that time, the fine for begging in a public street was 500 Rands. Those found to be illegal immigrants were taken to the Lindela Repatriation Camp for deportation. Mamonyane said the Metro Police had been informed that the reason why so many visually-challenged beggars had cropped up at intersections around the city was because of the influx of Zimbabweans (Ibid).

In late 2005, consequent upon police operations that cleared the major cities of undocumented immigrants, including beggars, the Lindela Repatriation Camp housed between 6 000 and 6 500 inmates, most of them Zimbabweans, per month with a daily intake of between 200 and 250 (SAMP, 28 October 2005). For the greater part of 2005, the camp was so overcrowded that 50 illegal immigrants sometimes shared a single room designed to accommodate 30 people. Outbreaks of diseases became common and sometimes resulted in fatalities. Between April and July 2005, for example, 43 immigrants, 28 of them Zimbabweans, died at the camp (Ibid).

The number of Zimbabwean deportees continued to soar as the police launched more operations to clear the streets of illegal immigrants, some of whom were beggars. The numbers of Zimbabweans deported from South Africa during the early 2000s were 26 742 in 2000, 19 932 in 2001 and 18 033 in 2002 (*News from Africa*, November 2003). The International Organisation for Migration estimated that 86 000 illegal Zimbabwean immigrants were deported from South Africa between January and May 2007

(Sokwanele, 20 July 2007).

Figure 12: Zimbabweans being herded to a deportation train in Johannesburg, September 2003

Source: Solidarity Peace Trust (21 November 2004)

In most cases, those who ended up being deported had not succeeded in bribing the law-enforcement agents to release them. During the deportation process, some deportees actually fled back to their begging points in South Africa, this being a clear indication that a considerable number of Zimbabweans opted for hardship in foreign land rather than hopelessness at home (Solidarity Peace Trust, 21 November 2004).

Figure 13: A Zimbabwean deportee flees from the shadow of the deportation train he had leapt from

Source: Solidarity Peace Trust (21 November 2004)

Constant fear of deportation characterised the lives of many Zimbabwean beggars, most of who were illegally residing in South Africa. Thus, with the help of NGOs, hundreds of visually-disadvantaged beggars in Johannesburg petitioned the South African government in 2010 for a special dispensation to regularise papers for their stay in the country. This was after South Africa's Ministry of Home Affairs had begun its Zimbabwe Documentation Project in late 2009 to regularise the stay of illegal Zimbabwean immigrants by issuing them with work, study or business visas. Since the visually-challenged beggars did not fit into these categories of permits, they applied for special consideration from the government. In January 2011, the Ministry of Home Affairs turned down their request and stated that all undocumented foreigners in South Africa would be treated in the same manner and would be deported in the event of being arrested by the authorities (Tolsi, 30 September 2011).

Social workers employed by the Johannesburg Municipality's Displaced Persons Unit also periodically picked up beggars at street intersections and sent them to Governor's House in the Hillbrow area in the city centre where they were subjected to various forms of abuse which included beatings and hosing them with cold water (*Irin News*, 13 June 2011). In September 2011, some visually-challenged beggars in Johannesburg complained of harassment by the government's social workers who they accused of being more brutal than the police. They alleged that after removing them from the streets, the social workers often detained them for the entire day without food or water. As if this was not enough, they were usually flogged with rubber pipes (Tolsi, 30 September 2011). Faith Mafa, a 22-year-old visually-challenged Zimbabwean woman, experienced such harassment together with other visually-challenged beggars after they had been rounded up in the Johannesburg city centre in 2012 (Solidarity Helping Hand, 4 March 2013).

Owing to the negative perceptions of the South African government and the generality of the population mentioned earlier on in this section, Zimbabwean beggars, particularly the disabled, subsequently suffered atrocious forms of discrimination in the provision of social services in South Africa. In February 2011, for example, Albertina Mukanhiri, a visually-impaired Zimbabwean woman who begged in Johannesburg, suffered gross ill-treatment at Johannesburg General Hospital after giving birth to a still-born child. According to Albertina, the nurses told her that:

> ...the baby had died because I was not supposed to give birth because it was very bad, unnatural for blind people to have babies. They would not feed me properly in hospital and then said I could not see the baby or bury it until I paid them R2 000 (US$200). The baby was only buried after a doctor stopped them...They tell us that we should go

back and get help from our government and hospitals (Tolsi, 30 September 2011: 1).

Where to stay and what to eat remained perennial headaches as most panhandlers could not afford to pay for decent accommodation and food. The living conditions of many Zimbabwean beggars in South Africa were deplorable. An example of such inhospitable conditions can be drawn from the northern margins of the Johannesburg CBD from the onset of the new millennium where many Zimbabwean beggars were concentrated in overcrowded dwellings in Hillbrow, Joubert Park and the buildings close to Ellis Park Stadium. In November 2004, a group of 31 visually-challenged Zimbabwean beggars whose ages ranged from two to more than 60 years was discovered staying in a one-room Hillbrow flat in Johannesburg. The occupants cooked on one double hot-plate stove. Ablutions were in a communal bathroom (*Zimbabwe Situation*, 21 November 2004). Similarly, in February 2005, Taimon Rukuni, a visually-challenged Zimbabwean man in Johannesburg, shared one room with 15 other visually-challenged beggars. Brighton Mkushi, another visually-challenged beggar in the same city shared a room with 30 visually-disadvantaged counterparts during the same period (SAMP, 5 February 2005). In February 2006, an average of eight visually-disadvantaged Zimbabwean beggars shared a two-bedroom flat in Hillbrow and Joubert Park in Johannesburg's city centre, paying between 65 and 200 Rands a week (SAMP, 26 February 2006).

By June 2011, several abandoned and neglected buildings in the Johannesburg city centre had become slum residences for thousands of immigrants, including Zimbabwean beggars. The squalid living conditions in these premises included over-crowdedness and limited or no access to electricity and water supplies. One such building near Ellis Park Stadium sheltered over 400 people, mostly Zimbabwean migrants, in rooms partitioned by cardboard or washing lines hung with sheets. Common health problems that emanated from such conditions included skin ailments, diarrhoea, respiratory tract infections such as tuberculosis, sexually-transmitted infections and stress-related complications (*Irin News*, 2 June 2011). Attempts by some beggars and other vulnerable tenants to maintain health standards and hygiene were frustrated when taps were often sealed to deny them access to water (Tipple and Speak, 2004).

Many Zimbabwean beggars lived in slum dwellings in various parts of South Africa. In Johannesburg during mid-2007, for example, the municipality identified 100 slum buildings, many of them abandoned by their white owners during the post-Apartheid exodus in the 1990s. Some of the buildings were taken over by criminals and slum landlords who charged rent but spent little or nothing to maintain them (*Irin News*, 2 June 2011). Considerable numbers of visually-challenged Zimbabwean beggars, together with their sighted counterparts, lived in five dilapidated buildings on the southern margins of the Johannesburg Central Business District. One such structure was Doorfontein Chambers which had been abandoned since the early 2000s when Zimbabwean beggars moved in and stayed for some years without paying rentals (*Irin News*, 2 June 2011; Tolsi, 30 September 2011). At Doorfontein Chambers, the living conditions for Zimbabwean beggars and other vulnerable tenants were extremely repulsive, as aptly described by one observer:

...There is no electricity- the darkness inside the hijacked building leaves anybody blind. Water is stolen from the fire extinguishers. Some walls are daubed with human faeces and the stench of urine permeates. The warehouse-like building has been almost entirely plundered of any metal that can be sold off and the elevator shaft is now completely exposed. In the pitch-blackness of the building, it is a danger to both the blind and the sighted. The labyrinthine floors have been individually partitioned using cardboard, bits of food and election posters, into small rectangular homes (Ibid: 1).

During the mid-2000s, some South Africans hijacked the building, declared themselves landlords and imposed a one-off monthly rental of 500 Rands (US$50). The resident visually- challenged beggars and incomers therefore contributed to pay that monthly rental. In mid-2011, new landlords came in and gave them notice to vacate the building by 10 October 2011. The beggars relocated to another building in the same area (Ibid).

Besides Johannesburg, the living conditions of many Zimbabwean beggars were also squalid in other South African urban centres. In Pretoria during December 2019, for example, more than 10 families of Zimbabwean beggars resided at an informal settlement in the centre of Boom Street in Marabastad. The settlement came to be popularly known as 'Little Zimbabwe' on account of the sizeable population of Zimbabwean nationals who were living there (Mutandiro, 19 December 2019). A description of the living conditions at Marabastad in late 2019 painted an absolutely inhospitable picture:

> Some live in shacks made from board and plastic which well-wishers have donated, while others live in shelters made of old plastic sheets and cloth. The conditions at the settlement are unhealthy because there are no toilets or taps for water. Clusters of rubbish are strewn across the settlement. There are puddles of stagnant water. Despite these conditions, residents here say they would rather live here than pay high rent elsewhere. Residents say Metro Police officers have regularly demolished their shacks but they rebuild soon after (Ibid: 1).

It is worth noting that there were indeed some destitute Zimbabwean immigrants who had nowhere to stay. Some newly-arrived Zimbabweans faced serious accommodation problems especially if they came into South Africa without making prior arrangements with those who were already there, or when trying to locate their acquaintances in various parts of the country. In late 2008 and early 2009, for example, scores of Zimbabwean beggars and other destitutes, including children, slept in pavements, ditches and under bridges in the South African border town of Musina (Bearak, 23 January 2009).

Figure 14: Homeless Zimbabweans sleeping outside Johannesburg Central
Methodist Church

Source: Jeffrey (undated)

Some destitute Zimbabwean immigrants who failed to secure
shelter and food approached church institutions where they begged
for assistance after unsuccessfully trying other options of survival. In
Johannesburg, for instance, many impoverished Zimbabweans
sought assistance at the Central United Methodist Church in the
Central Business District where Bishop Paul Verryn opened up the
premises for their overnight accommodation in the mid-2000s. Most
of the desperate Zimbabweans who slept at the church were single
women, young mothers and fathers, the visually-impaired and other
disabled persons (Immigrant for Social Justice, 31 August 2014). In
2007, for example, starvation forced more than 900 stranded
Zimbabweans, including little children, to take refuge at the Church
where they were given food and shelter (Sokwanele, 20 July 2007). In

179

November 2008, the centre was providing shelter to an average of 1 200 Zimbabweans every night (Sibeko, 27 November 2009). At some point in 2010, more than 2 000 Zimbabwean immigrants were sleeping in the church (Immigrant for Social Justice, 31 August 2014). Similarly, in January 2009, more than 100 Zimbabwean children were sleeping in a crowded tin-roofed garage at a Musina church. The church offered the garage to accommodate destitute Zimbabwean children most of who begged along the streets during the day (Gerardy, 11 January 2009).

Despite being sheltered and fed by charitable institutions such as churches, the problems of the downtrodden Zimbabwean immigrants were far from over as they were not immune from police clampdowns. During the night of 30 January 2008, the police raided the Central Methodist Church in Johannesburg and arrested undocumented Zimbabweans who congregated there to beg for food and accommodation. According to Bishop Paul Verryn, the police raid was carried out without a warrant, severely damaged Church property and ignited chaos among the refugees (Forster, 31 January 2008). Many sections of the public criticised the South African government and the police for being insensitive to the plight of Zimbabwean immigrants. Pamela, a Zimbabwean woman who was resident in South Africa at that time, lamented:

I am a Zimbabwean legally in South Africa and it breaks my heart. We have been reduced to beggars. We are constantly referred to as 'aliens'. In that church, there were fathers, mothers, brothers, sisters and children who have done nothing wrong but to seek refuge in the house of the Lord. Nothing was being done in secret; everyone knew of the existence of Zimbabwean refuges at the Methodist Church. By taking this action, the South African Police have shown the stand of the government on the mess that Zimbabwe has been reduced to. They are in denial of the suffering of the people. The church is under a biblical mandate to feed the hungry and shelter the homeless. It is a mandate from God and I do not care that the government may not subscribe to the authority of God but I and a whole lot of other people do. What has been done is to stomp upon holy ground, rip people out of their place of safety and throw them right back into danger of starvation and potential violence. The state has trespassed big time. Let me address the issue from a language that the state understands. We speak of the Bible, they speak of the Constitution as the supreme law of the land. Their supreme document states that citizens have the right to religion. Christian religion demands shelter and food for those in need. The church was exercising its right under the Constitution, its mandate from God and the urge of any sound human heart to help and the response of the state is to damage property and sanctity. It is a disgrace (Forster, 31 January 2008: 1).

On 31 January 2014, the Johannesburg's Central Methodist Church officially closed its doors to vulnerable immigrants. At the time of closure, the church had an estimated 500 residents. The reasons for the closure were not publicised but some reports pointed to the lack of funds and internal conflicts within the church over the accommodation of immigrants (Gumbo, 29 December 2014). Despite the official closure of the church, destitute immigrants, mostly from Zimbabwe, continued to seek assistance from the institution and were sometimes given food and shelter.

On 8 May 2015, at about 4am, the South African riot police and soldiers from the anti-crime unit raided the Central Methodist Church in Johannesburg and evicted about 1 000 Zimbabweans who took shelter there every night. The raid was part of Operation *Fiela* ('sweep out dirt') whose aim was to crack down on illegal immigrants and criminals (Laing, 8 May 2015). Renee Kilshaw, a 32-year-old South African resident at the church where she stayed with her partner, a former Zimbabwean soldier, and their four-year-old daughter Kristen, said they woke up to find the police pointing guns at them. She said: "It was so frightening. My daughter was just crying and asking who these soldiers were. I do not know what is going to happen to us now, [or] where we will go. I am so confused" (Ibid: 1). Some Zimbabwean migrants claimed that the police beat them up, while shouting: "*Kwerekwere*...get out, go home!" (Ibid: 1).

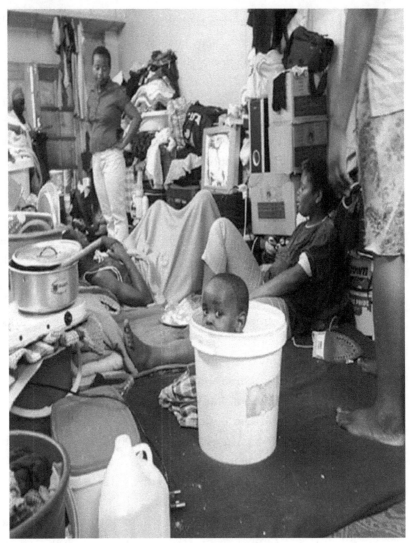

Figure 15: Zimbabwean immigrants sheltered in the Johannesburg Central Methodist Church, late 2014.

Source: Kandemiiri and Gumbo (3 January 2015)

Uncertainties pertaining to the provision of food and shelter were a major challenge for many Zimbabwean immigrants, including beggars. Some desperate Zimbabwean beggars became part, if not virtual slaves, of South African begging syndicates as a way of securing guarantees of accommodation and food. In most cases, it were the newly-arrived Zimbabwean beggars to South African cities who, out of insecurity, enrolled into syndicates run by South African nationals who allocated them spaces to operate in various localities (Bedfordview Residents Action Group, 19 October 2010). These South African syndicates became more visible in Johannesburg from the onset of the new millennium owing to the influx of wretched Zimbabweans into the country. The syndicate owners capitalised on the plight of desperate Zimbabwean refugees to assign them begging errands after which they demanded a portion of the proceeds and provided them with food and accommodation in return (*Financial Gazette*, 21 August 2016). In 2008, for example, Merlyn Ndou, a qualified teacher, fled economic turmoil in Zimbabwe anticipating greener pastures in Johannesburg. After failing to secure a job, Ndou was recruited into a Johannesburg group of beggars run by a South African national who provided shelter and food to desperate Zimbabweans. In return, the South African demanded from them part of whatever they obtained from panhandling. The South African benefactor, who had over 100 Zimbabwean panhandlers under his command, provided Ndou with food and shelter in a rundown squatter camp near Johannesburg's Alexandra Township. He set a target of 50 Rands per day for every beggar (Ibid). By August 2016, Ndou was still 'working' for the begging syndicate and had developed a rare skin disease which needed attention. Surprisingly, the skin ailment was a blessing in disguise to the syndicate leader who "used her health condition to draw public sympathy and boost alms" (Ibid: 1). Bemoaning how she was being exploited in South Africa, Ndou said: "I should have stayed home and continued as a teacher, because life here is not easy. I hear teachers are getting a decent salary these days" (Ibid: 1).

Pascal Mbedzi, a 24-year-old Zimbabwean man from Beitbridge, also fled Zimbabwe in 2008 and operated in the same begging syndicate with Ndou. The syndicate leader dropped his 'army' of beggars, including Mbedzi, at strategic points in Johannesburg every morning and collected them towards sunset. Mbedzi's begging zone was in Bramfontein Suburb where he got an average of 100 Rands per day (Ibid). The miserable predicaments of Tlou and Mbedzi clearly illustrate how some destitute Zimbabwean immigrants ended up as virtual chattels who begged on behalf of South African syndicate barons in return for accommodation and food.

While many undocumented Zimbabwean immigrants in South Africa in general and beggars in particular experienced a surfeit of tribulations throughout their stay, the beginning of the year 2020 coincided with the global spread of a ravaging pandemic in the form of the Coronavirus (COVID-19). Immigrants, particularly those who were undocumented, were hard hit by the pandemic with many Zimbabwean panhandlers plunging into abject poverty while some of their counterparts who previously survived from self-jobs turned to beggary.

In mid-April 2020, a visually-impaired Zimbabwean couple in the South African city of Louis Trichardt was reported to be in serious trouble as a result of the Coronavirus outbreak. Willie Chimuka and his wife, Fungai Pepukai, both of whom were visually-challenged, left Zimbabwe in 2018 for the South African town in the Limpopo Province where they begged outside local stores for a living (Chiguvare, 16 April 2020). In their daily begging pursuits, Chimuka usually sat near the entrance to Spar Supermarket while Pepukai positioned herself outside Jet Stores. The couple had four children, one of who came with them to South Africa while the other three remained in Zimbabwe with Chimuka's parents. During an interview in April 2020, the couple reported that before the lockdown, they were able to buy food and pay rent with the money they collected from begging. The couple complained that since the nationwide lockdown began in South Africa, they had not been able to collect enough money for food and rent (Ibid). Chimuka explained their dilemma as follows:

> We cannot sit at home and relax. All we need is permission to go back to our usual begging spots. If we do not, the family is going to go for days without food. Every month we send money and some food back home. Our parents are just peasant farmers and they cannot do much to support our children (Ibid: 1).

The couple went to Makhado Police Station in the city to request permission to return to their begging spots but were advised to stay home as movement would jeopardise their lives and those of others.

An official from the Limpopo Department of Social Development weighed in and said the department was running a programme of distributing food parcels to needy cases. The official advised the couple to visit a local councillor who would take their issue to social workers in the area (Ibid). The local social workers revealed that they were only allowed to assist people who stayed at a shelter in the Makhado Showground for the duration of the lockdown (Ibid).

In late April 2020, Inock Mukanhairi, a 58-year-old visually-challenged Zimbabwean beggar, was in a similar predicament in Johannesburg. Mukanhiri, together with his wife, who was also visually-handicapped, had been surviving from begging at traffic lights on Johannesburg's streets, relying on handouts from motorists, pedestrians and shop owners. Life became unbearable for the couple during the Coronavirus lockdown as they were required to remain indoors at their dilapidated flat in central Johannesburg which they rented together with more than 20 other visually-challenged beggars (Janssen, 29 April 2020). Mukanhiri lamented their plight as a result of the stringent lockdown conditions which barred them from scrounging for alms in the empty streets and barren sidewalks: "I really understand that the Coronavirus is killing a lot of people. But at the same time, I am locked inside my room. So death is death, due to Corona or due to hunger" (Ibid: 1).

As enunciated in this section, begging in South Africa by poverty-battered Zimbabweans was not an easy way of making money. Undoubtedly, it was an unenviable undertaking fraught with a plenitude of challenges and frustrations. In addition to the general problems faced by beggars since time immemorial, the peculiarities of begging in a foreign country, away from home, and among people of different nationalities, present more complications. Given the plethora of agonies of seeking livelihoods across national borders, many beggars would have opted to return home if survival prospects had been brighter.

Conclusion

This chapter examined struggles of survival by Zimbabweans in neighbouring countries, paying particular attention to South Africa.

It explored how Zimbabwean beggars exhibited a broad range of competencies in order to ensure maximum collection of alms that guaranteed sustenance for themselves while abroad and their dependants at home. The skilful negotiation of the physical and social terrain was of utmost importance as the beggars had to be at the right places at the right time, being ably assisted by the most suitable social partners. What emerges from this chapter is that home is not always the best for many of those marginalised people who have suffered years of neglect at the hands of family institutions, local welfare organisations and national governments. In addition, begging across national borders is an indictment on the part of home governments and local institutions for not putting in place elaborate and effective social welfare systems and mechanisms to cushion the poor.

Chapter 5

Counting the Costs: Blessing or Curse? Impact of begging on Zimbabwe's socio-economic landscape

Introduction

This chapter is preoccupied with counting the costs of begging in terms of credits and debits to a country's socio-economic fabric. In theoretical terms, the credits fall in the realm of Social Constructionism which argues that work is a broad phenomenon that can be interpreted differently depending on the social context, implying that begging can be productive in some sense since some panhandlers have managed to meet their basic necessities (Grint, 2005; Kassah, 2008). From the Social Deconstructionist Perspective, however, begging tends to be a short-term panacea to poverty for most people who survive from hand to mouth from the little financial and other proceeds they obtain, but this is largely at the expense of a bright future (Abebe, 2008). In taking stock of the issues, both quantitative and qualitative (phenomenological) analytic tools are employed. The chapter acknowledges that begging is a way of life and a critical survival option that has sustained the livelihoods of many vulnerable sections of the society where governments and welfare organisations have failed. It is being argued, however, that the benefits from begging are largely material (quantitative), personalised and/or localised. Otherwise, broadly and qualitatively, panhandling decimates a country's socio-economic fabric in the long term.

Begging as a survival initiative where governments have failed

From the Social Constructionist Perspective, the prevalence of begging by Zimbabweans from 2000 was one of the few realistic options of survival left to famished citizens, given the government's mismanagement of the economy, socio-economic degeneration, chronic poverty, and the absence of robust social welfare measures to cushion the poor. As Abbas (2008: 1) rightly notes, the increasing visibility of beggars is "an adversely gloomy reflection" of the administrative system. Thus, the overwhelming presence of beggars from the new millennium politically discredits Zimbabwean leaders and institutions in authority as this is clearly indicative of a dismal failure and an abrogation of their mandate to ensure social security of the generality of the population, and maintain law and order.

Elsewhere, Kaushik (2014: 14) also blamed the government of India for the prevalence of child beggars in that country: "It seems these children are visible to everyone but the government. There seems to be no initiative from the side of government to help these children lead a dignified life and to put them into schools". As far as Zimbabwe is concerned, Bourdillon (December 2001: 1) argued:

> A problem facing administrators is that if they are to be held responsible for the running of society, they need to be in control. Flagrant breach of law cannot be tolerated. Street children often do break the law. They are often involved in minor crime. They certainly do not respond well to attempts to control their activities especially where money is concerned. This leads to a…more serious problem for administrators: street children sometimes threaten the rights of other more law-abiding citizens. Apart from threat to people's property, street children sometimes harass the public, and can threaten their physical safety.

Indeed, begging can be an indirect form of political expression. It can be a disguised form of dialogue with fellow citizens on the failure by the state to provide basic necessities. As Cohen (2002: 14) notes, begging is in a way a political speech:

> By his tattered self-presentation in the public domain, and his supplication of passersby for assistance, the beggar's anomalous condition of dire want informs onlookers about, or at least suggests to them, the existence of social …disorder, and may disorient, or awaken from undesired complacency all who witness that soul's miserable penurious state. That is to say, in addition to his conscious, particular

188

message of want, the beggar conveys, however indirectly, an underlying message about society, and about life.

To many Zimbabweans, including some disabled citizens, the government is largely to blame for the upsurge in begging. In explaining the prevalence of begging by Zimbabweans within the country and abroad, various NGOs also castigated the government for impoverishing its citizens. In a strongly-worded statement in February 2005, for example, the Aroma Trust, a Zimbabwean-based NGO involved in welfare programmes for the country's visually-handicapped people, urged the government to redress the situation: "What we are now seeing in South Africa should not be allowed to continue. The government should move swiftly and bring back those blind people who have now become a nuisance on the South African roads. Those people should be adequately supported by the government" (*Daily News*, 11 February 2005: 1). Also speaking in 2006, as most rural San people in the settlements of Mgodimasili, Makhulela and Tjitatjawa in Matabeleland North Province resorted to begging as a result of Zimbabwe's economic ruin, Sol Ndlovu of the Zimbabwe Association of Minority Languages accused the government of negligence:

> [The San] are simply a misunderstood, discriminated-upon and despised people, but with sterling capabilities, and if adequately aided resource-wise, they can pull themselves out of the abyss of hopelessness they find themselves into today. Government should do just more than talk…NGOs have tried to help, but strictly speaking it is the duty of the government to see to it that people are equally catered for as other groups (*Irin News*, 26 September 2006: 1).

Many critics blamed the government for neglecting the poor, and failing to capacitate them to be productive and self-sustaining. In April 2010, Masimba Kuchera, a visually-challenged member of the National Disabled Council of Zimbabwe, lamented the government's failure to look into the welfare of disabled people, most of who had resorted to begging for survival: "The government has forgotten the disabled people. Nothing was mentioned in the country's 2010

189

budget. There are no projects or programmes whatsoever for disabled people" (Kwenda, 10 April 2010: 1). In 2010, Joshua Malinga, a disabled Member of Parliament and member of the ruling ZANU-PF's Politburo, the party's powerful decision-making body, also complained that the government's negligence had forced most disabled people into mendicancy. This motivated him to join the Disabled People's International, an NGO, in order to double up efforts to improve the welfare of the disabled people (Ibid).

What also irked many Zimbabweans was the government's financial extravagance on political expediency at the expense of the welfare of the vulnerable people. In August 2014, for example, there was public dismay in Zimbabwe after the ruling ZANU-PF held celebrations to mark the anniversary of their electoral victory on 31 July 2013 despite widespread poverty gripping the nation. The general public accused the ruling party of extravagancy and insensitivity by holding celebrations worth hundreds of thousands of American dollars at a time when the country was experiencing severe socio-economic infelicities that had reduced many people to panhandlers (*Zimbabwe Mail*, 1 August 2014). As Mbuso Fuzwayo, a Zimbabwean social commentator based in South Africa, also noted in 2014:

> The Zimbabwean government has destroyed the country. It does not care about its citizens who are now scattered all over the word as beggars. The government must create opportunities for the people. In 1980, Zimbabwe was the breadbasket for Africa but due to mismanagement, Zimbabweans are all over the world (*Radio Dialogue*, 30 April 2014: 3).

Given Zimbabwe's battered economy from the onset of the new millennium, and its financially-crippled and irresponsible government that plunged itself into bankruptcy largely through elite self-aggrandisement and politically-motivated extravagance while the majority of people languished in poverty, panhandling became one of the few options of salvaging sustenance. Having been dumped to fate by two successive egocentric political establishments, initially under Robert Mugabe and later under Emmerson Mnangagwa, many impoverished sections of the population resorted to begging in order to meet their subsistence needs rather than stare at hunger in the face and starve to death.

Begging for sustenance: A cushion from penury

Begging is an informal economic engagement that sustains the livelihoods of significant numbers of marginalised Zimbabweans. As will be noted in this section, testimonies from Zimbabwean beggars at home and abroad indicate that the proceeds from panhandling went a long way in meeting their subsistence needs and those of their immediate family members. More often than not, as Stones (2013: 158) notes, panhandling "provides cash income for immediate and urgent needs that cannot be satisfied by approaching welfare organisations". Indeed, as Swanson (2010) also noted in her study of urban societies in Equador, begging enables some impoverished people and their dependants to stay afloat.

Beggars from various parts of Zimbabwe revealed that even though life was tough in view of the economic meltdown since 2000, the alms they collected from well-wishers contributed significantly towards their upkeep (Charirwe, Chatindo, Mukondiwa, Nengomasha, Rangwanda, Ruwende, Sibindi and Sithole; Separate Interviews: 2014). In August 2011, some Harare beggars reported that one could collect between US$5 and US$10 every day (*Newsday*, 21 August 2011). There are also cases of child beggars who managed to sustain their poor families. This was the case of Tawanda, a five-year-old boy who begged in Harare along the stretch between Mbare Suburb and Samora Machel Avenue in the city centre in February 2011. His ailing 30-year-old HIV-positive single mother, Rudo Mugogi, and 21-month-old little brother solely depended on his proceeds of begging from motorists which averaged between US$5 and US$10 per day. His mother revealed that Tawanda had become their breadwinner through begging: "He [Tawanda] is the father of my house. I survive on the money he brings from begging to pay for our rentals and food. And sometimes I just do not know what to do when he refuses to come and beg saying he will be tired" (*Zimbabwean*, 16 February 2011: 1). Rudo was very ill and while Tawanda moved around begging, she slept on the pavement until sunset when they

191

travelled 12 kilometres to Epworth Suburb where they rented a room (Ibid). Despite benefitting in this manner, it is regrettable that children were being deprived of formal childhood activities, rights and protection, and were being inducted into a life of dependence and beggary.

A maintenance case heard at the Harare Civil Court on 6 January 2020 illustrates how, despite the country's prevailing socio-economic miseries, some disabled people earned substantial amounts of money from panhandling, part of which they could splash in luxuries. The court case involved Moses Ncube, a visually-challenged man who survived on begging in buses, who was being accused of pampering his girlfriend with money at the expense of his wife, Enerita Marindire, who was also visually-challenged. Ncube, who confessed to earning ZW$3 000 per month from begging, an amount that surpassed the salary of most civil servants such as teachers, nurses, soldiers and police details who were earning an average of ZW2500 per month, offered to pay ZW$900 as maintenance for his estranged wife and children. His wife had demanded ZW$1 500 but the court ordered him to pay ZW$1 200 per month as maintenance with effect from 31 January 2020 (*H-Metro*, 7 January 2020). What this case shows is that some beggars earned considerable amounts of money, much more than the salaries of most government employees. In addition, it can be noted that some disabled persons could even afford extravagant lifestyles, such as spoiling their concubines with goodies, from the proceeds of begging.

Some Zimbabwean panhandlers in South Africa acknowledged that the alms they got from begging were very helpful in sustaining their livelihoods and those of their dependents at home. Their daily collections tended to vary depending on where and when they operated. In February 2005, Brighton Mkushi, a visually-impaired Zimbabwean panhandler in Johannesburg, said that during month-end periods he earned about 120 Rands per day (SAMP, 5 February 2005). In February 2006, some Zimbabwean beggars in Johannesburg reportedly collected an average of 30 to 50 Rands a day (SAMP, 26 February 2006). Priscilla Sibanyoni who begged in central Johannesburg with her 15-month-old baby strapped to her back in 2007 earned an average of 30 to 100 Rands per day

(Mapumulo, 25 September 2007).

In September 2007, Shylet Madhabuya, a 38-year-old Zimbabwean woman who begged at the Park Central Mall, close to Noord Street taxi rank in central Johannesburg, said she collected between 50 and 180 Rands per day and average monthly earnings of 2 000 Rands which managed to sustain her family back home in Zimbabwe (Ibid). In June 2011, Emmanuel Runyanga, a visually-challenged Zimbabwean beggar in Johannesburg, said on a good day, he could get 50 Rands (US$5) and, together with his visually-handicapped wife, they regularly sent some of the money they would have begged to their two young children in Zimbabwe (*Irin News*, 13 June 2011).

Most Zimbabwean beggars interviewed by the *Mail and Guardian* in Johannesburg in September 2011 were in agreement that they eked out an existence in South Africa in order to send money home to support their children who they had left under the custody of their families and relatives. Ellen Ziya, a 46-year-old visually-impaired female beggar in South Africa since 2004, for instance, begged together with her two adult children in Johannesburg while the other seven younger ones stayed with her family in Bulawayo (Tolsi, 30 September 2011). She told the *Mail and Guardian* in 2011 that she supported her children in Zimbabwe through proceeds from begging: "Every two weeks I try and send about 300 Rands [US$30] home to my children. We usually send money or groceries with the bus drivers who are going to Bulawayo and they charge an extra 20 Rands [US$2] for every 100 Rands [US$10] we send, or depending on the size of the carrier bags" (Ibid: 1).

As noted in this section, begging is a livelihood initiative in which impoverished people seek alms to alleviate their dire conditions of deprivation. Some panhandlers managed to sustain their families at home and abroad from the proceeds of begging after the government had failed to cushion them. Ironically, the beggars were actually subsidising the Zimbabwean government by taking over its responsibilities of looking into the welfare of vulnerable sections of the society.

From rags to riches: Begging as an avenue of upward social mobility

From the social constructionist perspective, begging has seen some people making considerable progress in life and rising up the social ladder after putting the money they received to constructive use. Some panhandlers saved part of the money they had collected for other purposes and activities that enabled them to improve their living standards, for example, buying household property, educating themselves and their children, and starting income-generating projects. It is in this context that some panhandlers view begging as a means to an end and not an end in itself. As illustrated by some examples in this section, begging can be a steppingstone for better things to come, particularly in poverty-hit dispensations where opportunities and options of survival and progression are very limited.

It is important to note that the donation of alms, especially money, to poor people can be a great psychological boost, particularly to those who are on the margins of destitution. The handling of money empowers many beggars and invigorates them to be agents of their own destiny. According to Kassah (2008: 169):

> Feelings of devaluation, helplessness and powerlessness also seem to be reduced as they [beggars] earn their own money, which they disburse according to their wishes. Work in the form of begging may thus improve their self-image and change their devalued status to that of a socially-valued one. When begging assumes a valued status among disabled people recruitment may be facilitated. It may, therefore, be difficult, if not impossible, to ask beggars to stop their activities without any close substitute.

The acquisition of household property and other material possessions, among other things, is an index of progress and upward social mobility. It is in this context that when some of the beggars managed to buy household property and other valuables from the money they collected from well-wishers, it was a socio-economic success. In March 2007, for example, a driver of Tenda Buses, one of the public transport companies that plied the Johannesburg-Mutare route, stated that it was common during month-end periods for Zimbabwean beggars in South Africa to temporarily go back home with household items such as stoves, televisions and refrigerators (Marufu, 21 March 2007).

Some people are known to have raised money from begging which they reinvested to generate more income to sustain themselves and their dependents. In this sense, begging becomes "an entrepreneurial activity" by impoverished people (Swanson, 2007: 706). Malachias Mabate, a man from Karani Village in the Mutasa District of Manicaland Province, is an example of a visually-challenged beggar who rose to become an entrepreneur in his own right. He had lost sight in 1988 at the age of 16 years following a persistent eye infection which could not be medically treated since his parents had no money for the required eye operation. He began begging at the nearby Watsomba Business Centre in 1992 with the hope of raising money to start a small business. In 1998, he managed to buy two pigs, a bow and a sow, and went on to construct a pigsty, all from the proceeds of panhandling. By 2019, Mabate was running a very successful piggery project and was the major supplier of pork to several butcheries at Watsomba Business Centre (Mabate, Interview: 16 May 2019).

There are some panhandlers who managed to educate their children from the alms they had collected. John Sadutu, a visually-challenged man from Honde Valley in Manicaland Province, used the money he collected from begging to pay school fees for his son, Elliot, who did Forms 1-4 at a rural day secondary school from 1989 to 1992. The son got financial assistance from an NGO to pursue Advanced Level studies and later, a degree in Civil Engineering. In 2019, Elliot was employed as an engineer with a company in South Africa, and had managed to buy his parents a house in the low-density suburbs of Mutare where they were now staying (Sadutu, Interview: 26 August 2019).

Some future-oriented beggars used part of the money they got from well-wishers to further their own education. An illustrious example is Lwazi, a Zimbabwean street beggar who later became a university postgraduate. He was initially raised in Harare where he completed his Ordinary and Advanced Level studies after which he enrolled for a degree in Chemical Engineering at the Harare Institute of Technology. Since his parents were not employed, he struggled to raise fees for his studies by hawking through which he bought clothes and small electronic gadgets from Botswana and resold them in Zimbabwe. The hawking business ate a lot into his study time and made him to complete the four-year course in five years. Sadly, however, having graduated in 2014, Lwazi could not find a job in the field of chemical engineering, forcing him to become employed as a general hand at a farm for 12 months (Lindeque, 13 May 2019).

He moved to South Africa in July 2017 hoping to find a job in his field of study. Having failed to secure employment, he was advised by a Professor at the University of the Witwatersrand to enrol for diploma studies that specialised in petroleum, meaning that he had to do a Post-Graduate Diploma in Chemical Engineering (Oil and Gas) at the same university. Before enrolling, his Zimbabwean qualifications had to be evaluated by the South African Qualifications Authority (SAQA) and this needed money. In addition, the university needed 75% of the year's fees before lectures commenced. In an effort to raise the money, he found a job of handing out leaflets at traffic light intersections in Johannesburg's CBD, earning 80 Rands per day and managed to save 1 100 Rands that was required to submit his certificates to SAQA. Having been accepted for the Postgraduate Diploma Programme for 2018 by the University of the Witwatersrand, his next headache was the 75% of that year's fees, which amounted to 55 000 Rands, before lectures started. He resorted to begging in Johannesburg in order to raise the amount. He started by positioning himself at traffic light intersections in Fourways, begging for financial assistance to further his studies, using photocopies of his qualifications to authenticate his plea. By January 2018, he had managed to raise the amount needed. He then enrolled at the university and fortunately, some well-wishers availed scholarships to sustain his stay. In 2019, he completed his Postgraduate Diploma in Chemical Engineering (Ibid). What emanates from this example is that people do not become beggars out of choice, but by fate. Furthermore, the foregoing illuminates that begging can be a means to an end and not an end in itself for some beggars who became successful in life after investing the proceeds of begging towards a better career or other income-generating pursuits.

From the social constructionist perspective, the use of children can alternatively be understood positively given the limited survival options and inadequate state support services. It can be regarded as "the informal adoption" and "a sort of apprenticeship" for impoverished children which inducts them into the future experiences and challenges of adulthood and parenthood (Swanson, 2007: 715). It may also be viewed as one of the innovative means through which people in chronic need "maximise their families' earnings by incorporating children's labour on the streets" (Ibid: 715). Without underestimating the gravity of the beggars' plight, these arguments hardly hold any water. The use of children to beg is a gross violation of children's rights that also potentially plunges them into a vicious cycle of poverty in which they become perennial recipients rather than producers. Instead, what responsible adults should do is to mobilise resources, even through begging, and send children to school so as to open them up to a broad range of survival options in future.

It is a fact that begging is a way of life which most beggars do not cherish. Nonetheless, it is a way of life that has sustained the livelihoods of some marginalised Zimbabweans. Given the country's socio-economic quagmire from the onset of the new millennium, many poor people could have starved to death if they had not scrounged for a living from begging. As this section has demonstrated, there are exceptional cases, as also established by Abebe (2008), in which some downtrodden but resilient beggars achieved considerable progress from the alms they collected. It has become a rags-to-riches story for some panhandlers who have acquired property for themselves and their families. Others used the money they got from begging to start income-generating projects. In some cases, beggars managed to save money to pay school fees for themselves or their children, with some of them becoming very successful in life. Thus, as Swanson (2010) also noted in Equador, begging can be a path towards progress for some impoverished people. The cases of beggars who have made progress in life are, however, very few, understandably so because of Zimbabwe's numerous challenges since 2000, which incapacitated many potential well-wishers and plunged a significant section of vulnerable people into destitution.

Child begging and destruction of the social fabric

Social deconstructionist scholars have singled out child begging in general and forced child begging in particular as some of the most abominable and regrettable survival pursuits that have destabilised the social order of many countries (Ord, 2010). The involvement of children in begging presents "a sight that evokes an emotional response and an ethical dilemma, which is agonising for those with a conscience" (Botha, 9 April 2017: 1). Indeed, the prevalence of begging by children in any given community is a veritable manifestation of a "torn fabric of humanity" (Mbanje, 13 December 2015: 1).

Begging is inconsistent to, and an affront to, the normative discourse of child development. The primacy of contemporary 'global models' of childhood lies in the domesticity, dependency and protection of children under the care and supervision of parents (Abebe, 2009; Boyden, 1998). Many rights of children are violated if they become involved in panhandling. The rights to care, protection and education, for example, are often relinquished in the fierce contestations of survival along the streets.

Forced begging deprives children of the exposure to normal childhood recreational activities, among other things, which constitute one of the most important agents of socialisation that ensures them of healthy upbringing (Human Rights Watch, 2010; UNICEF, 2001) and normal life in society. The rights of children are protected by several international conventions. The United Nations Convention on the Rights of the Child (1989) and the African Charter on the Rights and Welfare of the Child (1990), for instance, forbid the practice of child labour, including the use of children to beg (Human Rights Watch, 2010; UNICEF, 2001). According to these statutes, "child-begging is a form of child labour" (Matikinye, 10 June 2015: 1). The United Nations International Children's

Emergency Fund (UNICEF) defines child labour as work performed by children who are under the minimum age legally specified for that kind of work, or work which, because of its detrimental nature or conditions, is considered unacceptable for children and is prohibited. This includes work which, by its nature or the circumstances in which it is carried out, is likely to harm the health, safety or morals of children. The International Labour Organisation (ILO) defines child labour as work that is mentally, physically, socially or morally harmful to children and that interferes with their schooling (Ibid).

Many countries around the world have also castigated the use of children to beg, with some of them criminalising the practice. In March 2013, Edna Mamonyane, a Johannesburg Metropolitan Police Spokeswoman, for example, condemned the use of children by adult beggars, mostly Zimbabweans, in the city as a violation of human rights and the law: "It is a very serious problem. We cannot let them [adult beggars] flaunt by-laws, especially when children are involved. This is abuse of the child (Solidarity Helping Hand, 4 March 2013: 1). Elsewhere, the Romanian Constitution, in fulfilment of the provisions of the European Convention of Human Rights, also criminalises the use of children to make profit. The penalty for recruiting or forcing a child to beg ranges from one to five years in prison. In the event of parents committing such a crime repeatedly, they risk losing parenthood and having their children put under the custody of orphanages (Mihalache and others, 2013).

In Zimbabwe, the Children's Protection and Adoption Act (1972) and the Labour Relations Act criminalise the use of children in begging pursuits (UNICEF, 2001). The Children's Protection and Adoption Act and its subsequent amendments criminalise the engagement of children in hazardous work that is likely to interrupt their education and expose them to injury, abuse and hazardous substances. The Labour Relations Act sets the minimum age for employment at 16 years and specifies that children between the ages of 16 and 18 years can only be employed as apprentices and only under special training conditions. The minimum age at which children can perform light work was set at 15 years. Young people below the age of 18 years are prohibited from doing work that can endanger their morals, safety and health (Defence for Children

International Zimbabwe, 14 March 2014). During an operation to clear Harare city centre of beggars and street kids in February 2013, Tadious Chibanda, a police spokesperson, stated that it was an offence under the Child Protection Act for an adult to use children to beg in the streets because it was a form of child abuse (Ncube, 3 February 2013). In 2014, Phillip Bhowasi, the Chairman of the Social Workers' Association of Zimbabwe, complained against the prevalent use of children in begging across the country and highlighted the manner in which the practice flouted human rights obligations and the law:

> Many children now miss their right to care and protection, thus all laws that protect the children need to be articulated and implemented. The implications remain severe because morality of any society is judged by the way we treat our children. Children are the future of a society and street children are the mirror to our future (Chifamba, 3 May 2014: 1).

Child begging is a very retrogressive livelihood option, given that it often deprives children of the right to education, an aspect of life in general and development in particular which deserves particular attention in this section. Through begging, some children who are supposed to be attending school are initiated into street life. As their education is disrupted by begging activities, the children's life is awkwardly guaranteed of "a bleak present and a murky future" (Abbas, 2008: 1). The United Nations Convention on the Rights of the Child (1989) and the African Charter on the Rights and Welfare of the Child (1990) emphasised that children are entitled to compulsory education that equips them with critical skills which make them useful to society (Human Rights Watch, 2010; UNICEF, 2001). The use of children to beg also impairs their educational and intellectual development because it leaves them with little energy to concentrate at school (UNICEF, 2001). It is for this reason, among others, that in late January 2013, as the Zimbabwean government launched an operation to clear the Harare CBD of child beggars and other vagrants, Tadious Chibanda, a police spokesperson, commented:

The child is supposed to be attending school like other children. Instead of being in class, the minor is now in the street assisting an old person to beg. Socially, it seems normal but it is illegal. The child is being deprived of his or her right to education and it is the duty of the police to protect those children and ensure that they determine their own future (Ncube, 3 February 2013: 1).

These sentiments were echoed by Caleb Mutandwa, the Programmes Director of Justice for Children, who cautioned that parents who use children to beg deprive them of decent education, good morals and prospects for a better future (Bwanya, 30 July 2013). In 2018, a survey of children begging and living on the streets of Harare conducted by UNICEF determined that about a third of the children had either never gone to school or had dropped out of school during the early primary years (Mwandiyambira, 26 September 2019). These findings were confirmed by Save the Children, a child rights organisation, which noted that many child beggars are excluded from mainstream education (Ibid).

Child-begging has a surfeit of disastrous psycho-social consequences that ruin the future of young generations (Ahamdi, 2010; Delap, 2009). The lack or absence of parental guidance, conditions of neglect and frustration emanating from despair make many child beggars susceptible to self-destructive and anti-social behaviour like alcoholism, drug addiction, violence and prostitution (*Newsday*, 21 August 2011). Ferguson (2006) noted that the impoverished condition of most street children tempts them to take part in criminal activities such as selling illegal substances, conniving with thieves, pick-pocketing and gambling (*H-Metro*, 23 March 2016). This resonates with the 2013 observations of Tadious Chibanda, the then Harare Provincial Police Spokesperson that some child beggars engaged in criminal activities such as associating with criminals, giving tips to robbers and providing information to carjackers (Ncube, 3 February 2013).

In addition, girl child beggars often get tempted into "survival sex" or "pseudo-prostitution" as they struggle to survive along the streets (Mtonga: 2011: 103). This activity, which is distinguishable from regular and conventional acts of prostitution or commercial sex work, is undertaken by young and inexperienced girls on an irregular basis as they seek money to meet their immediate subsistence needs such as the next meal (Ibid). Criminality becomes a survival option for considerable numbers of child beggars as they get older (Ibid). In addition, as Mtonga (2011) observed among street children in Zambian cities, as beggars grow older, they are often harassed by the police forcing them to seek livelihoods sometimes through criminal means such as theft. Yet at other moments the girl child beggars will be forced to provide sexual favours to the law enforcers in exchange for protection from harassment or for tip off information (Marjury, Tatenda, Mollen and Susan, Separate Interviews: 2020). Thus, as Scheper-Hughes and Hoffman (1994) argued, there can be a gradual progression from begging to criminality.

The desperate condition of many street beggars in Zimbabwean urban centres accounts for their propensity to commit several crimes in pursuit of livelihoods (Bwanya, 30 July 2013). In May 2013, for example, there was "hell on Harare's streets" as a result of criminal activities by street children, most of who were beggars. As the *Herald* (8 May 2013: 1) put it:

> There are many classes of street people traversing our streets as the scourge continues unabated. These are the people whom we see on the streets guarding our cars, washing the cars and soliciting for a few coins or spare change. However, there is a new scourge on the streets as we encounter, on numerous occasions, children who solicit for money and food. The children have also turned nasty as they target hapless women grabbing food and other stuff from the unsuspecting women. On numerous occasions, some have been apprehended for shoplifting in supermarkets. Some of them target women's handbags, phones, jewellery and other personal belongings. The police have also been forced to come hard on the street people as they try to deal decisively with the problem. While the raids have brought temporary relief to the problem, no lasting solution has been found as the street people emerge shortly after their release.

In Harare's Central Business District, as Lopez (1 February 2020) noted in February 2020, many young street beggars had turned to drugs and were often referred to as *zvigunduru*, which in Tsonga, a local minority language in Zimbabwe, means 'sleepers', as they spent most of their time sleeping or lying down on pavements or roadsides after taking drugs. Many *zvigunduru* could be seen lying down in the area around the Formula One Hotel, one of their favourite places. "It is better not to get lost inside that area, which is in fact the street children's territory, where laws are dictated by those who have nothing to lose," advised Lopez (Ibid: 1). Our investigations into the issue of taking drugs by young street children in most of Zimbabwe's cities revealed that most sniffed glue, drank a cough syrup called Broncleer, popularly known as *Bronco*, and smoked cannabis. While being very potent, these drugs were relatively cheap and readily accessible from local suppliers.

As children grow up begging in the rough life of the streets, the dividing line between criminality and beggary increasingly becomes blurred. In his characterisation of beggars in the United States of America during the late 19th century, Bentwick (1894: 127-128) said:

> Actually they are thieves themselves; for they take money for work which they have not done...Experience teaches that a man who will make a business of begging will steal. Professional beggars must therefore be hunted down and prosecuted just the same as any other sort of criminals...This being conceded, it follows that at least ninety-five out of every hundred habitual beggars are professional rogues, idle persons brought up to beggary, who cheat the good, prevent relief from coming into the hands of the needy, live a miserable, vicious, and wicked life, rob society of whatever each of them owes to God's world in return for the benefits that he gets, trouble society with infinite evils, and should be most severely punished, and by force exterminated, that is to say, converted into working members of the community by being set to some employment more or less profitable. The relation of the vagrant to the criminal class is of the closest character; it is hard to say where the one begins and the other ends. Every vagabond is an idle fellow, quite ready to turn his hand to the easiest way of getting money. When he cannot cheat, he steals; if stealing is beyond his reach, he begs in a whining tone.

Similarly, in many Western European countries such as Sweden and Finland, beggars from the minority Roma people are associated with criminal activities (Ahola, 2011; Phillips and Shah, 26 January 2016). In Zimbabwe, common observations associating beggars with criminality gathered from interviews include: that they start as innocent people in need but end up delinquents and criminals; they may begin by begging but end up stealing; they may begin by selling basic consumer items but end up peddling marijuana and other banned intoxicants; and they may originally be sober but end up drunkards from illicit Mozambican alcoholic spirits, drug addicts, and sniffers of glue (Mwasvipa, Piwa and Supani, Separate Interviews: 2020).

It is interesting to note, however, that what administrators and commentators may regard as problems associated with street beggars are, in many ways, solutions to challenges faced by this vulnerable section of the population. Hence, breaking the law in money-making rackets such as gambling, pickpocketing and theft are not a problem but a partial solution to the problems of poverty. Sniffing glue relieves the pain of cold and hunger. Alcohol and other forms of drug abuse relieve boredom, and enable a child beggar to become part of a supportive group (Bourdillon, December 2001). Thus, Bourdillon (December 2001: 1) raises the need to appreciate the challenges of street beggars before criminalising some of their activities outright:

> There may be other problems of which they [street beggars] are not fully aware, the danger of AIDS or other diseases, or of sniffing glue. But let us not confuse our problems with theirs. We need to remember that sometimes our problems are their solutions, and sometimes our solutions are their problems. If they are part of our problems; part of their problem is us!

Panhandling can ruin the future of young people by making their mindsets averse to creativity and production. As *The Newsday* (21 August 2011: 1) noted with most Zimbabwean street children: "While some of the children seem to enjoy it, darting from street to street, sometimes tripping passers-by, theirs is a sorry tale of lost childhood as they are initiated into the begging system early on in life". According to Jelili (2013), begging is definitely driven by socio-economic hardships but is socially destructive in that it destroys creativity and prevents child beggars from realising their potential and capabilities to do productive work. It waters down their self-esteem and dissuades them from engaging in productive investments. Added to that, it kills their initiative to exploit opportunities that may be available to alleviate poverty. As Stones (2013: 163) aptly noted:

> Issues such as self-concept, poor self-regard, and learned helplessness seem only to have become important features after an individual starts begging, and as such may tend to reinforce the practice...A sense of helplessness develops within a relatively short period of time, especially with regard to a future perspective. In this regard, it appears that the factors that lead someone to engage in begging tend to be the very factors that actually reinforce such a practice...It is apparent that [people] continue to beg because the factors that facilitate this practice...remain unalleviated, therefore con-tinuously supporting the practice of begging.

Inevitably, many beggars sink into a vicious cycle of poverty (Jelili, 2013). Thus, Jelili (2013: 57) proposed the "chronic poverty of begging" thesis which acknowledges that while begging is a product of poverty, chronic poverty is the outcome of begging. Similarly, according to Oscar Lewis (1959; 1998), poverty sometimes persists despite anti-poverty programmes. He argues that although some members of the society are systematically impoverished by complex structural processes, they in turn get socialised into a sub-culture of poverty which is passed from one generation to another. As children, for example, grow up in conditions of abject poverty, they get socialised into attitudes and behaviour that entrench their inability to escape from their impoverished condition. Such character traits include marginality, helplessness, pessimism, powerlessness and dependency. Thus, while the institutionalisation of poverty contributes towards begging, begging itself can perpetuate poverty by destroying creativity in children.

Robert Makura, a Zimbabwean social worker with Just Children Foundation, lamented that begging at an early age engenders in children a dependency syndrome that will persist in adult life, a problem that may need rehabilitation to be remedied (*Newsday*, 21 August 2011). In 2013, Patience Chiyangwa, the then Childline Zimbabwe spokesperson, discouraged people from giving money to beggars because it promoted a begging culture in children and prevented them from seeking sustainable solutions to their problems (Bwanya, 30 July 2013). In future, some children who grow up in these conditions of dependency may become part of a "floating population", a term that is frequently used in official circles around the world to characterise beggars as a parasitic and unproductive social group that contributes nothing to the economy (Ener, 1999: 338). John Maketo, the National Coordinator of CAZ, a local children's rights organisation, outlined some of the major psychological implications of using children to beg:

> Training children to become beggars and destitute while depriving them of an education and a prosperous future exposes them to a lot of indecent verbal and emotional abuse on the streets. Apart from this, such children end up being taunted by peers, causing serious psychological harm. We call upon Government, child welfare organisations and law enforcement agents to enforce the relevant regulations to protect children from this rampant exploitation. Children should grow up in a friendly environment in which they receive love, care and protection. Some parents are pushing children to the forefront so that they win the sympathy of passers-by (*Bulawayo24 News*, 10 December 2011: 1).

It is prudent to note that while child begging can realise material benefits that sustain livelihoods and alleviate poverty in the immediate term, the psychological implications on young minds in the long term may be catastrophic. Among other things, children develop dependency mindsets, a begging syndrome and a begging culture which may lead them into a parasitic adult life in future. Many child beggars may lack the creative instinct and in times of severe hardships, they lack resilience and easily get frustrated, leading some to develop anti-social behaviour and indulge in criminal activities.

The safety of child beggars is compromised since they are exposed to strangers and the harsh life of the streets. It is common for young boys to be sodomised while girl children are raped (Kembo and Nhongo, 2002; *Newsday*, 21 August 2011). In June 2007, Chipo Sithole, a 16-year-old female beggar in Harare, narrated the sexual abuses which children were usually subjected to along the streets:

> It is...tougher for the younger ones, both boys and girls, because they...have to deal with rape from fellow street kids and then also the elder men. Some of the kids are picked up while begging at street corners and others are raped where we sleep. But because we have no rights in this country, when we go and report to the police, they chase us away and do not take our cases seriously... (Gwara, 5 June 2007: 1).

In May 2013, a 17-year-old girl who begged in the Harare Central Business District, also recalled sorrowfully during an interview: "There was a time when I was forced to sleep with several boys living on the streets. These people move in groups. It is by God's grace that I did not fall pregnant from the abuse" (*Herald*, 8 May 2013: 1). In February 2019, Judith Ncube, Bulawayo's Provincial Affairs Minister, highlighted the vulnerability of young girls who begged along the streets to sexual molestation: "The girl child's life is fragile and should not be exposed to begging; they end up being abused..." (Chikiwa, 17 February 2019: 1).

The sexual abuses which many child beggars are exposed to also make them extremely vulnerable to Sexually Transmitted Infections (STIs) and HIV/AIDS (Bwanya, 30 July 2013). In addition, children are delicate to withstand hostile geographical landscapes and weather conditions which they often find themselves in when begging (Owusu-Sekyere, Jengre and Alhassan, 2018). Examples can be drawn from open and unfavourable spaces where children are unprotected from heat or cold. Exposure to heat, for example, can result in dehydration while extreme cold can cause influenza and pneumonia (Mwasvipa, Piwa and Supani, Separate Interviews: 2020). More still, street begging exposes children to many forms of physical harm and sometimes death. In March 2013, for example, Edna

Mamonyane, the spokesperson of the Johannesburg Metropolitan Police, cited an incident when a Zimbabwean beggar fell asleep on the roadside and her crawling child encroached into traffic and was killed (Solidarity Helping Hand, 4 March 2013).

Basically, this section has illuminated how child begging casts a dark cloud on the future of Zimbabwe in general and the prospects of development in particular. It is without doubt that the involvement of children in begging, whether voluntary or forced, is arguably one of the greatest tragedies of Zimbabwe. The right to education for many children remains a pie in the air and sometimes terminated by begging commitments. Begging itself inducts children into a culture of dependency in which they pursue lives largely characterised by receiving rather than initiating and producing. In addition, besides the health hazards encountered while operating in the streets, child beggars are exposed to many negative social experiences which ruin their prospects of becoming healthy, responsible and law-abiding adults in future. This follows from the plausible argument that children are "the fountain of life" (Abbas, 2008: 1), implying that they are the future of any society. Investing in children is one of the most important guarantees of a bright future. Child begging shatters all these hopes.

Image of the city and country at stake: Congestion, disorder and environmental pollution

The proliferation of beggars always worries administrators, both at the local and national levels. While beggars register their presence in public spaces in an effort to seek livelihoods, the authorities see problems with regards to the maintenance of public order, health standards and the image of the city and/ or country, among other things. From the view of the authorities, therefore, beggars are a menace. Ironically, what beggars view as solutions to their hardships become the problems for the administrators.

The congestion brought about by begging activities in some parts of the cities is a major concern for central government and municipal authorities. As already discussed in Chapters 1, 2 and 3, the strong presence of beggars is quite evident in most Zimbabwean towns and

208

cities, particularly on pavements, at street corners, traffic light intersections and outside supermarkets and restaurants. The appropriation of these public spaces by beggars is a worry for the administrators who see it "as an obstacle to the development of city centres, which must be 'positioned' in the 'city market place' through the 'selling' of images of themselves, as part of a process known as 'city branding'" (De Coulon, Reynold and Wiget, 2015: 193). Among other things, the congestion of beggars dents the image of cities and nations to the outside world, and may negatively affect tourism and foreign investment (Fawole, Ogunkan and Omoruan, 2011). This largely explains why, in the two months preceding the Soccer World Cup in South Africa in 2010, the South African authorities, for example, swooped on mostly Zimbabwean beggars who roamed the streets, vendors and prostitutes (*Zimbabwe Black Book*, 18 May 2010).

In addition, the activities of street beggars, including their jostling for alms from motorists at traffic light intersections, often disturbs the smooth flow of vehicular traffic and sometimes causes accidents, injuries and fatalities. In February 2006, for example, Joseline Shumba, a 44-year-old Zimbabwean mother who begged in South Africa, recalled how she was knocked down in a hit-and-run incident at an East Rand traffic light some time back. Even though most of the injuries she sustained took her a year to recover, she was left with a permanent limp as a result of the accident (Smith, 26 February 2006).

The influx of beggars in some urban spaces has negative implications for the city economy (Jelili, 2006). Their congestion of pavements often disturbs customers entering shops thereby disrupting the flow of business. In the Brazilian city of Bom Jesus during the 1990s, the mayor and the police were praised by shop owners, business people and middle-class residents for collaborating with death squads to clear the Central Business District of beggars and street people who they demonised as "human garbage" which caused "social anarchy" (Scheper-Hughes, 2008: 32). In the Zimbabwean city of Bulawayo in December 2007, most restaurants and hotels deliberately kept their rubbish bins clean and empty to discourage beggars from coming to search for food and at the same time pester their customers for alms. For the same reason, some lodges in the same city also locked their refuse bins inside their premises (*World Press*, 10 December 2007).

In many parts of the world, there has been a contest between middle-class dismay over the deteriorating hygienic standards and the image of the city on the one hand and subaltern socio-economic needs and livelihood activities on the other. In these discourses, begging activities are closely associated with environmental pollution. For most administrators, as Bourdillon (2001: 1) noted, beggars are an unwanted and problematic concern in various ways, including, being an environmental menace:

> One of these concerns is the image of the city or the country: street children are unsightly. They tarnish the image of a modern, well administered city. They offend middle and upper-class ideas of what life should be like in a city. The presence of street children offends particularly those administrators who are responsible for running the city properly: it looks as though they are incapable of doing their job properly. If this is the major problem, the solution is simply to round up the people concerned and put them out of sight.

Indeed, the high propensity of beggars to generate dirty materials in the form of waste or some of their material possessions has always been a nagging concern for municipal authorities (Jelili, 2006). Most spaces in city centres where beggars operate, particularly along streets and at traffic light intersections, neither have toilets nor refuse disposal facilities. As a result, it has always been common for many roadside beggars to relieve themselves of urine and other human waste behind shops and in sanitary lanes. The same applies to litter, some of which is dumped even along the streets and in pavements (Chako, Chatindo and Matereke, Separate Interviews: 2014).

The fact that most beggars who live in the streets have limited access to water and sanitary facilities has negative hygienic implications on them as individuals and the environment in general (Fawole, Ogunkan and Omoruan, 2011). Dirty water that is used by beggars to wash linen flows carelessly around public tapes, attracting swarms of flies, at most major marketplaces around the country (Chatindo, Matereke and Zenge, Separate Interviews: 2014). At

Mbare market in Harare in 2009, for example, beggars were a common sight at public water tapes washing their linen which included baby nappies (Chatindo and Zenge, Separate Interviews: 2014). Such situations and practices pose serious health risks of outbreaks of water borne diseases such as cholera and dysentery. The limited access to water facilities largely accounts for the unhygienic tendencies of most beggars some of whom rarely take a bath or wash their clothes (Chako, Chatindo and Matereke, Separate Interviews: 2014). As Tipple and Speak (2004) noted, most beggars are demonised by the generality of society for being scruffy, dirty and repulsive. Lamenting the prevalence of begging in the Nigerian city of Lagos, Fawole, Ogunkan and Omoruan (2011: 9) also castigated street beggars as "an eyesore or environmental nuisance", and a health hazard which contributed immensely towards the "social relegation of the city".

Beggars are known to have been an inconvenience to tourists in various parts of the world since time immemorial. Way back in 1878, for example, a handbook for foreign tourists to the Egyptian capital, Cairo, cited by Ener (1999: 320-321) alerted them of this problem:

> ...The cry 'Bakshish, bakshish ya khawagah' (oh sir! a gift!), with which Europeans are invariably assailed, is an insulting substitute for the good day of other countries. The Arab reserves his pious benedictions for his own countrymen, but never hesitates to take advantage of what he considers the folly of foreign travellers. The best reply to such applications is 'ma fish, ma fish' (I have nothing for you), which will generally have the effect of dispersing the assailants. Or the beggar may be silenced with the words 'Allahya'tik' (May God give thee).

Wijesiri (9 December 2018: 1) sheds more light on the incompatibility between beggary and tourism:

> ...Tourist agencies maintain that the problem of beggars is having a negative impact on the industry. From the standpoint of the tourist, encounters with beggars disrupt the habitual way of being a tourist and are viewed as an assault on the tourists' expectations of peaceful and uninterrupted sight-seeing.

In June 2012, Walter Mzembi, the then Zimbabwe's Minister of Tourism and Hospitality, argued that images of African beggars were used by the foreign media to discredit the continent's attractiveness as a tourist destination: "Images of street kids and beggars are shown to disparage Africa's brand whilst British adult street kids languishing at the entrance to Zimbabwe House on the Strand in London are never covered by the BBC" (*New Zimbabwe*, 26 June 2012: 1). In late April 2013, the World Economic Forum rated Zimbabwe 120 out of the 140 countries in terms of safety and security of tourists partly because of harassment by beggars (Bloch, 5 April 2013).

This section articulated how begging activities can put the future of any community, society and country at risk. It has shown how beggars are a menace to local and national authorities because of their interference with the proper running of many day-to-day aspects of public life, some of which are economically important to the survival of the country, for example, tourism and the retail business. In addition, most begging operations are not environmentally friendly and this poses numerous health hazards for the general public in many urban areas of the country. Despite beggars being problematic as discussed in this section, it is important to remind ourselves about the Social History approach in order to appreciate why they operate in this manner. Let us bear in mind that in circumstances of severe crises, people seek survival at any cost. In this case, beggars were seeking livelihoods in a country besieged by poverty and some of the solutions they sought to address their plight came to be viewed as problems by the government administrators and law enforcement agents.

Conclusion

This chapter has taken stock of begging activities in Zimbabwe in terms of their benefits and negative ramifications. It has been underlined that begging is indeed part of the struggle for survival for some downtrodden Zimbabweans who are wallowing in abject poverty without receiving deserving support from the government and other welfare stakeholders. Despite assisting vulnerable people from the jaws of death at the moment of need, the chapter noted that begging in itself is a parasitic way of life that signals a dark future if significant interventions are not made by the powers that be. It is the contention of this chapter, therefore, that while begging has sustained the livelihoods of some ordinary people in terms of their immediate material needs, critical interventions by the government and other welfare partners can actually assist, not only in meeting these needs, but also in capacitating and empowering them to look after themselves. Otherwise, in the long-term, panhandling is a survival mechanism that ruins future prospects of development in many ways.

Conclusions

This book has unravelled the rising problematiques of begging in Zimbabwe and beyond the country's borders, especially the southern African region, namely in South Africa, Botswana and Mozambique, by impoverished Zimbabweans since the turn of the 21st century. The book has focused on what begging entailed, who performed it, its dynamics, advantages and challenges. Critically, the book has troubled the fundamental drivers of beggary by Zimbabweans in the new millennium and identified the debilitating socio-economic crisis as the major contributing factor (Raftopoulos, 2009). The book has also contested the application of the political, economic as well as moral dimensions of begging. To further complicate the discussions, we contested the deliberations in this book against two main theories that undergird begging, namely Social Constructionism and Social Deconstructionism As theorists such as Grint (2005) and Kassah (2008) posit, the Social Constructionist narrative considers begging in the positive sense where it is perceived as productive in some sense since some panhandlers can manage to meet their basic necessities. On the polar end, Social Deconstructionism generally perceives panhandling as only providing short term benefits, which are obtained at the expense of better and more long-lasting gains both at the personal, community and national levels.

This contested terrain on the place of beggary, thus informs the larger body of discussions in the book. Indeed, there are some marginalised Zimbabweans who have managed to evade the incapacitating impacts of the new millennium socio-economic crisis that was informed by rampant poverty, widespread unemployment, insufficient food, and reduced livelihood alternatives through panhandling. However, what has also emerged from the book is that in the long term, these advantages are not self-sustaining and those that seek for alms have to continue begging otherwise they perish. This was amply illustrated in the era of the Covid-19, experienced from the start of the year 2020, which resulted in severe travel restrictions, both within Zimbabwe and across the borders. Under

215

Covid-19 induced travel restrictions, the capacity of most beggars to panhandle within Zimbabwe and abroad was nullified with many of them complaining of various inhibitions as they needed to travel to undertake their business. The text now winds up by highlighting the major contents and findings of each chapter, followed by the broad arguments emanating therefrom pertaining to begging as a livelihood dynamic and means for survival.

Chapter 1 contextualised the upsurge in begging in Zimbabwe in the socio-economic crisis that besieged the country from the onset of the new millennium and became characteristic of the successive reigns of presidents Robert Mugabe and Emmerson Mnangagwa. It illustrated that the proliferation of beggars from 2000 was largely rooted in escalating poverty levels that emanated from the crisis. Even though ecological disasters, particularly the droughts and floods from the turn of the millennium, played their part in aggravating Zimbabwe's socio-economic quagmire, it was proved beyond doubt that the ruling ZANU-PF government, in its desperate bid to cling to power, lit a fire that it subsequently failed to extinguish. Political expediency by ZANU-PF sacrificed the livelihoods of the majority of ordinary Zimbabweans. The pursuit of political currency by the ruling party was evident in the seizure of commercial white farms from February 2000. The seizures were a multi-pronged political mobilisation strategy improvised by ZANU-PF to spruce its waning legitimacy by using land as bait to win supporters from the MDC. Such a strategy also sought to depopulate MDC support bases, such as commercial farms, by displacing white farmers and their workers, most of who were alleged to be anti-ZANU-PF. In addition, land seizures also served as punishment to white farmers for financially backing the MDC. Operation *Murambatsvina* was another ploy by ZANU-PF to displace MDC supporters from urban and peri-urban areas. Again, this political gamble was done at the expense of the livelihoods of ordinary Zimbabweans. The operation left hundreds of thousands of people homeless and deprived millions of their sources of livelihood after their informal businesses had been destroyed. Such hardships, as shown in Chapter 1, tended to spur begging as survival options, both formal and informal, increasingly dwindled in the country.

It was also asserted in Chapter 1 that the land seizures failed to benefit the majority of ordinary Zimbabweans and instead, generated a multiplicity of life-threatening challenges for them. Food shortages became rampant as the commercial farming sector collapsed while the incoming new farmers, most of them amateurs, failed to fully utilise the land. The land seizures also left many former farm workers unemployed and homeless as the new farmers failed to engage most of them. In addition, some sections of the white community became destitute after their farms had been confiscated without compensation. This prompted some destitute whites and their former farm employees to seek livelihoods through begging. A number of examples which have been given in Chapter 1 attest to this. Indeed, droughts and floods did contribute in making Zimbabwe food-deficient but they did not cause farm workers to lose their jobs; neither did they leave others homeless and make begging to be an option of survival for many.

As noted in Chapter 1, land grabs triggered the socio-economic meltdown in Zimbabwe by isolating the country from the greater part of the international community, especially the West. It cannot be overemphasised how the West had traditionally been the key source of balance-of-payments support and funding for various economic projects. Land invasions were a gross violation of property rights and, together with the violent manner in which they were executed, severely eroded investor confidence. Companies closed down; others scaled down operations while many prospective investors avoided the country. In addition, the government increasingly became bankrupt as a result of limited revenue inflows due to lost production. Tax earnings from farmers and their workers, and agricultural export earnings plummeted as the commercial farming sector collapsed and many workers lost their jobs. The sources of government revenue shrank considerably as companies closed, scaled down production and retrenched workers while prospective investors shied away. Aggravating the cash-strapped position of the government was its extravagant spending, for example, its engagement in the DRC civil war from 1998 to 2002. These problems cascaded down to the ordinary people as the unemployment and poverty rates escalated. Chapter 1 ably articulated how bankruptcy rendered the government incapable of alleviating the plight of its poor citizens. As a result, the state failed to import adequate quantities of drugs, food and other basic necessities for the poor, many of whom became beggars who sought assistance from individuals, most of them strangers; international non-governmental organisations; and foreign governments.

Furthermore, as discussed in Chapter 1, the government worsened the situation by printing paper money in a vain attempt to cut the budget deficit. The period of hyperinflation up to 2009 witnessed untold suffering by the ordinary people. Prices of basic goods and services ballooned beyond the reach of the ordinary citizens, most of who were unemployed. Most children dropped out of school; many workers left employment as the local currency lost value; considerable numbers of the sick lost their lives because medicines were either in short supply or that they could not afford the costs; many became malnourished while others died of starvation. Under such conditions of abject poverty, begging became one of the realistic options of survival.

The first chapter also noted how the GNU and the introduction of a multi-currency regime from 2009 failed to adequately address the basic livelihood concerns of the people living in poverty. The political environment became relatively stable but investors largely remained speculative while awaiting an ultimate political solution. De-industrialisation remained problematic together with related challenges such as high unemployment rates and tight liquidity. As a result, the plight of the subaltern was hardly addressed and panhandling remained as one of the popular informal means of earning livelihoods. The coming to power of Emmerson Mnangagwa through a military coup assisted by a popular rising in November 2017 did not help matters as the socio-economic woes of many Zimbabweans continued, if not worsened. Chapter 1, therefore, established the primacy of chronic poverty in the upsurge in begging activities in Zimbabwe from 2000. In actual fact, poverty became endemic in the country, being evidenced, among other things, by high unemployment rates, food insecurity, hunger, starvation, homelessness and despair. Accordingly, Chapter 1 provided the book with a firm historical background that contextualises begging in the

Zimbabwean crisis with a view to showing its prevalence emanating from rising poverty and the malfunctioning of some institutions responsible for human welfare in the country of which the government is the major culprit.

Chapter 2 explored the broad range of strategies employed by beggars in Zimbabwe to collect as many alms as they could. The chapter argued that owing to Zimbabwe's desperate situation in view of grinding poverty, most beggars had to deploy a host of persuasive and at times desperate tricks to salvage sustenance from the ever-dwindling alms in a crisis-hit country. What made the Zimbabwean situation desperate for beggars was its plethora of challenges ranging from government mismanagement of the economy and socio-economic derangement to ecological disasters and epidemics. Owing to these multiple challenges, the plight of the marginalised sections of the population worsened as they were directly affected. To make matters worse, the number of potential domestic benefactors plummeted considerably while others either became incapacitated or generally unwilling to part with anything. Ultimately, the competition for alms became fierce as the ever-soaring number of panhandlers scrambled for the ever-shrinking population of potential alms-givers. Since begging relies on the mercy of well-wishers, most of who are strangers, the beggars had to be very innovative in terms of strategies of getting as much financial and material assistance as they could. As shown in this chapter, the management of space, time and the social terrain was critical in the operational strategies of beggars. The social landscape involved the general public, the major source of potential benefactors, and other individuals and groups they operated with. Various audio-visual mechanisms were devised to evince and evoke feelings of pity in an effort to woo public sympathy.

Even though some beggars solicit for donations in an intimidating or intrusive manner out of desperation and frustration, Chapter 2 has shown how many beggars exhibit manipulative potential that often appeals to the benevolence of people. Among other things, they develop special language abilities and adopt convincing persuasive styles to arouse the emotions of passers-by. Overall, the chapter has shown that most beggars are intelligent innovators and performers who employ a broad range of psychological and emotional tricks to make people feel sympathetic towards them. The surfeit of skills enlisted by beggars to solicit for alms include performing dramas and music that simultaneously entertain passersby as a way of drawing not only their attention but also sympathy to drop a few coins or other goods. At other times, however, some alms seekers blatantly lied about misfortunes that would not have befallen them to get some sympathy. Yet in other instances, some beggars made use of their disabled status to draw sympathy from the public. This sometimes involved foregrounding physical disabilities or hiring out children or relatives with severe physical disability in order to appeal more to potential alms-givers. Furthermore, the chapter has discussed how some women went to the desperate extent of hiring babies that they carried on their backs to enhance their status as better deserving beggars as they ventured into the streets of major cities to beg. Some physically-challenged beggars also sought the company of their children in begging escapades. The dynamics of child begging also involved some children who ventured into begging on their own to sustain their families in desperate situations, which not only compromised their education and affected their future but also exposed them to a number of potential abuses and violations of their rights as children. In addition to the above, begging for medical assistance became banal as the economic crisis worsened in the country. This followed the exodus of highly skilled medical personnel, the closure of specialised operations in the country and the prohibitive cost of specialised medical treatment, which led many patients to use the media to publicise their plight with the hope of getting assistance from well-wishers.

Chapter 3 explored the superfluity of hardships endured by beggars while scrounging for sustenance in Zimbabwe. As is the case in other parts of the world, the popular and official attitudes towards them are largely negative as they are often viewed as a nuisance. Consequently, they are frequently the target of official disapproval and legal restrictions of some kind. Thus, begging is part of the basket of the informal survival strategies that have been criminalised by both the central and local government structures in Zimbabwe, as in other countries of the southern African sub-region. From the year

2000, the plight of Zimbabwean beggars was exacerbated by grinding socio-economic hardships which included rampant inflation, tight liquidity, escalating poverty levels and the subsequent slump in the number of potential well-wishers that heightened competition and rivalry among them and caused a drastic reduction in the alms collected. To make matters worse, the Coronavirus outbreak and the various lockdown regulations effected from March 2020 in Zimbabwe, Mozambique, Botswana and South Africa pushed many beggars to the brink of starvation by restricting their movement as well as that of potential benefactors. As begging depends on mobility, the restrictions on travel meant that beggars were condemned to poverty and general shortages of basics they required to sustain their lives and their dependents.

What can be discerned from Chapter 3 is that panhandling is an undertaking that is often criminalised, looked down upon, demeaning, frustrating and exasperating. Given the hardships associated with the livelihood pursuit, it is largely without dispute that the decision to embark on begging is a difficult one. Such a decision is, in most cases, not a matter of choice but of dire necessity. In fact, begging can hardly be regarded as an occupation that a person would readily turn to. In the end, the gravity of the challenges outlined in Chapter 3, and the determination of beggars to soldier on illustrates that begging "is a last-resort practice for many people; it is commonly conceived as being a more acceptable option to providing for their basic needs than resorting to criminal activities, such as shoplifting, burglary, drug dealing, and prostitution" (Stones, 2013: 159). As the Zimbabwean crisis deepened over the years, many formal and informal livelihood undertakings dwindled. This reduction in the avenues of survival brought increased competition amongst the downtrodden, forcing many of them to embark on begging. What was even worse was that the heightened competition to seek alms well-wishers occurred at a time when the number of potential alms-givers was itself shrinking, which made begging a very difficult undertaking. The *coup de grace* as the third decade of the new millennium started seems to have been generated from the Covid-19 pandemic that literally brought travelling and seeking for begging opportunities from different spaces in Zimbabwe to a virtual standstill.

As noted in Chapter 4, the presence of Zimbabwean beggars in diasporic spaces eloquently articulates the magnitude of the country's socio-economic malaise and amply demonstrates that home is not always the best for many underprivileged people. The chapter explored the experiences of Zimbabwean beggars in neighbouring countries, paying particular attention to South Africa, Botswana and Mozambique. In this chapter, the strategies employed by Zimbabwean beggars in neighbouring countries were discussed in considerable detail. While the begging strategies share many similarities with those in Zimbabwe in terms of navigating space, time and the social landscape, the use of non-Zimbabwean assistants as well as the flighting of banners with heart-rending summaries of their plight is more noticeable, understandably so in view of the need to negotiate the language barrier with the nationals of neighbouring countries, among other things.

What Chapter 4 has also ably done is to demonstrate that the journey to the so-called greener pastures was not all rosy as most poverty-stricken Zimbabwean migrants had no official travel documents resulting in them using unofficial border-crossing means, most of which subjected them to a profusion of perils such as drowning in flooded rivers, attacks by wild animals, ambushes and sexual abuses by robbers; and arrest, detention and deportation by the authorities from the host countries. In addition to experiencing the general age-old problems caused by negative official and societal attitudes, Chapter 4 also identified several other miseries of Zimbabwean transnational beggars, most of which are linked to their citizenship. It was always problematic, for example, to get alms from strangers of different nationalities as most of them were not in a position to fully appreciate the plight of immigrants. In diasporic spaces, as also discussed in Chapter 4, the entrenchment of 'otherness' in discourses of citizenship has tormented many Zimbabwean immigrants in general and transnational beggars in particular. It has been shown, for instance, how Zimbabwean immigrants in South Africa and Botswana were pejoratively referred to as *makwerekwere* (unwanted foreign beggars). In addition, they have often been scapegoated in neighbouring countries for many socio-economic ills such as the upsurge in crime and the spread of diseases. The chapter also illuminated how, in South Africa, Zimbabwean beggars are resented by the general public as is the case with the Roma immigrant panhandlers in European countries such as Sweden and Finland.

National governments, the press and law-enforcement agents in neighbouring countries such as South Africa and Botswana have not helped the situation either. As noted in Chapter 4, both institutions have used terms such as 'influx' and 'waves' to refer to the movement of beggars, mostly Zimbabwean, into their countries. Besides being alarmist and loaded with stigmatising undertones, such references help to fuel populist anti-immigrant (xenophobic) and, specifically, anti-Zimbabwean sentiments. These miseries have also been exacerbated by generalised suspicions held by the press, law-enforcement agents and other official circles against immigrant beggars. Such suspicions, as shown in the fourth chapter, usually stigmatise, victimise and criminalise immigrant beggars in many ways. These generalised suspicions and allegations help to legitimise unequal treatment of immigrants in general and beggars in particular in the name of security and sanity, among other things. As a result, many transnational Zimbabwean beggars failed to benefit from the social safety nets offered by host governments even during the time of the worldwide Coronavirus outbreak from early 2020. They have also been discriminated against in the provision of basic social services meant for vulnerable sections of the population. More so, their general security is not guaranteed as the police often give low priority to attacks on immigrants in general and beggars in particular. Having gone through Chapter 4 and grasped the numerous tribulations encountered by Zimbabwean beggars, a question that may boggle the minds of many pertains to their continued stay in diasporic spaces. The answer, as noted in the chapter, is simple but tearful: the anguish at home was far worse than the agony abroad, this being clearly illustrative of the hollowness of nationalism in dispensations of uneven development, marginalisation and chronic poverty.

Chapter 5 took stock of begging in terms its repercussions on Zimbabwe's socio-economic fabric. In other words, the chapter examined the social and economic significance of begging for the beggars themselves and the country at large in terms of short-term and long-term implications. From the process of counting the costs, the complex and paradoxical nature of panhandling comes out very clearly as the practice has both positive and negative effects. In light of these effects, the chapter evaluated the overall impact of begging activities on Zimbabwe's socio-economic well-being.

As shown in Chapter 5, begging is a livelihood option that has sustained the livelihoods of many pauperised Zimbabweans, particularly from the onset of the new millennium. From a utilitarian perspective, it has been argued, panhandling became a necessity in the survival of some sections of the population who could otherwise have starved to death. Morally, the chapter acknowledged the sentiments of many beggars who averred that it was better to seek sustenance from panhandling than through criminal means such as pick-pocketing, theft and robbery. Added to that, by fending for their own livelihoods, the beggars were actually indirectly cushioning or subsidising the bankrupt Zimbabwean government, the very institution that had abrogated its constitutional mandate to provide safety nets that guarantee the welfare and sustenance of vulnerable people.

In Chapter 5, considerable attention was also devoted to the negative effects of begging. These include the disastrous implications, both in the present and in the future, of the involvement of children in begging as far as the beggars themselves and the country as a whole are concerned. Beggars have also been a concern to the authorities and the general public because of the congestion, disorder and environmental pollution that sometimes arise from their activities. That said, the central argument advanced in Chapter 5 is that while begging has proved to be an important source of immediate material needs of many vulnerable people, its long-term socio-economic effects for the beggars themselves and the society at large are dire.

Overall, this book has established that begging is a complex undertaking much to do with livelihood pursuits and survival behaviour. Largely rooted in poverty, it is in many ways a provisional livelihood option in which the alms obtained afford some hope and relief amid harsh realities of life. As noted in the foregoing discussion, many needy people regard begging as a means to an end and not an end in itself. In addition, it has been shown that begging is a degrading and frustrating experience which many poverty-stricken people would neither take as a matter of choice nor proudly regard as an occupation, but only as a desperate stopgap measure to meet urgent subsistence and welfare necessities. This is notwithstanding the fact that some desperate Zimbabweans have had begging as a long term 'career' that has sustained themselves and those close to them amidst threatening adversities posed by the ever-deepening crises in Zimbabwe.

The book also unravelled various ways which beggars have always used to negotiate vulnerable dispensations and salvage an existence. Characteristic of most impoverished people, beggars are a paradoxical phenomenon in that they are vulnerable but resilient and resourceful as they devise various mechanisms to mitigate the severe threats to their livelihoods.

In most cases, as emphasised in this book, begging is not a permanent solution to the problems of the people living in poverty; it only provides temporary relief. Thus, one major finding of this book is that begging is largely characterised by immediate gains and long-term losses. It has been proved that it is a survival mechanism that largely cannibalises from tomorrow (the future) in order to sustain today (the present). Last but not least, this book concluded that charity alone does not work in eradicating the plight of beggars. Instead, a holistic approach to the challenge of poverty and its manifestations must be worked out by national governments in consultation with other welfare stakeholders.

References

Abbas, S.N. (January 2008) 'Begging: A social evil', https://www.thenews.com.pk/archive/print/9014713, Accessed 10 May 2018.

Abebe, T. (2008) 'Earning a living on the margins: Begging, street work and the socio-spatial experience of children in Addis Ababa', in: *Geografiska Annaler: Series B, Human Geography*, Volume 90, Number 3, pp.271-284.

Abebe, T. (2009) 'Begging as a livelihood pathway of street children in Addis Ababa', in: *Forum for Development Studies*, Volume 36, Number 22, pp.275-300.

Addams, G. (10 September 2009) 'Border harassment deters tourists', www.theindependent.co.zw, Accessed 11 May 2018.

Adedibu, A. (1989) 'Begging and poverty in Third World cities: A case study of Ilorin, Nigeria', in: *Journal of Business and Social Sciences*, Volume 1, pp.25-40.

Africa Contact (26 May 2011) 'Background to political violence in Zimbabwe', www.akcampaign.worldpress.com, Accessed 12 July 2018.

Africa News (10 May 2016) 'New breed of beggars hit the streets of Harare', http://newsofthesouth.com, Accessed 8 May 2018.

African News Agency (19 March 2020) 'South Africa builds R37million fence at Beitbridge border to curb Corona Virus outbreak', https://www.iol.co.za/news/africa, Accessed 6 June 2018.

Agence France-Presse (24 September 2006) 'Brain drain cripples Zimbabwe's ailing health sector', www.reliefweb.int/report, Accessed 13 November 2018.

Ahamdi, H. (2010) 'A study of beggars' characteristics and attitude of people towards the phenomenon of begging in the city of Shiraz', in: *Journal of Applied Sociology*, Volume 39, Number 3, pp.135-148.

Ahola, V. (2011) 'The Roma: Thieves and beggars? Public attitudes towards the Roma in Finland displayed in Finnish newspaper articles in 2006-2011', Unpublished Bachelor of Social Services thesis, Diaconia University of Applied Sciences, Finland.

Aljazeera (15 March 2020) 'Cyclone Idai: One year on, Zimbabwe survivors losing hope', https://www.aljazeera.com/news, Accessed 12 August 2020.

Amnesty International (18 April 2008) 'Post-election violence increases in Zimbabwe', www.amnesty.org/org/en/news, Accessed 14 June 2019.

Aptekar, L. (1988) *Street children of Cali*, London: Duke University Press.

Arimenda, J. (11 December 2013) Interview: Odzi Township, Mutare District. Zimbabwe.

Arshad, M.R.M. Kamal, A.Z.M. and Arif, N.D. (2014) 'Street begging in Kuala Lumpur', in: *Journal of the Institute for Professional Development and Education*, Volume 78, Number 1, pp.1-5.

Associated Press (16 July 2003) 'More than 26 000 Zimbabweans repatriated from Botswana last year', www.highbeam.com, Accessed 28 July 2019.

Associated Press (3 November 2010) 'Red Cross: Zimbabwe on brink of food crisis', www.nbcnews.com, Accessed 1 August 2019.

Balarabe, A.H. Mahmoud, A.O. and Ayanniyi, A.A. (April-June 2014) 'The Sokoto blind beggars: Causes of blindness and barriers to rehabilitation services', in: *Middle East Africa Journal Ophthalmol*, Volume 21, Number 2, pp.147-152.

Bamu, R. (21 October 2019) 'Begging, an alternative for suffering citizens', http://www.zimsentinel.com, Accessed 11 August 2019.

BBC (31 May 2002) 'Zimbabwe turns away US food aid', www.news.bbc.co.uk, Accessed 2 June 2019.

BBC (29 April 2014) 'Zimbabwe: New era?' www.news.bbc.co.uk/news, Accessed 3 August 2019).

BBC News (21 November 2017) 'Grace Mugabe: Who is Zimbabwe's former first lady?' http://www.bbc.com/news/world-africa-30307333, Accessed 4 November 2018.

Bearak, B. (23 January 2009) 'Desperate children flee Zimbabwe for lives just as desolate', www.nytimes.com, Accessed 7 July 2019.

Bedfordview Residents Action Group (19 October 2010) 'Do not support beggars', www.bedfordviewrag.co.za/news, Accessed 22

June 2018.

Bell, A. (11 April 2014) 'Zimbabwe: 17 "Border jumpers" found dead in Limpopo River', https://allafrica.com/stories, Accessed 16 June 2018.

Benson, A. Kabonde, N. and Murawo, V. (28 January 2014) FGD: Spaceman Shopping Centre, Harare, Zimbabwe.

Bentwick, K.K. (January 1894) 'Begging as a fine art', in: *The North American Review*, Volume 158, Number 446, pp.125-128.

Beresford, P. (December 1996) 'Poverty and disabled people: Challenging dominant debates and policies', in: *Disability and Society, Special Issue: Disability, Development in the Changing World*, Volume 11, Number 4, pp.553-556.

Berger, S. (9 October 2008) 'Zimbabwe inflation hits 231 million per cent', www.telegraph.co.uk, Accessed 6 August 2018.

Betts, A. and Kaytaz, E. (2010) 'National and international responses to the Zimbabwean exodus: Implications for the refugee protection regime', Research Paper 175, Policy Development and Evaluation Service, United Nations High Commissioner for Refugees.

Bhoroma, V. (31 January 2020) 'Zimbabwean economy re-dollarising rapidly', in: *Zimbabwe Independent*, Harare: Zimbabwe.

Bhuke, S. and Ruzvezve, L. (12 September 2013) Joint Interview: Sakubva Bus Terminus, Mutare, Zimbabwe.

Blair, D. (10 July 2000) 'Children cast adrift with nothing but a begging bowl', https://www.telegraph.co.uk, Accessed 3 June 2018.

Blair, D. (19 August 2011) 'Children of the streets feel wrath of Mugabe', www.telegraph.co.uk, Accessed 4 June 2018.

Bloch, E. (5 April 2013) 'Urgent need for tourism turn around', www.theindependent.co.zw, Accessed 28 November 2018.

Bond, P. and Manyanya, S. (2002) *Zimbabwe's plunge: Exhausted nationalism, neoliberalism and the search for social justice*, Asmara: Africa World Press.

Bornman, J. (13 August 2019) 'Undocumented children face uncertain future', https://www.newframe.com, Accessed 22 March 2020.

Botha, M. (9 April 2017) 'Are begging women with kids of a lesser

God?' https://www.news24.com/Columnists/GuestColumn, Accessed 5 November 2017.

Botha, M. (24 April 2019) 'Where is caring government as women with kids beg in streets?' https://www.sowetanlive.co.za/opinion/columnists, Accessed 23 March 2020.

Bourdillon, M.F.C. (1991) *Poor, harassed but very much alive: An account of street people and their organisation*, Gweru: Mambo Press.

Bourdillon, M. (December 2001) 'The children on our streets', in: *CYC-Online: Journal of the International Child and Youth Care Network*, Issue 35, https://www.cyc-net.org/cyc-online/cycol-1201-bourdillon-I.html, Accessed 16 March 2018.

Bourdillon, M.F.C. and Rurevo, R. (2003) 'Girls: The less visible street children of Zimbabwe', in: *Children, youth and environments*, Volume 13, Number 1.

Boyden, J. (1998) 'Childhood and the policy makers: A comparative perspective on the globalisation of childhood', in: A. James and A. Prout (eds.) *Constructing and reconstructing childhood: Contemporary issues in the study of childhood*, London: Routledge Falmer.

Brown, M. (27 March 2020) 'South Africa begins nationwide Corona Virus lockdown', https://www.voanews.com, Accessed 12 August 2020.

Bulawayo 24 News (18 January 2011) 'Zimbabwe: December inflation slows to 3.2%', http://bulawayo24.com/index-id-business-sc-economy-byo-751-article, Accessed 12 June 2018.

Bulawayo 24 News (10 December 2011) 'Harare parents forcing children below the age of seven to beg: Study', https://bulawayo24.com/index-id-news-sc, Accessed 13 June 2018.

Bulawayo 24 News (8 February 2013) 'Judge castigates mums who forced their children into streets to beg', www.bulawayo24.com/index, Accessed 21 June 2018.

Bulawayo 24 News (22 April 2013) 'Zimbabwe's unemployment rate tops 70%', www.bulawayo24.com/index, Accessed 21 June 2018.

Bulawayo 24 News (24 June 2013) 'Man (33) seeks assistance to undergo brain surgery', www.bulawayo24.com/index, Accessed 21 June 2018.

Bulawayo 24 News (22 December 2013) 'Beggar arrested for posing security risk near Nkomo statue', www.bulawayo24.com/index, Accessed 21 June 2018.

Bulawayo 24 News (19 March 2020) 'South Africa to build 40-kilometre fence along Zimbabwe border', https://bulawayo24.com/index-id-news-sc-africa-byo-181570.html, Accessed 15 August 2020.

Bulawayo, P. (19 April 2020) 'COVID-19: Zimbabwe extends lockdown', https://www.enca.com, Accessed 14 August 2020.

Bulawayo Progressive Residents Association (30 July 2014) 'Social Welfare should take care of street kids', www.swradioafrica.com, Accessed 21 June 2018.

Bulter, D. (1 July 2013) 'Finance history: Zimbabwe economic collapse, 2000-2008', www.db.financial.reports.blogspot.com, Accessed 16 November 2019.

Burke, J. (10 August 2019) 'Hungry kids collapse as looters take millions: Life in today's Zimbabwe', https://www.theguardian.com/world/2019, Accessed 18 November 2019.

Burke, R.J. (1999) 'Tolerance or intolerance? The policing of begging in the urban context', in: H. Dean (ed.) *Begging questions: Street-level economic activity and social policy failure*, Bristol: The Policy Press.

Butcher, T. (11 July 2003) 'Instability spreads as thousands flee from Zimbabwe', www.freerepublic.com, Accessed 2 May 2019.

Bwanya, M. (30 July 2013) 'Hell on Harare's streets', www.harare24.com/index, Accessed 23 May 2018.

Chagonda, T. (20-21 December 2010) 'Dollarisation of the Zimbabwean economy: Cure or curse? The case of the teaching and banking sectors', Paper presented at *The Renaissance of African Economies*, Dar Es Salam : CODESRIA, http://www.codesria.org/IMG/pdf/papers14.pdf, Accessed 13 October 2019.

Chakanyuka, M. and Mhlanga, F. (16 April 2019) 'Year-on-year inflation rate jumps to 66.8%', in: *Newsday*, Harare: Zimbabwe.

Chako, R. (16 August 2014) Interview: Mucheke Bus Terminus, Masvingo, Zimbabwe.

Chambati, W. and Moyo, S. (2004) *Impacts of land reform on farm workers and farm labour processes*, Harare: African Institute for Agrarian Studies.

Chara, V. Manekeni, B. Mushanda, D. and Zangata, R. (14 February 2014) FGD: Total Service Station, Rusape, Zimbabwe.

Charirwe, N. (20 September 2014) Interview: Makoni Shopping Centre, Chitungwiza, Zimbabwe.

Chatikobo, J. and Chatikobo, T. (26 January 2014) Interview: Machipisa Bus Terminus, Harare, Zimbabwe.

Chatindo, Y. (26 January 2014) Interview: Machipisa Shopping Centre, Harare, Zimbabwe.

Chaunza, G. (14 December 2015) 'Street children dumped out of city', http://www.zimsentinel.com, Accessed 16 May 2019.

Chawasarira, J. (21 September 2014) Interview: Chikwanha Shopping Centre, Chitungwiza, Zimbabwe.

Chaza, N. (6 September 2014) Interview: Gaza Township, Chipinge, Zimbabwe.

Chaza, V. (17 August 2014) Interview: Civic Centre, Masvingo, Zimbabwe.

Chekai, L.R. (28 September 2017) 'Cash crunch blights beggars' plight', www.263chat.com, Accessed 11 May 2018.

Chellah, G. (5 December 2008) 'Khama likens Zimbabwe to a big refugee camp', www.maravi.blogspot.com, Accessed 19 July 2019.

Cheneso, I. (12 September 2013) Interview: Sakubva Bus Terminus, Mutare, Zimbabwe.

Chenje, L. Mupatsa, J. and Nyati S. (28 January 2014) FGD: Julius Nyerere Street, Harare, Zimbabwe.

Chibber, K. (26 July 2014) 'Zimbabwe's economy needs stabilising', www.qz.com, Accessed 8 December 2019.

Chifamba, M. (3 May 2014) 'Street children: A reflection of Zimbabwe's future', www.newsday.co.zw, Accessed 20 November 2019.

Chifera, I. (4 September 2015) 'White, coloured Zimbabweans reduced to beggars as economy falters', https://www.voazimbabwe.com, Accessed 3 January 2018.

Chigango, V. (13 February 2014) Interview: Vengere Suburb,

Rusape, Zimbabwe.

Chiguvare, B. (16 April 2020) 'Lockdown: A blind couple's battle to find food in Limpopo town', https://www.news24.com/SouthAfrica/News, Accessed 12 June 2020.

Chikiwa, K. (25 August 2018) 'Beggars resort to Ecocash', https://www.chronicle.co.zw, Accessed 15 November 2018.

Chikiwa, K. (17 February 2019) 'Education remains a dream for children of parents with disabilities', www.pressreader.com/zimbabwe/sunday-news, Accessed 6 April 2020.

Chikondo, E. Dhokoze, F. and Kodogwe, C. (16 August 2014) FGD: Mucheke Bus Terminus, Masvingo, Zimbabwe.

Chikwanha, T. (4 May 2014) 'Land seizures leave farm workers destitute', www.dailynews.co.zw, Accessed 27 November 2018.

Chimhete, C. (3 April 2005) 'Mbare vendors threatened with eviction', *Zimbabwe Standard*, Harare: Zimbabwe.

Chimhete, C. (1 May 2005) 'MDC decries ZANU-PF retribution', *Zimbabwe Standard*, Harare: Zimbabwe.

Chinenge, R. (16 August 2014) Interview: Mucheke Bus Terminus, Masvingo, Zimbabwe.

Chingoro, L. (12 September 2013) Interview: Sakubva Bus Terminus, Mutare, Zimbabwe.

Chingu, L. (19 September 2013) Interview: Forbes Border Post, Zimbabwe.

Chinyere, T. (17 August 2014) Interview: TM Supermarket, Masvingo, Zimbabwe.

Chipato, V. (13 October 2017) 'Hippo kills Zimbabwean border-jumper in Limpopo', http://www.allnetafrica.com, Accessed 22 August 2018.

Chipunza, P. (27 November 2013) 'Zimbabwe medical tariffs highest in the region', www.herald.co.zw, Accessed 8 October 2019.

Chipadze, S. (11 January 2020) Interview: Matongo Business Centre, Dangamvura Suburb, Mutare, Zimbabwe.

Chiriga, E. (16 April 2011) 'Unemployment still high in Zimbabwe', www.dailynews.co.zw, Accessed 14 May 2019.

Chirisa, S. (25 April 2019) 'Sad scenes in Gokwe as impoverished kids resort to lying across busy roads in order to beg for food', https://iharare.com, Accessed 27 April 2019.

Chitagu, T. and Matiashe, F. (17 February 2019) 'Mnangagwa issues chilling warning', www.thestandard.co.zw, Accessed 12 July 2020.

Chitemba, B. (1 November 2013) 'Zimbabwean businesses collapsing', www.theindependent.co.zw, Accessed 23 April 2019.

Chivango, P. (1 November 2013) 'The forgotten street children of Harare', http://newsofthesouth.com, Accessed 12 April 2019.

Chiweshe, M.K. (12 October 2017) 'Unaccompanied child migrants from Zimbabwe to South Africa', https://medium.com, Accessed 28 May 2019.

Chizunza, R. Rwenze, S. and Shawa, D. (26 January 2014) FGD: Department of Social Welfare, Harare, Zimbabwe.

Chronicle (24 April 2011) 'Man seeks US$80 000 to undergo surgery', www.chronicle.co.zw, Accessed 7 June 2020.

Churches in Manicaland (2006) *The truth will make you free: A compendium of Christian social teaching*, Mutare: Churches in Manicaland, 2006.

Civil Society Forum for East and Southern Africa (11-13 February 2002) 'Report on promoting and protecting the rights of street children', Nairobi: Civil Society Forum for East and Southern Africa.

Cohen, D.M. (2002) 'Begging the court's pardon: Justice denied for the poorest of the poor', in: *St. Thomas Law Review*, Volume 825, pp.1-16.

Corcoran, B. (28 November 2019) 'Zimbabwe struggling to feed itself as natural disasters wreak havoc', https://www.irishtimes.com/news/world/africa, Accessed 16 April 2020.

CNN (19 December 2006) 'Living off rats to survive in Zimbabwe', www.cnn.co/2006, Accessed 13 May 2019.

Crisis in Zimbabwe Coalition (7 February 2019) 'Darkness at noon: Inside Mnangagwa's new dispensation', www.kubatana.net, Accessed 18 September 2019.

Crisis UK (4 April 2003) 'Begging and anti-social behaviour: Crisis' response to the White Paper Respect and Responsibility - Taking a stand against anti-social behaviour', London: Crisis UK.

Cross, E. (4 February 2004) 'Fat cats feed on Zimbabwe's misery', www.eddiecross.africahead.com, Accessed 16 February 2019.

Daily News (11 February 2005) 'Calls for police restraint over blind beggars', www.queensu.ca/samp, Accessed 9 July 2019.

Daily News (21 August 2011) 'Vicious cycle breeds child beggars', https://www.newsday.co.zw, Accessed 21 October 2018.

Daily News (18 December 2018) 'Zimbabwe reeling from socio-economic challenges', Harare: Zimbabwe.

Daly, G. (1996) 'Migrants and gatekeepers: The links between immigration and homelessness in Western Europe', in: *Cities*, Volume 13, Number 1, pp.11-23.

Dancus, A.M. (2020) 'The art of begging', in: A.M. Duncan et.al (eds.) *Vulnerability in Scandinavian art and culture*, https://doi.org/10.1007/978-3-030-37382-5_11, Accessed 6 September 2020.

Dara, R. (16 September 2013) Interview: Barclays Bank, Mutare, Zimbabwe.

Davies, R. (18 July 2008) 'Braving peril to reach South Africa', https://www.aljazeera.com/focus, Accessed 9 July 2020.

De Coulon, G. Reynaud, C. and Wiget, A.C. (June 2015) 'Begging in Geneva in times of crisis: Multilayered representations of beggars, begging and cohabitation in the public space', in: *European Journal of Homelessness*, Volume 9, Number 1, pp.191-211.

Defence for Children International Zimbabwe (14 March 2014) 'Universal periodic review: Zimbabwe', Harare (Glen Forest Training Centre): Defence for Children International Zimbabwe.

Delap, E. (2009) 'Begging for change: Research findings and recommendations on forced child-begging in Albania/Greece, India and Senegal', Anti-Slavery International.

Dhliwayo, B. (18 January 2020) 'Beggars: The new street marshals', https://www.herald.co.zw, Accessed 12 July 2020.

Dier, A. (9 January 2015) 'Even beggars do not want Zimbabwe's new coins', https://www.newser.com/story/201062, Accessed 3 August 2019.

Disability Awareness in Action (March 1995) *Overcoming obstacles to the integration of disabled people*, UNESCO sponsored report as a contribution to the World Summit on Social Development, Copenhagen: Disability Awareness in Action.

Dixon, R. (16 August 2011) 'South Africa seizes babies of Zimbabwe beggars', www.latimes.com/articles, Accessed 21 June 2018.

Dongozi, F. (6 March 2005) 'Violence flares up', *Zimbabwe Standard*, Harare: Zimbabwe.

Dongozi, F. (5 June 2005) 'Public outrage at state brutality', *Zimbabwe Standard*, Harare: Zimbabwe.

Dube, G. (4 June 2006) 'Zimbabweans finding life tough in Botswana', www.thestandard.co.zw, Accessed 1 September 2018.

Dube, G. (8 April 2010) 'UNICEF says 6.6 million Zimbabweans living below food poverty line', www.voazimbabwe.com, Accessed 7 July 2018.

Dube, G. (12 June 2013) 'Zimbabwe workers living below breadline', http://m.voazimbabwe.com, Accessed 7 July 2018.

Dube, G. (8 November 2014) 'Desperate Zimbabweans living with disabilities begging for food', https://www.voazimbabwe.com, Accessed 18 August 2018.

Dube, M. (15 April 2013) 'Beggars turn to vending to survive', www.allafrica.com, Accessed 4 June 2019.

Dube, N. (17 August 2014) Interview: OK Supermarket, Masvingo, Zimbabwe.

Dugger, C.W. (4 June 2008) 'In a crackdown, Zimbabwe curbs aid groups', www.nytimes.com, Accessed 21 May 2019.

Dugger, C.W. (21 December 2008) 'In Zimbabwe, survival lies in scavenging', www.nytimes.com, Accessed 16 April 2019.

Duri, F.P.T. (2010) *The relentless governance by the sword: Situating Operation Murambatsvina in Zimbabwean history*, Saarbrucken: VDM Verlag.

Duri, F.P.T. (2012a) 'Negotiating the Zimbabwe-Mozambique border: The pursuit of survival by Mutare's poor, 2000-2008', in: S. Chiumbu and M. Musemwa (eds.) *Crisis! What crisis? The multiple dimensions of the Zimbabwean crisis*, Cape Town: Human Sciences Research Council.

Duri, F.P.T. (2012b) 'Antecedents and adaptations in the

borderlands: A social history of informal socio-economic activities across the Rhodesia-Mozambique border with particular reference to the city of Umtali, 1900-1974', Unpublished PhD thesis, Johannesburg: History Department, University of the Witwatersrand, South Africa.

Duri, F.P.T. (June-July 2014) 'Linguistic innovations for survival: The case of illegal panning and smuggling of diamonds in Chiadzwa, Zimbabwe (2006-2012)', in: *Africana*, Volume 7, Number 1, pp.41-60.

Duri, F.P.T. (2016) 'Touting for survival: The *hwindi* in Zimbabwe', in: F. Duri (ed.) *Resilience amid adversity: Informal coping mechanisms to the Zimbabwean crisis during the new millennium*, Gweru: Booklove Publishers, pp.51-80.

Duri, F.P.T. and Chikonyora, E. (2018) 'Seeing beyond national borders: Impoverished visually-impaired Zimbabwean beggars in Johannesburg, South Africa', in: M. Mawere (ed.) *The political economy of poverty, vulnerability and disaster risk management: Building bridges of resilience, entrepreneurship and development in Africa's 21st century*, Bamenda: Langaa Research and Publishing Common Initiative Group, pp.333-360.

Duri, F.P.T. Marongwe, N. and Mawere, M. (2020) 'Journeying through the First and Second Republics: Whither Zimbabwe?' in: F.P.T. Duri, N. Marongwe and M. Mawere (eds.) *Mugabeism after Mugabe? Rethinking legacies and the new dispensation in Zimbabwe's 'Second Republic'*, Masvingo: Africa Talent Publishers, pp.1-74.

Duri, F.P.T. Marongwe, N and Mawere, M. (eds.) (2020), *Mugabeism after Mugabe? Rethinking legacies and the new dispensation in Zimbabwe's 'Second Republic'*, Masvingo: Africa Talent Publishers.

Dzarowa, M. (22 April 2020) Interview: Dangamvura Shopping Complex, Mutare, Zimbabwe.

Dzimwasha, T. (13 January 2014) 'Zimbabweans migrating to South Africa at risk of abuse and exploitation', https://www.theguardian.com/global-development, Accessed 12 June 2018.

Dzinesa, A.G. (20 January 2000) 'Swords into ploughshares: Disarmament, demobilisation and re-integration in Zimbabwe, Namibia and South Africa', Occasional Paper 120, Institute of

Security Studies, http://www.iss.co.za/pubs/papers, Accessed 3
May 2020.

Dzirutwe, M. (29 October 2019) 'Zimbabwe hikes fuel prices 12%,
hitting inflation-weary consumers', https://www.cnbc.com,
Accessed 12 November 2019.

Economist (9 August 2007) 'Zimbabweans in South Africa',
https://www.economist.com/middle-east-and-africa, Accessed 5
May 2018.

Economy Watch Content (9 April 2010) 'Zimbabwe economy',
www.economywatch.com, Accessed 17 July 2018.

Elich, G. (14 February 2020) 'Mnangagwa's neo-liberal assault on
the Zimbabwean people', https://www.counterpunch.org, 10
August 2020.

Ener, M. (November 1999) 'Prohibitions on begging and loitering
in nineteenth-century Egypt', in: *Die Welt des Islams, New Series:
State, law and society in nineteenth-century Egypt*, Volume 39, Issue 3,
pp. 319-339.

Erasmus, S. (26 November 2017) 'Zimbabwe's top 10 economic
challenges', https://m.fin24.com, Accessed 20 January 2018.

Esan, O.I. (2009) 'Panhandlers as rhetors: Discourse practices of
peripatetic beggars in southwestern Nigeria', in: *California
Linguistic Notes*, Volume XXXIV, Number 2, pp.1-18.

Evans, R. (2006) 'Negotiating social identities: The influence of
gender, age and ethnicity on young people's "street careers" in
Tanzania', in: *Children's Geographies*, Volume 4, Number 1, pp.109-
128.

Eye Net (8 July 2004) 'Street children vulnerable to AIDS',
www.eye.net.org/features, Accessed 25 November 2019.

FAO (December 2001) 'Food supply situation tightening in
Southern Africa', in: *Africa Report*, Number 3, www.fao.org,
Accessed 19 July 2018.

Fawole, O.A. Ogunkan, D.V. and Omoruan, A. (January 2011) 'The
menace of begging in Nigerian cities: A sociological analysis', in:
International Journal of Sociology and Anthropology, Volume 3,
Number 1, pp.9-14.

Feltoe, G. (2004) 'The onslaught against democracy, and the rule of
law in Zimbabwe in 2000', in: D. Harold-Barry (ed.) *Zimbabwe:*

The past is the future: Rethinking land, state and nation in the context of crisis, Harare: Weaver Press.

Ferguson, K. M. (November 2006) 'Responding to children's street work with alternative income-generation strategies', in: *International Social Work*, Volume 49, Number 6, pp.705-717.

Feris, M. and Cox, A. (3 February 2005) 'Egoli police launch blitz on beggars', https://www.iol.co.za/news, Accessed 14 July 2019.

Financial Gazette (27 March 2009) 'Brain drain could risk economic revival', www.financialgazette.co.zw, Accessed 28 March 2019.

Fischer, L. (2010) *Pioneers, settlers, aliens, exiles: The decolonisation of white identity in Zimbabwe*, Canberra: Australian National University Press.

Financial Gazette (26 July- 1 August 2007) 'Price blitz devastates Zimbabwe's rural economy', Harare: Zimbabwe.

Financial Gazette (21 August 2016) 'Zimbabweans reduced to pathetic street beggars in South Africa', https://zimbabwenewsonline.com/index.php/top_news/3118.html, Accessed 8 September 2019.

Fitzpatrick, S. and Kennedy, C. (2000) *Getting by: Begging, rough sleeping and the big issue in Glasgow and Edinburgh*, Bristol: The Policy Press.

Fontein, J. (2009) 'Anticipating a tsunami: Rumours, planning and the arbitrary state in Zimbabwe', in: *Africa: The Journal of the International Africa Institute*, Volume 79, Number 3, pp.369-398.

Forster, D. (31 January 2008) 'Refugees arrested at the Central Methodist: Shame on the South African Police!' http://www.spirituality.org.za, Accessed 4 April 2018.

Fournier, C. (June 2009) 'When the affected state causes the crisis: The case of Zimbabwe', *Humanitarian Exchange Magazine*, Issue 43.

Fuller, A. (May 2012) 'Breaking the silence: Oppression, fear and courage in Zimbabwe', *National Geographic Magazine*, National Geographic.

Gerardy, J. (11 January 2009) 'Children flee Zimbabwe to uncertain future', www.mg.co.za/article, Accessed 1 April 2018.

Gilpin, R. (1 August 2008) 'Depoliticising Zimbabwe's economy', www.usip.org/publications, Accessed 21 January 2019.

Goba, C. (14 April 2020) 'Lockdown: Zimbabweans hit hard times in diaspora, a number of them turn to begging inside supermarkets', https://www.myzimbabwe.co.zw/news/63070, Accessed 17 September 2020.

Godwin, P. (2010) *The fear*, New York: Little Brown and Company.

Gomba, W. (12 September 2013) Interview: Sakubva Bus Terminus, Mutare, Zimbabwe.

Gona, S. (13 February 2014) Interview: Vengere Suburb, Rusape, Zimbabwe.

Gonzo, S. Nhova, L. and Senzeni, T. (26 January 2014) FGD: Machipisa Shopping Centre, Harare, Zimbabwe.

Goronga, L. (18 September 2013) Interview: Mudzviti Bus Terminus, Mutare, Zimbabwe.

Gossling, S. Schumacher, K. Morelle, M. Berger R. and Heck, N. 'Tourism and street children in Antananarivo, Madagascar', in: *Tourism and Hospitality Research*, Volume 5, Number 2, 2004, pp.131-149.

Grint, K. (2005) *The sociology of work*, Cambridge: Polity Press.

Groce, N. Murray, B. Loeb, M. Tramontano, C. Trani, J. F. and Mekonnen, A. (2013) 'Disabled beggars in Addis Ababa, Ethiopia', Employment Working Paper Number 141, Geneva: International Labour Office, Employment Sector, Skills and Employability Department.

Guerin, O. (10 May 2007) 'Zimbabwe's starving border jumpers', http://news.bbc.co.uk2/hi/africa/6642619.stm, Accessed 17 May 2018.

Gunda, T. (5 January 2012) 'World Remit raises funds for girl's heart surgery', www.zimdiaspora.com/index, Accessed 21 December 2019.

Gurusa, T. (3 November 2019) 'Fresh wave of border jumpers flood South Africa as Zimbabwe totters', https://www.newzimbabwe.com, Accessed 16 June 2020.

Gwara, J. (5 June 2007) 'Harare street life', www.streetkidnews.worldpress.com, Accessed 3 May 2019.

Gwaze, V. (24 November 2019) 'The definition of love?' https://www.sundaymail.co.zw, Accessed 13 February 2020.

Hakutangwi, P. Mashizha, S. Matanga, R. (14 August 2010) FGD:

Brakpan, East Rand, South Africa.

Hammar, A. and Raftopoulos, B. (2003) 'Zimbabwe's unfinished business: Rethinking land, state and nation', in: A. Hammar, B. Raftopoulos and S. Jensen (eds.) *Zimbabwe's unfinished business: Rethinking land, state and nation in the context of crisis*, Harare: Weaver Press.

Hanchao, L. (1999) 'Becoming urban: Mendicancy and vagrancy in modern Shanghai', in: *Journal of Social History*, Volume 33, Number 1, pp.7-36.

Hannan, M. (1959) *Standard Shona Dictionary*, Salisbury: College Press.

Harare 24 News (20 August 2014) 'Blind beggars worry senator', www.xijmbdf.harare24.com, Accessed 24 February 2018.

Harare 24 News (6 September 2014) 'Zimbabwe records 75 company closures, over 9 000 job losses', www.zncc.co.zw, Accessed 24 February 2018.

Harawa, F. (20 August 2013) 'Food used as political weapon', www.dailynews.co.zw, Accessed 7 November 2019.

Hasazi, S.B. Gordon, L.R. and Roe, C.A. (1985) *Factors associated with the employment status of handicapped youth exiting high school from 1979 to 1983: Exceptional children: An introductory survey of special education*, New York: Maxwell Macmillan.

Hawkson, E.E. (2015) 'Trained beggars with parents as teachers', https://www.graphic.com.gh/features, Accessed 19 June 2019.

Heal Zimbabwe Trust (28 July 2013) 'The 2013 pre-election political environment analysis', www.healzimbabwe.co.zw, Accessed 14 May 2020.

Hill, G. (2003) *The battle for Zimbabwe: The final countdown*, Cape Town: Zebra Press.

H-Metro (23 March 2016) 'Dilemma of the blind on Christmas', https://www.hmetro.co.zw, Accessed 4 October 2018.

H-Metro (7 January 2020) 'Blind beggar gets ZW$3 000 per month from buses', https://news.pindula.co.zw, Accessed 17 July 2020.

Human Rights Watch (25 October 2003) 'Zimbabwe: Food used as political weapon', www.hrw.org/news, Accessed 16 August 2019.

Human Rights Watch (2010) *Off the backs of children: Forced begging and other abuses against Talibes in Senegal*, New York: Human Rights

Watch.

Humanium (6 November 2011) 'Children of Zimbabwe: Realising children's rights in Zimbabwe', www.humanium.org/en, Accessed 12 May 2020.

Hunga, V. (26 January 2020) Interview: Max Business Centre, Mutare, Zimbabwe.

Hungwe, C. (August 2012) 'The migration experience and multiple identities of Zimbabwean migrants in South Africa', in: *Journal of Social Sciences Research*, Volume 1, Issue 5, pp.132-138.

Hunt, G. (3 August 2011) 'From bread-basket to a basket-case: Land seizures from white farmers cost Mugabe's Zimbabwe £7 billion', www.dailymail.co.uk/news, Accessed 23 May 2018.

Immigrant for Social Justice (31 August 2014) 'Zimbabwean, blind, hungry and homeless in South Africa', www.socialjusticeimmigrant.blogspot.com, Accessed 5 February 2018.

Independent Online (18 January 2006) 'Border jumpers swept away in Limpopo River', https://www.iol.co.za/news/africa, Accessed 10 June 2020.

Independent UK (7 December 2008) 'UN forced to cut food aid to Zimbabwe's starving people', www.independent.co.uk, Accessed 18 April 2019.

Inflationomics (27 March 2008) 'Insights from Zimbabwe', www.inflationomics.com, Accessed 2 June 2019.

Irin News (26 September 2006) 'Zimbabwe: The continent's original people survive by begging', www.inflationomics.com, Accessed 10 August 2020.

Irin News (13 March 2008) 'Zimbabwe: More food shortages anticipated', www.irinews.org/report, Accessed 12 June 2018.

Irin News (23 May 2008) 'South Africa: Xenophobic attacks spreading', www.irinews.org/report, Accessed 18 December 2019.

Irin News (29 January 2009) 'Zimbabwe: Three-quarters of the people need food aid', www.irinnews.org/report, Accessed 12 June 2018.

Irin News (26 May 2010) 'South Africa: Troops reinforcing a porous

and dangerous border',
https://www.refworld.org/docid/4c0367c91a.html, Accessed 6
November 2018.

Irin News (31 January 2011) 'Zimbabwe: New surge in political
violence', www.irinnews.org/report, Accessed 1 Julu 2019.

Irin News (2 June 2011) 'Slumming it in Johannesburg',
www.irinews.org/report, Accessed 26 September 2019.

Irin News (13 June 2011) 'South Africa: Blind beggars go south',
www.irinews.org/report, Accessed 26 September 2019.

Isilow, H. (9 April 2015) 'Johannesburg's blind beggars',
https://www.aa.com.tr/en/life, Accessed 12 April 2019.

Jakado, L. (12 July 2019) Interview: Mutare CBD, Zimbabwe.

Janssen, B. (29 April 2020) 'Virus lockdown worsens suffering for
Johannesburg beggars',
https://www.islandpacket.com/news/health-
care/article242365491.html, Accessed 30 April 2020.

Jeffrey, P. (n.d.) 'Refugees in South Africa sleep on the street',
https://www.google.co.za, Accessed 18 March 2019.

Jelili, M.O. (2006) 'Environmental and socio-economic dimensions
of begging in Ilorin and Ogbomoso', Unpublished Masters in
Technology thesis, Ogbomoso: Department of Urban and
Regional Planning, Ladoke Akintola University of Technology,
Nigeria.

Jelili, M.O. (2013) 'Street-begging in cities: Cultural, political and
socio-economic questions', in: *Global Journal of Human Social
Science, Sociology and Culture*, Volume 13, Issue 5, pp.53-58.

Jena, R. (22 November 2019) Interview, Mutare CBD, Zimbabwe.

Johwa, W. (10 September 2004) 'Zimbabwe/DRC: The war that
might not have been', www.africa.no/Detailed/5990.html,
Accessed 22 January 2018.

Jombe, F. (19 September 2013) Interview: Forbes Border Post,
Zimbabwe.

Kadirire, H. (9 July 2017) 'Children forced to beg at road
intersections', https://www.zimbabwesituation.com/news,
Accessed 29 September 2019.

Kaelbe, H. (2003) 'Social history in Europe,' in: *Journal of Social
History*, Volume 37, Number 1, pp.29-35.

Kahiya, V. and Mukaro, A. (22 July 2005) 'Kondozi Farm seized in latest farm raid', www.theindependent.co.zw, Accessed 13 March 2018.

Kahwema, T. (6 September 2014) Interview: Gaza Township, Chipinge, Zimbabwe.

Kamasah, A. (14 December 2018) '"Blind" beggar regains eyesight after she was threatened with tear-gas', https://www.pulse.com.gh/filla, Accessed 15 June 2019.

Kandemiiri, J. and Gumbo, T. (3 January 2015) 'Ray of hope as Zimbabwean refugees prepare to leave South Africa church', https://www.churchtimes.co.uk/articles, Accessed 24 May 2020.

Kanongo, R. (13 September 2013) Interview: Main Street, Mutare, Zimbabwe.

Kaonde, E. (14 September 2013) Interview: TM Supermarket, Mutare, Zimbabwe.

Kariati, M. (19 May 2014) 'A city of vendors, beggars, and conmen', https://www.thezimbabwean.co, Accessed 30 July 2019.

Kasamba, R. Nedzoyi, M. and Sande, B. (15 September 2013) FGD: Fidelity Building, Mutare, Zimbabwe.

Kassah, A.K. (March 2008) 'Begging as work: A study of people with mobility difficulties in Accra, Ghana', in: *Disability and Society*, Volume 23, Number 2, pp.163-170.

Kativhu, T. (14 September 2013) Interview: Meikles Park, Mutare, Zimbabwe.

Kaushik, A. (March 2014) 'Rights of children: A case study of child beggars at public places in India', in: *Journal of Social Welfare and Human Rights*, Volume 2, Number 1, pp.1-16.

Kazore, M. and Pachije, W. (7 September 2014) Interview: Birchenough Bridge Shopping Centre, Buhera District, Zimbabwe.

Keepile, K. (18 March 2010) 'Single mothers' struggle for survival on Johannesburg's streets', www.mg.co.za/article, Accessed 2 July 2019.

Kembo, J. and Nhongo, K. (2002) 'The phenomenon of child trafficking in Zimbabwe', Harare: Unpublished Research Report.

Kennedy, C. and Fitzpatrick, S. (2001) 'Begging, rough sleeping and social exclusion: Implications for social policy', in: *Urban Studies*,

Volume 38, Number 11, pp.2001-2016.

Kesani, M. (16 July 2019) Interview: Mutare CBD, Zimbabwe.

Khumalo, T. (29 July 2014) 'Blind Zimbabwe beggars try their luck in South Africa', http://www.rnm.nl/africa/article, Accessed 19 March 2019.

Khupe, W. (19 April 2010) 'Disabled people not cash cow products', https://www.thezimbabwean.co, Accessed 10 May 2018.

Kitsepele, N. (25 November 2013) 'Botswana kicks out more illegal Zimbabwe immigrants', www.africareview.com, Accessed 27 March 2020.

Koinage, J. (19 December 2006) 'Living off rats to survive in Zimbabwe', http://edition.cnn.com/2006/WORLD/africa, Accessed 12 April 2020.

Kondonge, W. (16 August 2014) Interview: Mucheke Bus Terminus, Masvingo, Zimbabwe.

Kopoka, A. (2000) *The problems of street children: An ignored tragedy*, Dar-es-Salaam: Institute of Development Studies, University of Dar-es-Salaam.

Kriel, M. (22 September 2009) 'Letters from Zimbabwe', www.morningmirror.africanherd.com, Accessed 6 February 2019.

Kros, C. (July 2007) 'Considering the legacy of radical/social history in South Africa,' in: *African Historical Review*, Volume 39, Number 1, pp.41-58.

Kumarappa, J.M. (2007) *Our beggar problem and how to tackle it*, Bombay: Peffer Press.

Kurewa, C. (6 September 2014) Interview: Gaza Township, Chipinge, Zimbabwe.

Kusena, V. (16 August 2014) Interview: Mucheke Bus Terminus, Masvingo, Zimbabwe.

Kwaramba, F. (23 November 2013) 'White community falls on hard times', www.weekendpost.co.zw, Accessed 3 June 2019.

Kwaramba, F. and Mtimba, G. (31 October 2013) 'Hunger grips rural Zimbabwe', www.dailynews.co.zw/articles, Accessed 3 June 2019.

Kwase. L. (11 November 2019) Interview: Mutare CBD, Zimbabwe.

Kwenda, S. (10 April 2010) 'Africa's disabled will not be forgotten', www.un.org/africarenewal, Accessed 30 August 2018.

Laing, A. (8 May 2015) 'South African church sanctuary for refugees targeted in police raid', https://www.telegraph.co.uk/news/worldnews/africaandindiano cean/southafrica/11593301, Accessed 17 March 2020.

Levin, N. (4 December 2017) 'Grace Mugabe: Zimbabwe's Lady Macbeth', http://uchicagogate.com/articles, Accessed 17 February 2018.

Lewis, O. (1959) *Five families: Mexican case studies in the culture of poverty*, New York: Basic Books.

Lewis, O. (1998) 'The culture of poverty', in: *Society*, Volume 35, Issue 2, pp.7-30.

Limpopo Mirror (8 June 2012) 'Notorious robber shot by border police', https://www.limpopomirror.co.za, Accessed 24 November 2019.

Lindeque, B. (13 May 2019) 'From beggar to postgraduate: This is Lwazi's incredible story!' https://www.goodthingsguy.com/people, Accessed 29 May 2019.

Lloyd-Roberts, S. (13 September 2007) 'Zimbabwe families forced to beg for scraps', https://www.telegraph.co.uk, Accessed 4 July 2019.

Lopez, X. (1 February 2020) 'Zimbabwe: Street children in Harare', https://www.southworld.net, Accessed 12 February 2020.

Ma, A. (24 November 2017) 'Who is Emmerson Mnangagwa? Meet Zimbabwe's new president', http://uk.businessinsider.com, Accessed 19 December 2017.

Mabate, M. (16 May 2019) Interview: Watsomba Business Centre, Mutasa District, Zimbabwe.

Mabhiza, L. (16 February 2020) 'Man drowns crossing Limpopo River into Zimbabwe', https://mbaretimes.com, Accessed 4 April 2020.

Machamire, F. (9 January 2017) 'South Africa warns Zimbabwean border jumpers', https://nehandaradio.com, Accessed 15 March 2018.

Madhuveko, E. (12 September 2013) Interview: Sakubva Bus Terminus, Mutare, Zimbabwe.

246

Madima, A. (21 August 2019) 'Four machete border jumper robbers busted', http://beitbridge24.com, Accessed 6 September 2019.

Madzamba, R. (17 October 2009) 'Man seeks funds for son's South Africa treatment', www.zimbabwenewsonline.com, Accessed 11 July 2018.

Mafarachisi, L. (17 September 2013) Interview: Sakubva Suburb, Mutare, Zimbabwe.

Mafingenyi, D. (15 July 2004) 'Botswana', www.swafrica.net/archives, Accessed 1 June 2019.

Mafu, S. (11 December 2011) 'Bulawayo girl (11) seeks funds to undergo heart surgery', www.bulawayo24.com/index, Accessed 18 May 2019.

Magumbo, N. Rwasunda, F. and Sigogo, Z. (13 September 2014) FGD: Jairos Jiri Centre, Mutare, Zimbabwe.

Mahlangu, I. Dlomo, L. Makhetha, T. and Dhlamini, P. (24 March 2020) 'President declares virus lockdown for South Africa', https://wwwsowetanlive.co.za, Accessed 10 April 2020.

Mail and Guardian (29 January 2009) 'Zimbabwe's unemployment skyrockets', www.mg.co.za/index, Accessed 16 March 2020.

Makoni-Muchemwa, U. (7 April 2011) 'Zimbabwe through a lens', http://www.kubatanablogs.net, Accessed 21 November 2019. Accessed 3 June 2019.

Makunike, C. (27 September 2002) 'Zimbabwe: What lies beneath the mask of normality', https://mg.co.za/article, Accessed 24 July 2020.

Makuyana, I. and Diale, L. (7 January 2015) 'Two Zimbabwean border jumpers drown trying to cross into South Africa', https://www.zimbabwesituation.com/news, Accessed 8 January 2018.

Mamdani, M. (December 2008) 'Lessons from Zimbabwe', in: *London Review of Books*, Volume 31, Number 23, pp.17-21.

Mamimine, S.P. (12 August 2019) 'Forced child begging vs ignorance of the law,' https://www.newsday.co.zw, Accessed 19 May 2020.

Mangoma, T. (29 May 2002) 'Zimbabwe: More children forced to beg', https://allafrica.com/stories, Accessed 2 June 2019.

Manwere, O. (14 September 2007) 'Over 3 million need food aid', www.theindependent.co.zw, Accessed 12 May 2019.

Manyukwe, C. (17 May 2005) 'ZANU-PF youths chase teachers', in: *The Daily Mirror*, 17 May 2005.

Mapumulo, Z. (25 September 2007) 'Beggars are driven by hunger to flee Zimbabwe', www.sowetanlive.co.za, Accessed 14 July 2020.

Marapa, R. (15 August 2014) Interview: Mucheke Bus Terminus, Masvingo, Zimbabwe.

Marima, R. Jordan, J. and Cormie, K. (1995) 'Conversations with street children in Harare, Zimbabwe', in: *Zambezia*, Volume 22, Issue 1, pp.1-24.

Marima, T. (19 August 2019) 'In Zimbabwe, an economic crisis with 175% inflation drives discontent', https://www.npr.org, Accessed 2 January 2020.

Marongwe, N. (2013) 'Rural women as the invisible victims of militarised political violence: The case of Shurugwi District, Zimbabwe, 2000-2008', PhD thesis, Cape Town: University of the Western Cape.

Marongwe, N. and Moyo, K. (2016) 'By hook or crook: Illegal mechanisms for survival at the Beitbrigde Border Post', in F.P.T. Duri, (ed.) *Resilience amid adversity: Informal coping mechanisms to the Zimbabwean crisis during the new millennium*, Gweru: Booklove Publishers.

Marongwe, N. and Muguti, T. (2017) 'Problematising the developmental potential of Community Share Ownership Trusts (CSOTs) in Zimbabwe: The case of the Tongogara CSOT, 2011-2014', in: M. Mawere (ed.), *Development perspectives from the South: Troubling the matrices of [under]development in Africa*, Bamenda: Langaa Research and Publishing CIG.

Marozva, F. (28 January 2014) Interview: First Street, Harare, Zimbabwe.

Marufu, N. (21 March 2007) 'Blind cross border to make a living', www.thezimbabwean.co.uk, Accessed 13 May 2020.

Masapa, R. (14 September 2013) Interview: TM Supermarket, Mutare, Zimbabwe.

Mashinya, F. and Gwaze, V. (15 December 2019) 'Child beggars for hire,' https://www.sundaymail.co.zw, Accessed 27 June 2019.

248

Masiyiwa, G. (10 November 2016) 'Invisible children beg, sell on Zimbabwe's streets to aid families in economic turmoil', https://globalpressjournal.com/africa/zimbabwe, Accessed 19 June 2019.

Masunungure, E. (2004) 'Travails of opposition politics in Zimbabwe since independence', in: D. Harold-Barry (ed.) *Zimbabwe: The past is the future: Rethinking land, state and nation in the context of crisis*, Harare: Weaver Press.

Masunungure, E. (4-7 June 2009) 'Zimbabwe's agonising but irreversible political transition', Paper presented at the Institute of African Studies, University of Leipzig, Leipzig, Germany.

Matereke, E. (28 August 2014) Interview: Civic Centre, Masvingo, Zimbabwe.

Mathuthu, M. (10 October 2009) 'Doctor warns as tumour girl undergoes surgery', www.newzimbabwe.com, Accessed 23 June 2018.

Matikinye, R. (21 September 2007) 'Blitz exposes flawed state welfare system', www.theindependent.co.zw, Accessed 17 May 2019.

Matikinye, R. (11 December 2009) 'Political patronage threatens Zimbabwe's mines', www.newzimbabwe.com, Accessed 4 February 2019.

Mawere, M. (2017) *Theorising development in Africa: Towards building an African framework of development*, Bamenda: Langaa Research and Publishing CIG.

Mawire, W. (7 February 2017) 'Zimbabwe's tourism minister urges government to act on street child beggars', https://panafricanvisions.com, Accessed 18 September 2018.

Mayaya, R. (17 September 2013) Interview: Nyamauru Suburb, Mutare, Zimbabwe.

Mazuru, N. (2016) 'Blessing or curse? Impact of cross-border mobility and migration by Zimbabwean parents on their children during the new millennium', in: F.P.T Duri and N. Marongwe (eds.) *Contested spaces, restrictive mechanisms and corridors of opportunity: A social history of Zimbabwean borderlands and beyond since the colonial period*, Gweru: Booklove Publishers.

Mbanje, P. (13 December 2015) 'Life on the streets: A 12-year-old's story', https://www.thestandard.co.zw, Accessed 15 November 2019.

Mbanje, P. (13 April 2019) 'Zimbabwean students reduced to beggars in Algeria', https://www.zimbabwesituation.com/news, Accessed 26 April 2019.

McFadden, P. (30 July 2014) 'Homeless in Harare another day', www.wworld.org/programs, Accessed 19 August 2019.

Meldrum, A. (4 February 2004) 'Mugabe seizes largest sugar producer', www.theage.com.au, Accessed 16 November 2019.

Meldrum, A. (1 June 2005) 'Mugabe allows UN to increase food aid', www.theguardian.com, Accessed 9 May 2018.

Meredith, M. (2002) *Mugabe: Power and plunder in Zimbabwe*, New York: Public Affairs.

Merton, P.K. (1957) *Social theory and social structure*, London: Free Press of Glencoe.

Mhiko, J. (14 September 2013) Interview: Meikles Park, Mutare, Zimbabwe.

Mhizha, S. (November 2010) 'Self-image of adolescent street children in Harare', Master of Philosophy in Social Studies (Psychology) dissertation, Department of Psychology, Faculty of Social Sciences, University of Zimbabwe.

Mhlanga, P. and Mangudhla, T. (15 April 2020) 'Zimbabwe losing inflation battle', https://businesstimes.co.zw, Accessed 13 July 2020.

Mhlanga, T. (26 January 2020) 'ZIMCODD bemoans inequality in Zimbabwe,' in: *The Zimbabwe Standard*, Harare: Zimbabwe.

Mihalache, C. Matei, E. Manea, G. Cocos, O. and Dumitrache, L. (2013) 'Begging phenomenon in Bucharest City: Dimensions and patterns of expression', in: *Review of Research and Social Intervention*, Volume 43, pp.61-79.

Mlambo, D. (7 September 2014) Interview: Birchenough Bridge Shopping Centre, Buhera District, Zimbabwe.

Moshenberg, D. (28 January 2009) 'Bordering on peace: Save Zimbabwe now', www.womeninandbeyond.org, Accessed 20 September 2019.

Moyo, J. (5 May 2014) 'Disabled Zimbos forced into cheap labour', www.radiovop.com/index, Accessed 12 May 2019.

Moyo, J. (18 August 2014) 'South Africa: No Canaan for young Zimbabweans', www.mw.nl/africa/article, Accessed 3 September 2019.

Moyo, L. (1 April, 2020) 'Vanorarama nekukumbira rubatsiro vovhiringwa neCovid-19 muZimbabwe', https://www.voashona.com, Accessed 20 April 2020.

Moyo, S. (19 August 2012) 'Beggars cannot be choosers', www.com, Accessed 2 June 2019.

Moyo, S. (September 2000) 'The interaction of market and compulsory land acquisition processes with social action in Zimbabwe's land reform', Paper presented at the SAPES Trust Annual Colloquium, Harare.

Mswazie, W. (7 March 2019) 'Mum "sells" three-year-old daughter', https://www.chronicle.co.zw, Accessed 19 July 2019.

Mtonga, J. (December 2011) 'On and off the streets: Children moving between institutional care and survival on the streets', Master of Philosophy in Childhood Studies, Faculty of Social Sciences and Technology Management, Norwegian University of Science and Technology, Norwegian Centre for Child Research.

Muchairi, H. (22 November 2013) 'Of beggars and the streets', www.deckmagazine.com/opinion, Accessed 7 June 2020.

Muchenje, R. (1 March 2019) 'Basic freedoms diminish under Mnangagwa's reign', in: *The Zimbabwe Independent*, Harare: Zimbabwe.

Mudahondo, T. (29 March 2020) 'Beggars blast Zimbabwe lockdown', https://bulawayo24.com/news, Accessed 2 April 2020.

Mudzonga, N. (28 January 2014) Interview: First Street, Harare, Zimbabwe.

Mudzungairi, W. (19 September 2013) 'Agriculture: The tale of Zimbabwe's sleeping giant', www.newsday.co.zw, Accessed 4 May 2019.

Mugabe, R. (2001) *Inside the Third Chimurenga,* Harare: Department of Information and Publicity, Office of the President and Cabinet.

Mugabe, T. (12 April 2019) 'Mnangagwa in big trouble over failure to fix economy; military hardliners push him into tight corner', www.myzimbabwe.co.zw, Accessed 14 May 2019.

Mugoti, R. Samson, T. and Wakota, V. (27 September 2014) FGD: Nyika Business Centre, Bikita District, Zimbabwe.

Mugwengwendere, F. (13 September 2013) Interview: Dangamvura Shopping Complex, Mutare, Zimbabwe.

Mukaro, A. (3 June 2005) 'Retributive hand seen in police blitz', in: *The Zimbabwe Independent*, Harare: Zimbabwe.

Mukonda, V. (17 August 2014) Interview: Mucheke Bus Terminus, Masvingo, Zimbabwe.

Mukondiwa, S. (20 September 2014) Interview: Makoni Shopping Centre, Chitungwiza, Zimbabwe.

Mukumbira, R. (1 May 2003) 'Citizens turn on Zimbabwean migrants', www.thefreelibrary.com, Accessed 27 May 2019.

Mukumbira, R. (20 May 2003) 'Botswana-Zimbabwe: Do new fences make good neighbours?' www.africafiles.com/articles, Accessed 27 May 2019.

Muleya, D. (8 April 2005) 'MDC supporters suffer ZANU-PF retribution', in: *The Zimbabwe Independent*, Accessed 2 September 2020.

Muleya, T. (8 April 2014) 'Four border jumpers drown in Limpopo River', https://www.chronicle.co.zw, Accessed 4 June 2020.

Muleya, T. (30 May 2015) 'Border jumpers kill charging crocodile', https://nehandaradio.com, Accessed 15 July 2020.

Muleya, T. (17 April 2016) 'Risking life, limb at Beitbridge', https://www.sundaymail.co.zw, Accessed 10 May 2020).

Muleya, T. (12 October 2018) 'Limpopo River toy gun robbers arrested', https://www.chronicle.co.zw, Accessed 20 September 2019.

Muleya, T. (24 January 2019) 'Border jumpers kill robber', https://www.herald.co.zw, Accessed 21 September 2019.

Munanavire, B. (8 November 2013) 'Stray children invade pavements', www.weekendpost.co.zw, Accessed 21 September 2019.

Munemo, E. and Tom, T. (April 2013) 'Problems of unemployment faced by visually-impaired people', in: *Greener Journal of Social Sciences*, Volume 3, Number 4, pp.203-219.

Munhendo, L. 22 (March 2019) 'Zimbabwe ranked among

unhappiest countries in the world,' https://allafrica.com, Accessed 20 July 2020.

Munnion, C. (3 July 2008) 'Botswana troops mass on Zimbabwe border', www.telegraph.co.uk, Accessed 14 July 2019.

Muranduko, T. (17 September 2013) Interview: Mutare Railway Station, Mutare, Zimbabwe.

Murigo, D. (6 September 2014) 'The impact of the economic crisis in Zimbabwe, 2000-2009', www.academia.edu, Accessed 12 September 2019.

Muronzi, C. (6 September 2019) 'Robert Mugabe leaves a legacy of economic mismanagement', https://www.aljazeera.com/ajimpact, Accessed 19 November 2019.

Muronzi, C. (27 September 2019) 'IMF: Zimbabwe has the highest inflation rate in the world', https://www.aljazeera.com/ajimpact, Accessed 19 November 2019.

Murwira, L. (17 August 2014) Interview: Civic Centre, Masvingo, Zimbabwe.

Mushava, E. and Nleya, F. (25 February 2013) 'Political violence returns', www.newsday.co.zw, Accessed 18 May 2019.

Mutandiro, K. (19 December 2019) 'Grim life of families living in Pretoria's "Little Zimbabwe"' https://www.news24.com/SouthAfrica/News, Accessed 1 January 2020.

Mutandwa, G. (16 July 2012) 'Beggars slowly becoming a menacing reality', www.allafrica.com, Accessed 14 August 2018.

Mutenga, T. (3 July 2014) 'Zimbabwe: A nation of buyers, sellers', www.financialgazette.co.zw, Accessed 21 April 2019.

Mwandiyambira, N. (26 September 2019) 'Spare a thought for child beggars,' https://www.thepatriot.co.zw, Accessed 6 November 2019.

Mwasvipa, L. (25 February 2020) Interview: Dangamvura Shopping Complex, Zimbabwe.

My Zimbabwe News (25 August 2013) 'ZANU-PF has killed the country', www.myzimbabwe.co.zw, Accessed 7 October 2019.

Nanga, Y. (16 July 2019) Interview: Mutare CBD, Zimbabwe.

Nation Master (4 February 2010) 'Zimbabwe's economy statistics', www.stationmaster.com, Accessed 18 July 2019.

Namwata, B.M.L. Mgabo, M.R. and Dimoso, P. (June 2012) 'Categories of street beggars and factors influencing street begging in central Tanzania', in: *African Study Monographs*, Volume 33, Number 2, pp.133-143.

Ncube, X. (3 February 2013) 'Police swoop on street kids', www.dailynews.co.zw, Accessed 15 August 2019.

Ncube, X. (19 February 2017) 'How Zimbabweans risk life and limb to cross into South Africa', https://www.thestandard.co.zw, Accessed 20 July 2018.

Ndlovu, I. (6 April 2014) 'Liquidity crunch in Zimbabwe', www.southerneye.co.zw, Accessed 4 May 2020.

Ndlovu, M. (28 May 2019) 'Zimbabwe has second highest inflation rate in the world', https://bulawayo24.com, Accessed 1 June 2019.

Ndlovu, R. (17 February 2019) 'Nearly 100 Zimbabwe companies close down', https://www.timeslive.co.za, Accessed 3 March 2019.

Nengomasha, V. (17 August 2014) Interview: OK Supermarket, Masvingo, Zimbabwe.

Netsianda, M. (12 October 2012) 'Jail time for two border robbers', https://www.zoutnet.co.za/articles/news/15367, Accessed 19 March 2020.

Netsianda, M. (18 March 2018) 'Limpopo smugglers up the game with new boats', https://www.sundaynews.co.zw, Accessed 11 April 2018.

New Humanitarian (18 March 2018) 'Undocumented kids alone in a new country', https://www.thenewhumanitarian.org/fr/node/235901, Accessed 21 April 2020.

New Humanitarian (9 February 2012) 'One of the many holes in the 250km razor wire fence along the Zimbabwe-South Africa border which allow easy access to would-be intruders,' https://www.thenewhumanitarian.org/photo/201202090759150 656, Accessed 3 June 2019.

New Zimbabwe (22 June 2012) 'Multi-million dollar tourism blitz planned', www.newzimbabwe.com, Accessed 28 July 2020.

New Zimbabwe (10 July 2016) 'Protests and the growing risks for Mugabe', www.newzimbabwe.com, Accessed 11 September 2019.

New Zimbabwe (16 October 2016) 'Zimbabwe: Visually-impaired beggars besiege toll gates', https://allafrica.com/stories/201610150289.html, Accessed 11 September 2019.

New Zimbabwe (20 May 2019) 'Zimbabwe economy pronounced dead; set to contract 20% in 2019', https://www.newzimbabwe.com, Accessed 11 November 2019.

News from Africa (November 2008) 'Neighbours react to economic refugee influx', www.newsfromafrica.org, Accessed 13 July 2019.

Newsday (21 August 2011) 'Vicious cycle breeds child beggars', www.newsday.co.zw, Accessed 6 December 2019.

Newsday (30 March 2020) 'Inflation shoots to 560%', Harare: Zimbabwe.

Nhongonya, D. (18 September 2013) Interview: Mudzviti Bus Terminus, Mutare, Zimbabwe.

Ntali, E. (9 January 2020) 'Tales of Zimbabwe's invisible children', www.263chat.com, Accessed 10 February 2020.

Nungu, R. (21 September 2014) Interview: Chikwanha Shopping Centre, Chitungwiza. Zimbabwe.

Nyamnjoh, F.B. (2006) *Insiders and outsiders: Citizenship and xenophobia in contemporary Southern Africa*, Dakar: Zed Books.

Nyathi, K. (4 January 2020) 'Once solid Zimbabwe economy is in free fall', https://www.theeastafrican.co, Accessed 2 February 2020.

Nyatsanza, P. (22 April 2009) 'Street children need families', www.allafrica.com/stories, Accessed 14 May 2019.

Nyikadzino, G. (10 June 2015) 'Children bear brunt of parents' disability', https://www.newsday.co.zw, Accessed 7 July 2019.

Ogunkan, D.V. and Jelili, M.O. (April 2010) 'The influence of land use on the spatial variation of begging in Ogbomoso, Nigeria', in: *Journal of Geography and Regional Planning*, Volume 3, Number 4, pp.73-83.

Ord, C. (9 November 2010) 'Begging the question: The dilemma of tourism and street children', in: *The International Ecotourism Society*

Research Corner.

Organisation for Economic Cooperation and Development (OECD) (2004) *African economic outlook 2003-2004: Country studies: Zimbabwe*, Paris: OECD.

Orme, J. and Seipel, M. (July 2007) 'Survival strategies of street children in Ghana: A qualitative study', in: *International Social Work*, Volume 50, Number 4, pp.489-499.

Osa-Edoh, G. and Ayano, S. (2012) 'The prevalence of street begging in Nigeria and the counselling intervention strategies', in: *Review of European Studies*, Volume 4, Number 4, pp.77-83.

Otoole, S. (9 July 2013) 'Three men, a fence and a dead body', https://chimurengachronic.co.za, Accessed 21 October 2019.

Otoole, S. and Botes, P. (4 April 2011) 'Porous border is smugglers' paradise', https://mg.co.za/article, Accessed 13 June 2020.

Ottey, M. (16 May 2013) 'Brother, can you spare me a penny? How about 50 dollars?' www.miketendstotravel.worldpress.com, Accessed 12 June 2019.

Owolabi, E.F. (2012) 'Child abuse and sustainable development in Nigeria', in: *African Journal of Social Sciences*, Volume 2, Number 2, pp.108-119.

Owusu-Sekyere, E. Jengre, E. and Alhassan, E. (2018) 'Begging in the city: Complexities, degree of organisation, and embedded risks', in: *Hindawi: Child Development Research*, Volume 2018, pp.1-8, https://doi.org/10.1155/2018/98634102018, Accessed 17 February 2019.

Oxfam (10 June 2002) 'Fighting off starvation in Zimbabwe', www.oxfamamerica.org, Accessed 11 July 2018.

Oxfam International (12 August 2020) 'After the storm: One year on from Cyclone Idai', https://www.oxfam.org/en/after-storm-one-year-cyclone-idai, Accessed 19 August 2020.

Padya, S. (16 July 2019) Interview: Mutare CBD, Zimbabwe.

Patel, D. (1988) 'Government policy and squatter settlements in Harare, Zimbabwe', in: R.A. Obudo and C.C. Mhlanga (eds.) *Slum and squatter settlements in sub-Saharan Africa: Towards a planning, strategy*, New York: Praeger, pp.205-218.

Perryer, S. (7 October 2019) 'Lacking common sense: How Zimbabwe went from economic star to financial basket case', https://www.worldfinance.com/special-reports, Accessed 12 December 2019.

Peta, B. (4 February 2005) 'Blind Zimbabweans coining it in Johannesburg', https://www.iol.co.za/news/south-africa, Accessed 16 April 2020.

Phillips, B. and Shah, K. (26 January 2016) 'Begging for life: From Manila to Malmo', https://www.aljazeera.com/programmes/peopleandpower-160126130424263.html, Accessed 29 March 2020.

Phiri, G. (14 January 2015) 'Roadblocks to "destination Zimbabwe"', https://www.aljazeera.com/indepth/features/zimbabwe-2015113783123763.html, Accessed 2 November 2019.

Pigou, P. (18 January 2019) 'Revolt and repression in Zimbabwe', www.crisisgroup.org, Accessed 18 September 2019.

Pilossof, R. 1 (December 2010) 'The Commercial Farmers Union of Zimbabwe and its politics after *Jambanja*', www.solidaritypeacetrust.org, Accessed 5 November 2018.

Pindula News (2 May 2019) 'Workers blast government's neoliberalism and austerity policies', https://news.pindula.co.zw, Accessed 21 May 2019.

Pindula News (4 June 2019) 'Zimbabwe slowly ditching RTGS dollar', https://news.pindula.co.zw, Accessed 8 June 2019.

Pindula News (December 2019) 'Vendors reportedly hiring out their children to beggars handlers for a commission', https://news.pindula.co.zw, Accessed 19 April 2020.

Pindula News (15 April 2020) 'Higher Life Foundation donates 362 food hampers to people living with disabilities', https://news.pindula.co.zw, Accessed 21 April 2020.

Pindula News (17 April 2020) 'The food rations were too little: Homeless kids now back on the streets after escaping lockdown safe houses', https://news.pindula.co.zw, Accessed 19 April 2020.

Piwa, V. (13 January 2020) Interview: Mangenje Business Centre, Dangamvura, Mutare, Zimbabwe.

Plentive, C. (26 October 2007) 'Botswana, a bittersweet Eldorado for Zimbabwean refugees', www.mg.co.za/article, Accessed 12

June 2018.

Potts, D. (2006) 'Restoring order? Operation Murambatsvina and the urban crisis in Zimbabwe', in: *Journal of Southern African Studies*, Volume 32, Number 2, pp.272-291.

Poverty Reduction Forum Trust (2011) 'Urban poverty in Zimbabwe: The case of Mutare', Field Research Report, Harare: Poverty Reduction Forum Trust.

Poverty Reduction Forum Trust (2013) 'Study of poverty in Manicaland: The case of Mutare rural', Research Paper, Harare: Poverty Reduction Forum Trust.

Press Reader (19 January 2009) 'Living as beggars here is better than working life in Zimbabwe', www.pressreader.com/south-africa/the-star, Accessed 25 June 2019.

Puture, N. (26 February 2020) Interview: Chikomo Tavern, Dangamvura, Mutare, Zimbabwe.

Quidiz, B. (2005) 'Poverty and hunger: A race against the clock', in: *The International French News Magazine*, Volume 57, pp.45-46.

Quist-Arcton, O. (25 November 2008) 'Food crisis expands in tumultuous Zimbabwe', www.npr.org, Accessed 15 February 2019.

Radio Dialogue (30 April 2014) 'Mixed feelings over complaints of foreigners causing unemployment in South Africa', http://www.channelzim.net/news, Accessed 4 May 2019.

Radio VOP (24 December 2010) 'Zimbabwe: Difficult Christmas for Zimbabwean beggars', www.radiovop.com/index, Accessed 6 January 2020.

Raftopoulos, B. (2001) 'The labour movement and the emergence of opposition politics in Zimbabwe', in: B. Raftopoulos and L. Sachikonye (eds.) *Striking back: The labour movement and the post-colonial state in Zimbabwe, 1980-2000*, Harare: Weaver Press.

Raftopoulos, B. (2003) 'The state in crisis: Authoritarian nationalism, selective citizenship and distortions of democracy in Zimbabwe', in: A. Hammar, B. Raftopoulos and S. Jensen (eds.) *Zimbabwe's unfinished business: Rethinking land, state and nation in the context of crisis*, Harare: Weaver Press, 2003.

Raftopoulos, B. (2009) 'The crisis in Zimbabwe, 2000-2008', in: B. Raftopoulos and A. Mlambo (eds.) *Becoming Zimbabwe: A history from the pre-colonial period to 2008*, Harare: Weaver Press.

Ranga, J. (13 September 2013) Interview: Main Street, Mutare, Zimbabwe.

Rangwanda, W. (17 August 2014) Interview: OK Supermarket, Masvingo, Zimbabwe.

Relief Web (22 November 2006) 'Australia provides emergency food aid to Zimbabwe', www.reliefweb.int/report, Accessed 12 June 2019.

Relief Web (25 February 2008) 'Zimbabwe hospital stops surgical operations', www.reliefweb.int/report, Accessed 21 May 2020.

Reuters 25 (September 2008) 'Zimbabwean children eating toxic roots, rats, says aid agency', www.theepochtimes.com, Accessed 2 December 2018.

Reuters Alert (20 March 2007) 'Zimbabwe says drought will worsen food shortages', http://www.ReutersAlertNet.org, Accessed 16 June 2019.

Richardson, C.J. (2005) 'The loss of property rights and the collapse of Zimbabwe', in: *Cato Journal*, Volume 25, Number 3, pp.541-565.

Roberto, Z. (7 September 2014) Interview: Chimanimani Town, Chimanimani District, Zimbabwe.

Roblee-Hertzmark, A. (2012) 'Beggars in three countries: Morocco, India and the United States',

Undergraduate Honours Thesis, Boulder: University of Colorado, 2012.

Rugoho, T. and Siziba, B. (2014) 'Rejected people: Beggars with disabilities in the city of Harare', in: *Developing Country Studies*, Volume 4, Number 26, pp.51-56, www.iiste.org, Accessed 5 July 2019.

Runyanga, N. (19 November 2018) 'The new dispensation: One year on', www.bulawayo24.com, Accessed 21 December 2018.

Rurevo, R. and Bourdillon, M. (2003) *Girls on the street*, Harare: Weaver Press.

Rusiro, P. (12 September 2013) Interview: Sakubva Suburb, Mutare, Zimbabwe.

Ruwende, D. (20 September 2014) Interview: Makoni Shopping Centre, Chitungwiza, Zimbabwe.

Sachikonye, L. (May 2003) 'The situation of commercial farm workers after land reform in Zimbabwe', Report prepared for the Farm Community Trust of Zimbabwe, Harare: Farm Community Trust of Zimbabwe.

Sachikonye, L. (2011) *When a state turns on its citizens: 60 years of institutionalised violence in Zimbabwe*, Auckland Park: Jacana.

Sadutu, J. (26 August 2019) Interview: Dangamvura Shopping Complex, Mutare, Zimbabwe.

Salami, K.K. and Olugbayo, A.O. (2013) 'Health-seeking behavior of migrant beggars in Ibadan, Southwestern Nigeria', in: *Health*, Volume 5, Number 4, pp.792-804.

Samakande, L. (15 February 2014) Interview: Vengere Hall, Rusape, Zimbabwe.

SAMP (5 February 2005) 'South African police round up Zimbabwe's blind beggars', www.queensu.ca/samp, Accessed 12 November 2018.

SAMP (8 September 2005) 'Beggars blockade border post', www.queensu.su/samp, Accessed 12 November 2018.

SAMP (3 October 2005) 'Taxi-load of blind Zimbabwean beggars stopped', www.queensu.su/samp, Accessed 12 November 2018.

SAMP (28 October 2005) 'Inter-departmental approach to address challenges at Lindela'; and 'Lindela horror revealed', www.queensu.su/samp, Accessed 12 November 2018.

SAMP (28 February 2006) 'Blind beggars and human trafficking', www.queensu.su/samp, Accessed 12 November 2018.

SAMP (8 November 2006) 'Botswana hunts down illegal immigrants', www.queensu.su/samp, Accessed 12 November 2018.

Sanderson, S. (1 March 2020) 'Getting soaked in Victoria Falls', https://www.thestandard.co.zw, Accessed 11 March 2020.

Sandton Chronicle (25 August 2016) 'Using children as begging pawns', https://sandtonchronicle.co.za/163245, Accessed 16 June 2019.

Sangati, T. (16 May 2016) Interview: Gweru CBD, Zimbabwe.

Savides, M. (9 April 2020) 'South Africa lockdown extended by two more weeks', https://www.timeslive.co.za, Accessed 28 April 2020.

Saxon, T. (11 July 2002) 'Search for survival: Disabled begging on the increase', www.thezimbabwean.co, Accessed 21 May 2018.

Schaefer, B.D. (23 March 2007) 'The crisis in Zimbabwe: How the US should respond', www.heritage.org/research, Accessed 4 November 2019.

Scheper-Hughes N. (March 2008) 'A talent for life: Reflections on human vulnerability and resilience', in: *Ethnos*, Volume 73, Number 1, pp.25-56.

Scheper-Hughes, N. and Hoffman, D. (May-June 1994) 'Kids out of place: Street children, Latin America and the Caribbean', North American Congress on Latin America and the Caribbean Report, New York: North American Congress on Latin America and the Caribbean.

Scoones, I. (5 August 2013) 'Zimbabwe: Confusion and aftermath of elections', www.thinkafricapress.com, Accessed 17 September 2019.

Scoop Independent News (15 January 2010) 'Cablegate: 2010 investment climate- Zimbabwe', www.scoop.co.nz>scoop>wikileaks, Accessed 25 November 2019.

Scott, B. (2 November 2009) 'Unaccompanied children flee Zimbabwe in growing numbers', https://www.voanews.com/archive, Accessed 5 April 2020.

Sengere, N. (17 September 2013) Interview: Mutare Railway Station, Zimbabwe.

Sesedzayi, C. (13 September 2013) Interview: Main Street, Mutare, Zimbabwe.

Sguazzin, A. Latham, B. and Bax, P. (24 January 2019) 'Chilling analysis: Mugabe beat protestors; Mnangagwa shoots', www.biznews.com, Accessed 1 February 2019.

Shato, J. (14 September 2013) Interview: Meikles Park, Mutare, Zimbabwe.

Sibanda, T. (1 May 2006) 'Zimbabwe refugees turn to begging in Johannesburg streets', http://www.swradioafrica.com/News_archives/files, Accessed 20 August 2020.

Sibeko, S. (27 November 2009) 'Zimbabwean refugees face crime, harassment in South Africa', www.globalpost.com, Accessed 9

December 2019.

Sibindi, R. (26 January 2014) Interview: Machipisa Shopping Centre, Harare, Zimbabwe.

Sigauke, S. (24 March 2015) 'Zimbabwe is burning everyone: Destitute white people increasing on the streets,' https://iharare.com, Accessed 2 September 2020.

Silape, S. (1994) 'How people with disabilities can strive in the labour market', Harare: Unpublished Research Paper.

Simati, J. (22 April 2020) Interview: Dangamvura Shopping Complex, Mutare, Zimbabwe.

Sithole, J. (7 February 2007) 'More white Zimbabwean farmers expelled', www.ens.newswire.com, Accessed 10 July 2018.

Sithole, M. (7 September 2014) Interview: Birchenough Bridge Shopping Centre, Buhera District, Zimbabwe.

Sithole, Z. (28 March 2012) 'Inflation, land seizures impoverish whites', www.thezimbabwean.co/news, Accessed 16 April 2019.

Smith, A.D. (6 July 2008) 'Zimbabwe: Refugees defy crocodiles to cross border', https://www.theguardian.com/world/2008/jul/06/zimbabwe.so uthafrica, Accessed 19 July 2020.

Smith, C. (26 February 2006) 'Blind beggars, the visible face of human trafficking', http://www.zwnews.com/issuefull.cfm?ArticleID=13895, Accessed 27 June 2019.

Sokwanele (20 July 2007) 'Zimbabwean refugees suffer in Botswana and South Africa', www.sokwanele.com/articles, Accessed 11 January 2020.

Solidarity Helping Hand (4 March 2013) 'Johannesburg's begging question', www.helpendehand.co.za, Accessed 14 March 2018.

Solidarity Peace Trust (21 November 2004) *No war in Zimbabwe*, www.zimbabwesituation.com, Accessed 18 July 2019.

Sotwa, V. (13 June 2015) Interview: Masvingo CBD, Zimbabwe.

Standard (16 January 2005) 'Poverty drives many onto the streets', www.queensu.ca/samp, Accessed 18 September 2019.

Standard (6 March 2005) 'SADC protocol watch', Harare: Zimbabwe.

Standard (3 April 2005) 'Soldiers accused of intimidating voters',

Harare: Zimbabwe.

Standard (12 June 2005) 'Clampdown', Harare: Zimbabwe.

Standard (14 August 2005) 'Survey exposes evils of *Murambatsvina*', Harare: Zimbabwe.

Stearns, P.N. (2003) 'Social history: Present and future,' in: *Journal of Social History*, Volume 37, Number 1, pp.9-21.

Stone, D.A. (1984) *The disabled state*, Philadelphia: Temple University Press.

Stones, C.R. (2013) 'A psycho-social exploration of street begging: A qualitative study', in: *South African Journal of Psychology*, Volume 43, Number 2, pp.157-166.

Sundai, L. (13 June 2015) Interview: Masvingo CBD, Zimbabwe.

Sunday Mail (15 July 2012) 'Know your Indigenisation and Empowerment Act', www.sundaymail.co.zw, Accessed 10 October 2018.

Supani, L. (10 January 2020) Interview, Dangamvura Shopping Complex, Mutare, Zimbabwe.

Swanson, K. (2007) 'Bad mothers and delinquent children: Unravelling anti-begging rhetoric in the Ecuadorian Andes', in: *Gender, Place and Culture: A Journal of Feminist Geography*, Volume 14, Number 6, pp.703-720.

Swanson, K. (2010) *Begging as a path to progress: Indigenous women and children and the struggle for Ecuador's urban spaces- Geographies of justice and social transformation*, London: University of Georgia Press.

Takawira, S. (26 March 2015) 'The plights of a child beggar', www.263chat.com, Accessed 24 October 2019.

Tanquintic-Misa, E. (31 January 2013) 'Zimbabwe: Bankrupt, appeals for electoral funding', www.au.ibtimes.com/articles, Accessed 9 January 2020.

Taremba, L. (13 September 2013) Interview: Main Street, Mutare, Zimbabwe.

Thomson Reuters Foundation (13 July 2014) 'Zimbabwe crisis', www.trust.org, Accessed 9 July 2019.

Tibaijuka, A. (2005) *Report on the fact-finding mission to Zimbabwe to assess the scope and impact of Operation Murambatsvina by the UN Special Envoy on the human settlement issue in Zimbabwe*, New York : United Nations.

Tignor, R.I. (2005) *Oscar Lewis and the birth of development economics*, Princeton: Princeton University Press.

Tipple, G. and Speak, S. (24-27 June 2004) 'Attitudes to and interventions in homelessness: Insights from an international study', International Conference Paper on adequate and affordable housing for all, Toronto: Centre for Urban and Community Studies.

Tobias, D. and Duri, F.P.T. (2017) 'Panhandling across national borders: Zimbabwean beggars in South Africa, Botswana and Mozambique during the new millennium,' in: F.P.T. Duri and N. Marongwe (eds.) *Contested spaces, restrictive mechanisms and corridors of opportunity: A social history of Zimbabwean borderlands and beyond since the colonial period*, Gweru: Booklove Publishers, pp.349-392.

Tolsi, N. (30 September 2011) 'Blind beggars search for a better life in Johannesburg's darkest corners', www.mg.co.za/article, Accessed 12 January 2020.

Tondi, C. (12 September 2013) Interview: Sakubva Bus Terminus, Mutare, Zimbabwe.

Trade Mark Southern Africa (1 July 2011) 'Zimbabwe monthly economic review', www.trademarksa.org.news, Accessed 12 May 2019.

Tripathi, S.C. and Arora, V. (2010) *Law relating to women and children*, Allahabad: Central Law Publications.

Tshabalala, X. (2017) 'Hyenas of the Limpopo: The social politics of undocumented movement across South Africa's border with Zimbabwe', PhD thesis Number 729, Linköping University, Faculty of Arts and Science.

Umtali Advertiser (1 July 1949) 'Control of begging wanted: Umtali Council seeks powers', Mutare: Turner Memorial Library, Zimbabwe.

Umtali Advertiser (2 October 1951) 'Beggars again frequenting Umtali', Mutare: Turner Memorial Library, Zimbabwe.

UN (12 August 2005) 'Report of the UN special envoy, Anna Tibaijuka, on the scope and impact of Operation *Murambatsvina*, 2005', reproduced by the *Zimbabwe Independent*, Harare: Zimbabwe.

UN (September 2008) 'Southern Africa: Mozambique-Zimbabwe:

The commodities lifeline', http://www.allAfrica.com, Accessed 12 January 2019.

Unedoro, B. (11 April 2008) 'Poor Zimbabwean whites hit hard times', https://iwpr.net/global-voices, Accessed 10 May 2018.

UNICEF (2001) 'A study on street children in Harare', New York: UNICEF.

US Government (8 March 2006) *Human rights reports, 2005: Country reports on human rights practices*, Washington DC: United States Department of State Bureau of Democracy, Human Rights and Labour.

US Government (2009) *2008 country reports on human rights practices*, Washington DC: Bureau of Democracy, Human Rights and Labour.

US Government (2014) *CIA world fact book 2014*, Washington DC: CIA Publications.

Vantu News (29 October 2019) 'A suspected Zimbabwe border jumper killed by hippos while crossing Limpopo River', https://www.vantunews.com/news, Accessed 4 November 2019.

Vheremu, N. (14 February 2014) Interview: Rusape Bus Terminus, Rusape, Zimbabwe.

VOA (18 January 2006) 'Seeking to escape Zimbabwe: "Border Jumpers" find death in the Limpopo River', https://www.voazimbabwe.com, Accessed 20 July 2018.

VOA (31 December 2009) 'Zimbabwe military deploys to remove country's remaining white farmers', www.voazimbabwe.com, Accessed 21 July 2018.

VOA (20 November 2011) 'One million Zimbabweans need food aid', www.voanews.com, Accessed 20 July 2018.

VOA News, 18 March 2020 'Zimbabweans still recovering a year after Cyclone Idai', https://www.voanews.com/africa, Accessed 2 April 2020.

VOA Studio 7 News Bulletin (31 October 2005) 7pm News.

Wabudabu, M.W. (11 December 2009) 'Jokonia is doomed', www.newzimbabwe.com/pages, Accessed 15 August 2019.

Wanga, C. (18 September 2013) Interview: Mudzviti Bus Terminus, Mutare, Zimbabwe.

Wasosa, M. (28 January 2005) 'ZDI admits involvement in Charleswood seizure', www.theindependent.co.zw, Accessed 16 October 2018.

Watson, F. (1 March 2003) 'Understanding the food crisis in Zimbabwe', www.ennonline.net/fex, Accessed 12 December 2018.

Welthagen, N. (January 2013) 'White beggars in South Africa', Research Report, Pretoria: Solidarity (South Africa).

WFP (13 September 2012) 'Starvation stalls Zimbabwe', www.wfp.org, Accessed 26 September 2019.

WFP (14 March 2013) 'Grim food security outlook', www.wfp.org, Accessed 26 September 2019.

WFP (22 March 2013) '1.4 million Zimbabweans', www.wfo.org, Accessed 26 September 2019.

Wijesiri, L. (9 December 2018) 'Beg to live or live to beg?' http://www.sundayobserver.lk, Accessed 24 December 2018.

Wines, M. (2 May 2006) 'How bad is inflation in Zimbabwe?' www.nytimes.com, Accessed 8 June 2019.

Women News Network (29 May 2013) 'Disability and hardship work as stepping stone to creativity in Zimbabwe, Africa', www.womennewsnetwork.net, Accessed 14 February 2020.

Women's Coalition of Zimbabwe (30 June- 6 July 2005) 'Women's Coalition condemns Operation *Murambatsvina*/ Restore Order', in: *Financial Gazette*, Harare: Zimbabwe.

World Bank (19 September 2019) 'Restoring Zimbabwe's livelihoods, infrastructure after Cyclone Idai', https://www.worldbank.org/en/news/feature, Accessed 12 August 2020.

World Press (10 December 2007) 'One-way street to despair: Life for Zimbabwe's street kids', www.streetkidnews.worldpress.com, Accessed 2 June 2018.

World Press (23 May 2008) 'Makwerekwere', www.khanya.wordpress.com, Accessed 27 May 2018.

World Press (4 June 2008) 'Zimbabwe: Politics and food aid', www.gowans.worldpress.com, Accessed 2 July 2018.

Wozemwa, F. (26 November 2019) Interview, Mutare CBD, Zimbabwe.

Yarns and Fibres (15 April 2011) 'Zimbabwe: Textile and clothing industry', www.yarnsandfibres.com, Accessed 6 May 2020.

Zaba, F. and Mazulu, P. (1 November 2013) 'Cancer fight hamstrung by steep costs', www.theindependent.co.zw, Accessed 10 July 2020.

Zeilig, L. (Spring 2002) 'Crisis in Zimbabwe', in: *International Socialism*, Issue 94.

Zenge, M. (28 January 2014) Interview: Spaceman Shopping Centre, Harare, Zimbabwe.

Zhou, T. (22 September 2016) 'Zimbabweans are beggars in South Africa - Tito Mboweni', https://bulawayo24.com/index-id-news-sc-africa-byo-96884.html, Accessed 11 February 2019.

Zikina, S. (26 January 2014) Interview: Machipisa Shopping Centre, Harare, Zimbabwe.

Zimbabwe Black Book (18 May 2010) 'South Africa rounds up poor, prostitutes ahead of World Cup', www.zimbabweblackbook.worldpress.com, Accessed 18 September 2018.

Zimbabwe Herald (8 May 2012) 'Burnt victim seeks help', www.herald.co.zw, Accessed 5 June 2019.

Zimbabwe Herald (8 May 2013) 'Hell on Harare's streets,' https://www.herald.co.zw, Accessed 2 February 2020.

Zimbabwe Herald (15 February 2015) 'Cyclone Eline ghost haunts Zimbabwe', Harare: Zimbabwe.

Zimbabwe Herald (6 July 2017) '"Roadblocks… Zimbabwe not a war zone", Mzembi tells ZRP', Harare: Zimbabwe.

Zimbabwe Human Rights NGO Forum (2010) 'The land reform and property rights in Zimbabwe, Volume 1', Harare: Zimbabwe Human Rights NGO Forum.

Zimbabwe Independent (3 June 2005) 'Blitz seeks to mask government ineptitude', Harare: Zimbabwe.

Zimbabwe Independent (17 June 2005) 'Government, NGOs clash over blitz', Harare: Zimbabwe.

Zimbabwe Independent (20 March 2006) 'Sugar production hits new lows', www.theindependent.co.zw, Accessed 10 November 2019.

Zimbabwe Independent (6 January 2011) 'How can we forget the empty shelves?' https://www.theindependent.co.zw, Accessed 12 July

2020.

Zimbabwe Independent (10 January 2020) 'Gloomy economic outlook for 2020', Harare: Zimbabwe.

Zimbabwe Institute (13 November 2007) 'Mugabe government admits Zimbabwe white farmers were wronged', www.zimbabweinstitute.net, Accessed 30 October 2019.

Zimbabwe Mail (1 August 2014) 'Mugabe parties while Zimbabwe burns', https://thezimbabwemail.com, Accessed 4 October 2019.

Zimbabwe Mail (22 May 2019) 'When will Zimbabwe's fuel and power blues end?' www.thezimbabwemail.com, Accessed 29 May 2019.

Zimbabwe News Live (7 August 2016) 'Zimbabwean women fake destitution in South Africa', http://www.thezimbabwenewslive.com, Accessed 17 July 2019.

Zimbabwe News Live (24 July 2018) 'Hippo kills Zimbabwean border jumper', http://www.thezimbabwenewslive.com, Accessed 30 July 2018.

Zimbabwe Situation (21 November 2004) 'Hillbrow horror: 31 blind people in one room', www.zimbabwesituation.com, Accessed 20 April 2019.

Zimbabwean (19 April 2010) 'Zimbabwean beggars trek to Beira', www.thezimbabwean.co/news, Accessed 3 October 2019.

Zimbabwean 14 August 2010 'Many disabled people in South Africa resort to begging to survive', www.media-dis-n-dat.blogspot.com, Accessed 3 October 2019.

Zimbabwean (16 February 2011) 'The life of a child beggar', www.thezimbabwean.co/news, Accessed 1 March 2019.

Zimbabwean (22 August 2011) 'Global action against Zimbabwe's political rape horror', www.thezimbabwean.co/news, Accessed 6 March 2019.

Zimbabwean (26 August 2019) 'Desperate Zimbabweans use cell phone transfers to get cash', http://www.tsazim.com, Accessed 14 May 2019.

Zim-Eye (28 July 2015) 'Unemployed Zimbabwean migrants flood South Africa's streets', https://staging.zimeye.net, Accessed 16 June 2019.

Zimunhu, T. (18 February 2014) 'Street kids an eye sore in Harare', www.thezimmail.co.zw, Accessed 12 January 2020.

Zirongo, L. (21 September 2014) Interview: Chikwanha Shopping Centre, Chitungwiza, Zimbabwe.

Zvayi, C. (7 June 2005) 'Reports on clean-up vindictive', in: *Herald*, Harare: Zimbabwe.

Zvofa, R. (12 June 2015) Interview: Masvingo CBD, Zimbabwe.

Zvobgo, C.J. (1990) 'Education and employment of the blind in Zimbabwe, 1981-1987', in: *Journal of Educational Research*, Volume 2, pp.164-203.

Zwinoira, T. (26 March 2019) 'UN survey shows Zimbabwe worse off under Mnangagwa', in: *Newsday*, Harare: Zimbabwe.